T0301419

Managing Transaction Costs in the Era of Globalization

ADVANCES IN NEW INSTITUTIONAL ANALYSIS

Series Editor: Claude Ménard, *Professor of Economics and Director, ATOM (Center for Analytical Theory of Organizations and Markets), University of Paris Panthéon-Sorbonne, France*

Understanding the nature and role of institutions in the dynamics and failures of modern economies is an increasing concern among scholars and policy-makers. Substantial progress has been made in economics as well as in other social sciences, particularly political science, history, sociology and the managerial sciences. New institutional scholars have been, and remain, at the forefront of this movement. Alternative views have also been proposed that deserve consideration. This series intends to promote the development and diffusion of these analyses with books from leading contributors as well as younger up-and-coming scholars.

The series will include topics such as:

- Institutions and growth
- Transaction cost economics
- The role of formal rules and legal institutions
- Regulation and deregulation
- Political institutions and the state
- Institutions and modes of governance
- Contracting issues
- Customs, beliefs and institutional changes.

The series will be essential reading for researchers in economics, the social and managerial sciences, as well as policy-makers.
   Titles in the series include:

Institutions and Development
Mary M. Shirley

Regulation, Deregulation, Reregulation
Institutional Perspectives
Edited by Claude Ménard and Michel Ghertman

Managing Transaction Costs in the Era of Globalization
Frank A.G. den Butter

Managing Transaction Costs in the Era of Globalization

Frank A.G. den Butter

VU University Amsterdam, The Netherlands

ADVANCES IN NEW INSTITUTIONAL ANALYSIS

Edward Elgar

Cheltenham, UK • Northampton, MA, USA

Published by
Edward Elgar Publishing Limited
The Lypiatts
15 Lansdown Road
Cheltenham
Glos GL50 2JA
UK

Edward Elgar Publishing, Inc.
William Pratt House
9 Dewey Court
Northampton
Massachusetts 01060
USA

A catalogue record for this book
is available from the British Library

Library of Congress Control Number: 2012939107

ISBN 978 1 78100 130 1

Typeset by Servis Filmsetting Ltd, Stockport, Cheshire
Printed and bound by MPG Books Group, UK

Contents

Abbreviations

AEO	Authorized Economic Operator
AMD	Advanced Micro Devices
B2B	business to business
BIS	Bank for International Settlements
BRIC	Brazil, Russia, India, China
CBA	cost–benefit analysis
CBS	Centraal Bureau voor de Statistiek (Statistics Netherlands)
CEE	Central and Eastern Europe
CELENEC	European Committee for Electronical Standardization (Comité Européen de Normalisation Electrotechnique)
CEO	Chief Executive Officer
CM	crude materials
CO_2	carbon dioxide
CPB	Central Planning Bureau
CRP	chemical and related products
DCA	direct cost of acquisition
DNB	de Nederlandsche Bank (The Dutch Central Bank)
DIN	Deutsches Institut für Normung
EIB	Economisch Instituut voor de Bouw (Economic Institute for the Building Industry)
EU	European Union
FASB	Financial Accounting Standards Board
FDI	foreign direct investments
G2B	government to business (between government and business)
G2G	government to government (within the government)
GDP	gross domestic product
GM	genetically modified
GPS	global positioning system
GSM	global system for mobile communications
HK	Hong Kong
HRM	human resource management
IASB	International Accounting Standards Board

ICT	information and communication technology
IHC	IHC Holland Merwede
ISO	International Organization for Standardization
IT	information technology
JIT	just in time
MMA	miscellaneous manufactured articles
MNC	multinational operating corporations
MSD	Merck, Sharpe & Dohme
MTE	machinery and transport equipment
NA	National Accounts
NGO	non-governmental organization
OECD	Organisation for Economic Co-operation and Development
pm	pro memori
ppp	people planet profit
PTA	preferential trade agreement
R&D	research and development
RC	recurring costs
RFID	Radio Frequency Identification
RFT	Right First Time
RtP	Requisition to Pay
SCM	supply chain management
SER	Sociaal Economische Raad (Social and Economic Council)
SFI	special financial institution
SITC	Standard International Trade Classification
SMEs	small and medium-sized enterprises
SWIFT	Society for Worldwide Interbank Financial Telecommunication
SWOT	Strengths, Weaknesses, Opportunities, Threats
TC	transaction costs
TCA	Tax and Customs Administration
TCA	total cost of acquisition
TCO	total cost of ownership
TPM	total preventive maintenance
TPS	Toyota Production System
TQM	total quality management
UK	United Kingdom
USA	United States of America
UTA-personnel	Personnel in executive, technical and administrative staff functions

VOC	Verenigde Oost-Indische Compagnie (United East India Company)
WCO	World Customs Organization
WRR	Wetenschappelijke Raad voor het Regeringsbeleid (Scientific Council for Government Policy)
WTO	World Trade Organization
XBRL	eXtensible Business Reporting Language

About the author

Prof.dr. Frank A.G. den Butter (1948) is a policy-oriented economist. He studied econometrics at the University of Amsterdam and obtained his PhD from Erasmus University Rotterdam. From 1973 to 1988 he worked at the Netherlands Central Bank and was involved in economic modelling, policy analysis and research management. Since 1988 he has been professor of economics at the Vrije Universiteit Amsterdam and has founded the research team ALERT (Applied Labour Economics Research Team), which has meanwhile obtained an excellent international reputation in its field. From 1989 to 1996 he was a director of the Tinbergen Institute, the Netherlands Research Institute and the Graduate School for Economics and Business of the Amsterdam and Rotterdam Universities. From 1998 to 2002 he was a member of the multidisciplinary Scientific Council for Government Policy at the Prime Minister's office in The Hague. As a member of the council, he was responsible for the report on 'The Netherlands as a trading nation', which was published in 2003 and which initiated the research reported in this book.

Moreover, Frank A.G. den Butter was the chairman of the Royal Netherlands Economic Association (the oldest economists' association in the world) from 1997 to 2003 and was a member of the Central Statistical Committee (the supervisory committee of the Central Bureau of Statistics) from 1998 to 2004. He has also been a member of the economic policy committee of the Social Economic Council and has chaired various academic and governmental committees and bodies. He has served in various committees of the Dutch National Science Foundation, among which was a committee that promoted research in environmental economics in the Netherlands. He is the chairman of the supervisory committee of the Economic Institute for the Building Industry. Outside the Netherlands, he has been a member of the board of the European Association of Labour Economists and has acted as a consultant for the OECD, ILO, the World Bank, the government of Ethiopia and the IAB.

Frank A.G. den Butter has published about 300 articles, both in international and in Dutch journals, and about 20 books. See website http://staff.feweb.vu.nl/fbutter/.

Preface and acknowledgements

The inspiration for this book comes from two experiences. First, a flower merchant who, in the mid 1990s, I overheard in the departure lounge of Heathrow Airport. With inimitable charm he phoned a British customer to sell a batch of flowers available in Aalsmeer. A good example of a Dutch tradesman's skill. The second experience was the ado of my sons, and many other children, with Flippos, the cartoon disks collected from chip packets. That made me think back to the barter with pictures of football quartets during my own schooldays. The latter experience made me write a column ('Little traders') which is included in this book in Box 1.1.

When the Scientific Council for Government Policy (WRR) in the Netherlands in 2000 planned a new report, I suggested 'the Netherlands as a Trading Nation' as a subject. It resulted in a report to the government which was published in 2003. The question is how the Netherlands and similar trade-oriented modern open economies can keep up and strengthen their positions as a trading nation in the globalizing world. This book stems from a recommendation in the WRR report, namely that there is a need for further research on that question and for an institute that facilitates that research and disseminates knowledge. With that purpose, the foundation *Handelsland.nl* was created. This foundation is a sponsor of the newly-founded *Research Institute for Trade and Transaction Management* (RITM) at the VU University Amsterdam. The book is an outcome of the research programme of RITM.

Parts of the text of this book are based on research conducted with others. I would like to acknowledge their help and cooperation. They are Robert Mosch (trust), Ok van Megchelen (construction industry), Stefan Groot and Farouk Lazrak (standards), Daniel Leliefeld (IHC Holland Merwede), Patrik Corveleijn (financial asset transactions in Europe), Raphie Hayat (China), Kees Linse (procurement), Andre Nijsen (implementation costs of government regulation), Peter Risseeuw and Marcel van den Berg (trust offices), Ebel Berghuis and Christian Pattipeilohy (trade in tasks), Seung-Guy Jo (picking winners), Marcel Boons (Lean) and Jianwei Liu (AEO certificates). George Dujardin, Nanko Boerma and Harry Starren were, as members of the board of the 'Handelsland. nl' foundation, excellent promoters and sponsors of this research project on transaction management. Useful comments and suggestions by Albert Koers and Peter Jöbsis on previous drafts of the Dutch version of the book are acknowledged. Erik Zonneveld and Abdessalam Es-Saghir proved to be very helpful research assistants. Finally the editor of this series published by Edward Elgar, Claude Ménard, provided extensive and excellent comments on previous English versions of the book.

Frank A.G. den Butter
Ouderkerk a/d Amstel
March 2012

1. Introduction

This chapter gives a first impression of the increasing importance of managing transaction costs in the era of globalization. It defines the skill of keeping transaction costs low as transaction cost management, or shortly, *transaction management,* and explains its role in transaction economies. By keeping the costs of trade transactions as low as possible, the value creation from these transactions is optimized. Here, trade transactions are defined in the broadest sense, including all kind of transactions which specialization and the resulting need for coordination bring about. This chapter also contains a reading guide for the book.

1.1 GLOBALIZATION AND THE ORGANIZATION OF PRODUCTION

In this era of globalization and computerization, the division of labour and specialization in production and services are the main sources of economic prosperity. Specialization uses economics of scale and the skills and tools of others to reduce total production costs and/or to improve the quality of products and services. This was already true in 1776 when Adam Smith wrote about the gains from specialization in *The Wealth of Nations.* It is much truer in these modern times where production chains are split up further and further so that there is more and more fragmentation of production. In contrast to producers who make all the parts and components of the product themselves, specialization in the manufacturing and service of parts and components has become standard. Nowadays, there are numerous examples of hiring staff and the outsourcing of tasks, especially outside the core business of the organization (such as catering or maintenance in an office building or the outsourcing of administrative work). Trade in products in the traditional sense, driven by the Ricardian principles of comparative advantages, has now gradually been transformed to a trade in tasks.

These developments, which the globalization and new possibilities of information and communication technology (ICT) have brought about, also deeply change the way production of goods and services is organized.

Instead of executing all tasks themselves, the producers of a final product or service have now become the orchestrators who successfully connect the individual parts of the production chain to each other. The focus now has come to lie in the orchestrating function, which aims to fully exploit all the advantages of this specialization and the fragmentation of production. That is why modern economies, where economic activity is more and more directed towards this orchestrating function, can be characterized as *transaction economies*. Hence, a transaction economy is focused on the organization of production and can, therefore, also be labelled as an *orchestration economy*. This transition from production to orchestration is also reflected in the statistics of such economies: agricultural and industrial production are losing their shares of the domestic product in favour of services.

The scope of the trade transactions, which this new way of organising production brings about, can be very broad. The transactions may take place within the organization (for example, between offices or business units) or outside the organization (outsourcing, procurement, supply chain management (SCM)). They may take place at home or abroad. They may take place only once, be recurrent or take place very frequently.

With respect to all these different types of transactions, the orchestrator seeks to exploit the advantages of specialization (higher quality and/ or lower production costs) as much as possible by keeping transaction costs as low as possible. Of course, these transactions differ from case to case. Cost saving can relate to the preparation of a transaction or to implementation and enforcement. The costs are often difficult to trace in an organization, because it is sometimes rather fussy to register which workers are involved in preparing, implementing or monitoring transactions, and which are involved in the pure production process. Think of a farmer: when he is feeding his animals, cleaning the stable or collecting his crop, he is engaged in production, but when he takes his cow or crop to the market or is doing his accounting to adhere with government regulation, he is involved in managing transaction costs.

Being successful in orchestration, and thereby being good at managing transaction costs, requires (superior) knowledge of markets, products, production technologies and supply industries and services. It also requires strategies to cash in on the created added value. In addition, ICT and advice from professionals such as lawyers, management consultants and tax experts can be important to controlling transaction costs. All this is very knowledge-intensive and can, in one way or another, be supported by innovation policy.

This book takes this management of transaction costs as a guiding principle. Apart from comparative advantages in production, transaction costs are the main determinant of (international) trade flows. Similarly, differences in transaction costs are crucial for the location and investment decisions of firms on where to produce and on where to organize and orchestrate production in their headquarters. Therefore, knowledge on transaction costs, and on how to manage transactions, is vital for these trade and investment decisions.

This book labels the skill of managing transaction costs in an efficient way as transaction cost management, or more briefly as *transaction management*. It must be admitted that this label of transaction management is used in a much broader sense than in the accustomed case where advisors in transaction management are mainly concerned with monetary and contractual matters in conducting transactions. Within the broad scope of managing transaction costs, efficient transaction management that reduces transaction costs will make existing trade more profitable and will lead to more trade. It strengthens the competitive position of individual firms and, through spillover effects, of the whole nation, so that it enhances welfare. In this way, a reduction of transaction costs creates value for firms and society. The conundrum is that with lower transaction costs total transactions will rise more than proportionally so that transaction costs will take a larger share of total costs. This enhances the importance and profitability of transaction management. Hence, briefly stated, *transaction management is the ability to keep the costs of trade transactions as low as possible so that the value creation from these transactions is optimized*.

The more knowledge there is on these aspects, which is partly tacit knowledge, the better the management of transactions can be strengthened. In the world of globalization and global (out)sourcing, it is vital for firms to preserve the orchestrating function in the production, demand and supply networks. Major questions in this respect are: where and how can we buy ideas for new products and services; how do we obtain knowledge on making these products and providing these services; where do we find labour; and where and how can we continue and improve selling these products and services at the highest margins? Financing and risk management are an important part of that management function. It is this new role for professional businesspeople that is a key component to transaction cost management. Therefore, another major focus of how to manage transaction costs is to cope with cultural diversity. The ability to work with different cultures is a vital skill for a good trader. Transaction management is about all these aspects of a modern knowledge economy. That is why this book considers transaction management as a main road to value creation in this era of globalization.

From the theoretical perspective this book looks at transaction management from the viewpoint of transaction cost economics and new institutional economics. These theories are concerned with the organization of production and with the governance of the firm. The question is what governance structure – via the market, hierarchy or some hybrid form in between – brings about the lowest transaction costs in production. From this perspective, transaction management is about selecting the best governance structure for value creation. The skill of selecting the optimal governance structure is not only relevant for a firm being competitive but also for the welfare of a nation.

All in all, it implies that managing transaction costs efficiently is a key competency in the globalizing world of today and tomorrow. The purpose of this book is to investigate and elaborate this argument, and make it operational for practical purposes. The upshot is that efficient transaction management, and finding new ways to reduce transaction costs, will enhance the profits from the fragmentation of production and global outsourcing of tasks. It will bring about an increase in the productivity and competitive position of orchestrating firms and nations. Eventually it will add to consumer welfare, not only through lower product prices and quality improvements, but also through enhanced diversification of products. The latter aspect brings an important addition to consumer surplus. Moreover, tailored production also emphasises the importance of good transaction management as more diversity makes control over transaction costs even more significant for competing firms. For those reasons, the book also discusses the mutual relationship between transaction management and knowledge and innovation policy. As this book is explicitly based on modern theories of transaction cost economics and new institutional economics, and provides examples for applying these theories in practice, transaction management should not be regarded as another heuristic management tool.

1.2   CONTENTS OF THE BOOK

The contents of the remainder of the book are as follows. The underlying argument of transaction management is that much of the wealth in the world comes from specialization and the division of labour. That is what makes modern fragmentation of production pay off, and that is why the focus of value creation lies more and more in the efficiency of coordination (Chapter 2).

This fragmentation of production and value creation through efficient coordination characterizes the position of what this book calls transaction or orchestrating economies. It also plays a pivotal role in the relationship between the new, emerging economies (Brazil, Russia, India and China, usually termed BRIC countries) and the European economies. From that perspective it is useful to obtain a quantitative impression of the position of a number of transaction economies as a 'hub' in world trade using data on trade flows (Chapter 3).

The globalizing world of more and more specialization and an extended division of labour brings about more transactions. Therefore, transaction costs play a crucial and ever-increasing role. The economic theory of transaction costs teaches us about which types of transaction costs are involved and how these transaction costs affect the working of the economy. It is this theory of transaction cost economics, and more generally the links between this theory, modern trade theory, new institutional economics and economic theory of the organization of production, which provide the key scientific underpinnings of transaction management. It appears that transaction management can and will be applied to a much broader range of 'transactions' than one is initially inclined to think (Chapter 4).

Thanks to the reduction of transaction costs, more parts of the production chain can be outsourced to suppliers, subcontractors or specialized plants of firms. Sometimes outsourcing is in the home country, but more often it is abroad. This implies that outsourcing and offshoring are becoming important strategic decision tools in the transaction management of businesses. As mentioned before, this transforms internationally-operating firms in the home country from a manufacturing-oriented industry to one based on orchestration and transaction management. This transition is very much what can be observed in reality in the globalizing world. Characteristic of this is to let others perform various tasks in the production chain, both within a developed economy but more so in major emerging economies (including the BRIC countries) where, for the time being, wages are low. In Chapter 5, some examples are given of this increasing emphasis on the orchestrating function.

Computerization and globalization seem to be important determinants of trade flows. The empirical analyses of trade flows use so-called gravity equations, which include various determinants for transaction costs. Trust is one of these determinants and another one is the extent to which specialized knowledge is needed to execute outsourced tasks. This trade in tasks is illustrated with data on trade between the Netherlands and China (Chapter 6).

An important but perhaps somewhat undervalued part of transaction management is standardization. Standards that reduce transaction costs come in many forms. It is likely that still much efficiency is to be gained from further standardization, for example in the handling of the trade of European assets. By contrast, established standards carry the danger of being inflexible and underutilizing new technological opportunities. Another aspect linking standardization to transaction management is that consumers are more and more interested in diversity of goods and of services by asking for tailored products. It makes standardization more complex and it influences transaction costs (Chapter 7).

This illustrates the link that exists between transaction management and innovation. Innovation does not only relate to new technologies that enhance productivity by the design of new products or by a more efficient technical production process: innovation can also contribute to the increased efficiency of conducting transactions. When innovation is targeted towards reducing transaction costs and thereby on value creation through better transaction management, it will contribute much to increasing competitiveness in transaction economies. In particular this means open forms of innovation that contribute to value creation through the better organization of production. This illustrates how the transaction economy and the knowledge economy are two sides of the same coin. Because transaction management is internationally-oriented in the globalizing world, excellent skills on how to cope with cultural diversity are key components to this discipline (Chapter 8).

Innovations in transaction management are not only valuable for firms that implement them, but also other firms, and more generally society as a whole, can benefit. This means that these transaction innovations – or trade innovations – bring about so-called positive externalities. The theory of public sector economics points out that the role of government is to exploit these externalities: in linking innovation policy to trade policy, the government should facilitate and stimulate knowledge investments, which in turn enhance the efficiency of conducting transactions. It should also avoid negative externalities playing a role. A major question in this respect is whether the government should conduct an active industrial and innovation policy by 'picking winners' – that is, by selecting key economic sectors that will obtain government support to enhance their competitive positions. This targeted policy has its pros and cons (Chapter 9).

However, transaction costs are also important in the implementation of government policy. Here, implementation costs are made up both by the government itself and by the citizens and businesses who are subject to government policy, which in most cases will relate to some kind of government regulation. Various institutional arrangements, which facilitate discussions and finding compromise agreements between stakeholders with different and sometimes conflicting interests, and a good use of modern technology, can help make the implementation of government policy efficient and avoid unnecessary transaction costs (Chapter 10).

Finally Chapter 11 summarizes in a number of key statements the significance and meaning of an efficient management of transaction costs. It describes the steps to be taken in the practical application of transaction management.

1.3 ORIGIN AND BACKGROUND OF THE BOOK

This book originates from a research programme which was a follow-up to a policy advice to the Dutch government by the Scientific Council for Government Policy (WRR, 2003). Therefore, there are ample examples and case studies relating to the Netherlands. Yet, the general philosophy of transaction management is applicable to firms and government policies in all modern welfare states with open economies.

As a trading nation, the Netherlands has certainly, since the Golden Age or even before (think of the Hanseatic League), been good at keeping the costs of transactions low – that is, good at transaction management. The painting 'The Syndics' (Staalmeesters) by Rembrandt (Figure 1.1) symbolizes that, as early as the seventeenth century Dutch traders realized the importance of keeping transaction costs low. The syndics controlled and categorized the quality of 'laken', a fine woollen fabricate, so that it was unnecessary for traders to control for quality before every transaction. By trusting the hallmark of the syndic, buyers and sellers of this fabricate

Source: Reprinted with permission of Rijksmuseum Amsterdam.

Figure 1.1   The painting 'The Syndics' (Staalmeesters) by Rembrandt symbolizes good management of transaction costs in the seventeenth century

did not incur high costs in each transaction because they had come to an agreement on the quality of the 'laken'. Moreover, traders could rely on realized prices for standards of various qualities. This shows how important it is for traders to be able to rely on standards, which are preferably uniform and valid throughout the world. This facilitates transactions and promotes trade (Chapter 7). Moreover, the quality standards set by the syndics were trusted because they were a forerunner to the famous Dutch polder model of consultation. All members of the standard-setting committee came from different religious backgrounds. A painting, made by a well-known painter and that shows distinguished gentlemen, can help establish trust, which is a major device in transaction management. These aspects of trust and keeping transaction costs low by good consultation and organization of discussion between various interest groups are of major importance both for implementation of strategic plans and joint ventures in the business sector and for finding societal support for policy plans by the government (Chapter 10).

The hypothesis of the WRR report is that as a trading nation the Netherlands has a comparative advantage in keeping transaction costs low. This book poses the same hypothesis for similar transaction economies. These comparative advantages can be exploited further in the future through good transaction management. It will enhance the competitive position of these transaction economies. However, it is difficult to test and support this hypothesis in a direct way scientifically. For such an analysis comparative data on transaction costs and value creation through a reduction of transaction costs should be available on a time series basis for several relevant competitor countries of the transaction economies. Yet, one could argue that a mercantilist and commercial tradition of these nations may constitute a guarantee for obtaining and maintaining these comparative advantages. This commercialism, or to formulate it differently, being a good tradesman, is a skill that is not entirely based on good education and that cannot be obtained by studying books. It is a form of entrepreneurship, which is partly innate and must partly be learned in practice by trial and error (see Box 1.1). The story in this box, published in 1999, provided the inspiration to start this book on transaction management (Den Butter, 1999).

Given the origin and scope of this book, it is inevitable to look back at the glorious past of the Netherlands as a trading nation in the assessment of present and future transaction management. In fact, the United East India Company was the first internationally-operating modern enterprise where the importance of transaction management was recognized, although without naming it as such. Today the good parts of the United East India Company mentality are to be cherished, but the bad parts

BOX 1.1   LITTLE TRADERS

Economists have the most ingenious theories to explain economic phenomena. However, when it becomes important to understand practice, learned economists remain silent and ignorant. Take entrepreneurship for example. There is a need for good businesspeople, or entrepreneurs, who dare to take risks and who intuitively know the right business strategy to choose. They are good for the country because a climate where new businesses flourish brings much profit, employment and welfare. Economic theory has, however, only shaped a colourless, representative rational entrepreneur. He or she will, given the available information, always make the best decisions, but has, furthermore, just a random chance of bad or good luck. The unlucky entrepreneur goes bankrupt, whereas the lucky one makes huge profits. There is no place in the theory for intuition or for the enforcement of good luck.

According to the theory, investments in knowledge make firms profitable. These investments comprise both investments in research and technological development, which may result in new products or making production more efficient, and investments in human capital. In the latter case, knowledge is acquired through education, but also through work experience. These investments in knowledge are again based on rational considerations: the proceeds from using the acquired knowledge has to make investments profitable. This rational theory of knowledge investments, therefore, has little to do with intuition and 'Fingerspitzen Gefuhl', which distinguishes the good entrepreneur from the bad. One does not become a good entrepreneur or a good trader – which is more relevant in trading nations – by means of sheer rational calculations. Such skill is culturally determined, almost innate, and anyhow obtained by playful learning, preferably when one is young and in the streets, just like the top football players.

The craze of collecting Flippos has been over now for some time. The successful Flippo campaign was launched by Smiths Chips, a firm selling potato chips, in the spring of 1995. Flippos are small round plastic disks with Warner Bros cartoons on them that are put in the bags of chips. Collecting and exchanging Flippos became popular among children, teenagers and young adults.

The commotion of my sons with Flippos made me realize that this kind of epidemic collecting and exchanging among youngsters can contribute to the formation of what we may label the entrepreneurial spirit of a tradesman. It reminded me of a collecting craze from my own primary schooldays. In this case, the items to collect were cards with cartoon drawings of football players. For each country, there was a quartet of cards with the four most known internationals of those days. Therefore, the aim was to collect the full game of quartet cards of international football. It was only a small inconvenience that, to obtain cards, you had to buy pieces of awful-tasting pink chewing gum.

Therefore, a lively barter trade in these football cards developed among my schoolmates. By coincidence, or perhaps the cleverness of the chewing gum marketer, not all players were equally available. Therefore, for some players you soon had a duplicate, while other players were very scarce. It resulted in a lively market mechanism with the formation of relative barter prices. For example, the value of the Dutch player Van der Hart was three times that of the Austrian player Happel (it had nothing to do with the true skills of the players). This process of price formation was complicated by the fact that you had an extra interest to get a full quartet. Therefore, you were willing to pay a relatively high price for a player who completed the quartet. Moreover, it was more difficult to obtain a complete quartet for one country than for another. The result was that, in this barter trade, a network of information developed about who had specific cards for exchange, and about which were the current exchange conditions. I remember that the last quartet that I had to complete was Brazil, as one player, Garrincha, was very scarce. Of course I told my friends that I wanted that card desperately and that I was ready to exchange that card for many other cards – even for a full quartet of another country. Eventually, this information had become so far spread that one of my friends brought me into contact with a boy from another school who was interested in the exchange. I forget whether I had to give this friend a commission in the form of some pink chewing gum, or even a number of football players.

At the risk of repeating that everything was better in the olden days, the collecting craze with Flippos unfortunately contributed less to developing the entrepreneurial spirit of the trader. My sons made me understand that in the case of Flippos, trade was confined to a simple barter of double Flippos. Yet, in the Flippos craze, a game element was introduced, where, by taking risks, Flippos could be won or lost. However, this element of a game in the Flippo entrepreneurship only mimicked the standard economic theory of random chances where entrepreneurs with good luck make profits but those with bad luck may lose all of their Flippos. In the Flippo craze, there was no reward for intuition or for the good interpretation of price signals and other information. The only other mirror of the real world in the Flippo game was that the biggest risk-takers ended up with a large gambling debt and stole Flippos to pay off the debt. That can hardly be regarded as a positive contribution of the Flippo craze to the formation of a sound commercial spirit. However, maybe I paid too high a price for Garrincha in my schooldays as well.

should be avoided. The Chinese witnessed these good and bad parts as early as the seventeenth century:

> The Hollanders are greedy and cunning, have a lot of valuable knowledge and were clever in the pursuit of advantage, for profits they even risk their lives and there are no places where they do not dare to go. . .. These people are also very capable and resourceful, they make sails as spider webs, which they can turn to all sides to catch the wind, so they manage to sail with the wind in every direction. (Zandvliet and Blussé, 2002, pp. 19–20)

Overconfidence and greed have no place in modern times. However, the tradition of a trading nation using technical knowledge and product knowledge for profitable trade still has a place. Discovering and exploiting all new opportunities at a global scale is a key ambition in the transaction economy. That is the essence of transaction management as a key competency for a modern open economy where trade transactions are drivers of economic welfare.

2.   Specialization and coordination

This chapter describes how an increase in specialization leads to the fragmentation of production so that more and more of the comparative advantages of countries can be exploited. On the one hand, it is the reduction of transaction costs that allows for more specialization but, on the other hand, it leads to more transactions. Therefore, it enhances the role of transaction costs and consequently that of transaction management. Moreover, it implies that supply chains become more complicated, which is accounted for by developments in supply chain management (SCM).

2.1   COMPARATIVE ADVANTAGES

Most developed countries, especially when they can be characterized as open economies with a high amount of trade, witness an increasing trend in jobs related to trade and services. Gradually, production jobs are replaced by what can be regarded as transaction jobs. A major cause of this trend is the increasing *division of labour and specialization* both within national economies and in the world as a whole. Specialization means the exploitation of economies of scale and using the diversification of skills and availability of resources in the production of goods and services. Production takes place where it is cheapest. Availability in a country of raw materials and of capital, both physical capital and human capital, determines what is produced and what is traded. These are the *comparative advantages* of a country in international trade. Traditional Ricardian trade theory explains the goods and services trade flows from such comparative advantages. A country with rich natural resources has a competitive advantage and it will be able to sell these resources, whether or not processed, profitably in world markets. The same applies to a country where labour is relatively cheap because of low wages or, to be more precise, where the productivity of labour is high relative to wages. Then, the exports of labour-intensive products and services are relatively profitable.

Yet, these differences in available resources between countries – labour, capital and raw materials – only partially explain international trade. If all comparative advantages were fully exploited, world trade flows would be far greater than they actually are (see, for example, Trefler, 1995). The explanatory power of this type of comparative advantage seems limited in the modern world economy. In international trade, and especially in those countries where trade and transactions are a driving force in the economy, other aspects play a more important role. Here, it is essential to realize that *trade is not for free*, but brings about all sorts of costs. Indeed, the division of labour and specialization, on the one hand, has the effect that the production of goods and services becomes more efficient. This holds true both for the division of labour and for specialization within firms, and between firms and countries. On the other hand, the division of labour and specialization also imply that the various activities are to be coordinated.

All the costs of this coordination can, in a broad sense, be regarded as *transaction costs*. In the case of coordination between firms through the market, these (business) transactions imply a transfer of property rights. In this case of market transactions, we have horizontal transaction costs. But in a modern economy a large number of transactions take place within firms. Part of these is intracompany trade, where, if possible and appropriate, market mechanisms for making the transactions cost-efficient can be simulated, which is also a form of transaction management. However, many transactions occur within the hierarchy of the firm. Here, we have vertical transaction costs. Another part of the transaction costs of firms in a modern society is related to the labour market, such as search costs, hiring costs, firing costs and the costs of building up firm-specific human capital.

The balancing of efficiency gains and transaction costs because of specialization can be illustrated using the traditional Edgeworth box diagram from the economic textbooks. The diagram provides a stylized illustration of the welfare gains of exchange. The diagram box in Figure 2.1 distinguishes between two different goods (X and Y) and two different persons (or firms) (A and B). The box shows which exchange possibilities A and B have in the case of an initial distribution (endowment) of goods X and Y. For person A the origin is OA and for person B it is OB. In origin OA, the initial endowment is that person A owes nothing, whereas person B owes the total available amount of goods X and Y. In origin OB, person A owes everything and person B nothing. From OA the indifference curves UAI, UAII and UAIII indicate which combinations of X and Y yield the same amounts of utility (welfare) for A. The further the indifference curves are located from the origin, the higher the utility (welfare) for A. For person B the mirror image holds true from origin OB with indifference curves UBI, UBII and UBIII. The further UB is away from the origin OB, the higher is the utility and welfare for person B.

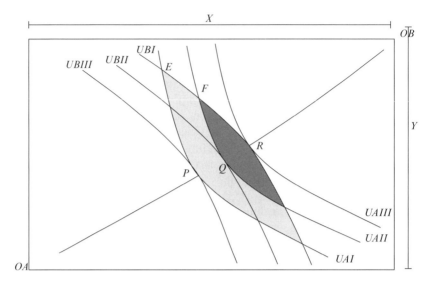

Figure 2.1   Edgeworth box

Now suppose that point F represents the initial distribution of X and Y. This means that A owes a lot more of good Y than B and B initially has about the same amount of good X as A. Note that the total amount of goods X and Y determines the size of the box. The figure shows that the initial endowment in point F allows for a welfare improvement of both persons – or at least not a reduction of welfare for one of the persons – when exchange takes place so that the distribution of goods X and Y moves to the area between the indifference curves UAII and UBI. In this *Pareto improvement* an exchange increases total wealth in such a way that none of the persons loses wealth (Box 2.1).

The actual amount of the exchange of goods X and Y, and thereby their relative prices, will depend on the bargaining powers of both persons. Ultimately that bargaining power determines which point on the contract curve QR is reached. If the initial endowment were more unequal in the sense that one person has more of X and the other more of Y (point E in the figure), then the potential for exchange to be welfare-enhancing becomes larger. Now the area between UAI and UBI offers the possibility for a Pareto improvement. The outcome of an efficient exchange contract is now on the PR curve. The intuition is that specialization, where A produces one good and B the other good, represents a situation where there will be more exchange and thereby the welfare effects of that exchange will be higher than in a situation where both persons are producers of both goods.

BOX 2.1 A PARETO-OPTIMUM OUTCOME IN WELFARE ECONOMICS

According to economic welfare theory, a Pareto-optimal situation is one where the wealth (the 'individual utility') of one person can only be increased at the cost of the wealth of another person. If not, there is a win–win situation. Where through an exchange of goods or services, as illustrated in the Edgeworth box, two persons can increase their wealth, there will be a strong economic incentive to act and exploit the win–win situation. The result will be that a Pareto-optimal situation is reached. Pareto-optimum outcomes yield the maximum wealth from the perspective of individual welfare. By contrast, from the perspective of social welfare, the situation of the Pareto-optimum may be improved, for example in the case that the distribution of individual wealth is very uneven. In that case, the redistribution of wealth may lead to higher social welfare. When redistribution takes place from a Pareto-optimal situation, it implies that there is always one person or group of persons ('the rich') that lose welfare for another person or group of persons ('the poor') to gain welfare.

It should be noted that such a Pareto improvement does not bring about a redistribution of welfare and that the government should not interfere with the exchange for that reason. It only brings about more welfare, and the relative bargaining power solves the distribution problem (which is different from the redistribution problem).

In the traditional description of barter exchange, the Edgeworth box assumes that exchange is for free and that the negotiation about the exchange between the two parties does not affect their production possibilities or endowment (the total amount of X and Y is equal for any exchange). In other words, in the Edgeworth box, there are no transaction costs.

The question now arises about how the existence of efficiency gains due to specialization, but also the transaction costs that the exchange will bring about, can be included in this simple economic analysis of barter. Efficiency gains because of economies of scale in specialization mean that A will be able to produce more of the good where they have comparative advantages and B more of the other good. So in total more of X and Y becomes available. This means that specialization makes the surface of the box bigger. By contrast, increased specialization means that there will be more exchange and that, therefore, transaction costs increase. The time and effort that A and B have to spend on the exchange, and the consequent transaction costs, will result in less of X and Y being produced. Therefore, the surface of the box becomes smaller. It is of importance to the welfare gain specialization yields that the increase of the surface of the box, because of efficiency gains, outweighs the decrease due to higher transaction costs.

That is exactly what good transaction management should do: keep transaction costs low so that the opportunities to benefit from specialization can be exploited as much as possible. Moreover, keeping transaction costs low will also reduce as much as possible the distortion in the allocation of goods and services that transaction costs bring about. For that reason one role of the government is to facilitate good transaction management (for example, through a good system of legal protection of property rights – see Chapter 9).

The trend of a continuous increase in the division of labour and in specialization is not one of just today or tomorrow. As mentioned in the Introduction, Adam Smith noted how the division of tasks greatly increases productivity; and he used his famous pin factory example as an illustration. This increase in productivity can eventually translate into higher wages or lower prices and thereby into more purchasing power. It is no overstatement to say that wealth, measured by material wealth, has in the past century increased significantly, mainly because of productivity improvements that were the result of labour division and specialization.

Clearly, transaction costs and the ability to reduce them have contributed to these developments. The upshot here is that transaction costs can be too high, so that no (business) transactions take place. In that case, the benefits of division of labour and specialization are not sufficient to outweigh the disadvantages, namely the coordination costs that specialization brings about. In that case, a reduction of transaction costs may imply that further specialization is profitable and the amount of exchange (trade) increases, which is illustrated above in the Edgeworth box diagram. It also means that existing trade becomes cheaper. In both cases, the reduction in transaction costs increases *welfare.* In the context of the debate on globalization, an important question is who receives most of the benefits of this welfare increase. So solving part of the coordination problem evokes a distribution problem of welfare.

From the perspective of the national interest, it seems desirable that the benefit of this reduction of transaction costs accrues to the home country. In the long-run equilibrium situation with well-functioning markets, the domestic consumer will eventually gain all of the benefits. However, from the perspective of international solidarity, it may be desirable for others to profit from the welfare gain as well, preferably to alleviate poverty in the world. In that sense, good transaction management does not only improve prosperity at home, but it can also contribute to the welfare gains in the poor regions of the world. It should be mentioned, however, that there are still some snags to resolve – with respect to the global distribution problem – of exploiting increased trade opportunities, such as negotiations in the WTO (Doha Round) show.

2.2 FRAGMENTATION OF PRODUCTION

The trend of ongoing global specialization and the division of labour has the effect that production chains are more and more split into various parts. The result is an increasing *fragmentation of production*. Those parts of the chain that can be produced elsewhere at a lower price become outsourced. In fact, this fragmentation of production has so drastically changed the nature of trade that a different approach to trade theory is needed. No longer do comparative advantages in the production of goods and services explain trade flows. Instead, comparative advantages in performing tasks are the dominant determinant of international trade flows. World trade has become a *trade in tasks* as Grossman and Rossi-Hansberg (2006, 2008) argue (see also Chapters 4 and 6).

This fragmentation of production takes place both nationally and globally. At the national level, there is an increasing use of specialist subcontractors and suppliers. The number of self-employed people without personnel has significantly increased in the recent period in the Netherlands: from 397000 in 1996 to 705000 in 2010. This is an increase of almost 80 per cent in 14 years. At the global level, the fragmentation of production and ongoing specialization is a major characteristic of the process of globalization. Thanks to a steady reduction of transaction costs it has become increasingly attractive to produce or buy components of products abroad. Outsourcing and the establishment of foreign branches (in the statistics recorded as FDI) are its visible effects. Here, the strategic decisions of whether to 'make or buy' and where to locate production – the location decision – are made by comparing lower production costs with higher transaction costs (see also Section 5.2).

Globalization and the increasing share of transaction costs in total costs make it possible for an individual firm, but also for a country as a whole, not only to specialize in the field of production, but also in the field of fostering transactions and the coordination that is needed for these transactions to become and remain profitable. The latter is what happens in a transaction economy, assuming that it has a comparative advantage in making profitable transactions. In other words, it has a comparative advantage as a trading nation. Good and innovative *transaction management* – that is, always finding new ways to create value in transactions – is needed to safeguard the comparative advantage in this field. This 'specialization' of a transaction economy (or orchestration economy) implies that other countries, because of their specific comparative advantages such as the availability of raw materials, cheap labour and/or specific technical knowledge, will specialize in certain types of production or assembly. Of course, this is not a static situation. For instance, countries that are now specializing in assembly may acquire knowledge that allows them to fulfil the role of orchestrator at a later stage. In that case, comparative advantages will relate more and more to the specific type of orchestration a country has knowledge about.

2.3   SUPPLY CHAIN MANAGEMENT

The splitting of the production chain into various component parts is relevant for what in a broad sense is labelled supply chain management (SCM). As a matter of fact, due to the fragmentation of production induced by changes in transaction costs, supply chains become longer and longer. They also become more complex. On the other hand, good management of supply chains, where transaction costs are kept as low as possible, allows an enhanced complexity of supply chains. That is why this section pays attention to SCM. The question is what role SCM plays in a transaction economy where creating value in transactions is a key factor to the competitive position of the firm and/or the country.

2.3.1   SCM is not just Logistics

This role reflects what activities can and cannot be considered the essence of SCM. In other words, how SCM is defined. The literature provides various definitions of SCM that do not explicitly demarcate this concept. In any case, SCM is more than just the logistics that aim at handling the flow of goods at the lowest possible costs. Today a very broad view dominates of what activities should be part of SCM. The relationship between distribution and logistics, and the legal, financial and business services are essential elements in this view of SCM. Innovative techniques in the field of ICT should also be used in support.

This broad description of what SCM can and should do fits perfectly with the ideas of this book on transaction management. It is not sufficient just to have the physical flows of goods well organized. Additionally, the whole process of buying, selling and transit in all links of the chain should be analysed in an integral way with respect to transaction costs. This can then take into account that a forced reduction of costs in a particular link of the chain, for example because of strict delivery requirements, may bring about unnecessarily high costs in the next link of the chain.

It is also important from the policy and strategic management perspective that SCM includes more than just transportation and logistics. In other words, SCM encompasses all the economic activity of firms that aims to connect the various parts in the production and value chain at the lowest possible transaction costs. This includes not only the activities of the firms themselves, but also the services to those firms.

A problem with this broad definition is that it is difficult to statistically calculate the contribution of SCM to total economic activity at the macro level. Of course, it is possible to measure the flow of goods in and out of a country and how much the distribution function adds value. However, the physical flows of goods, and the use of infrastructure to transport these goods, only represent the tip of the iceberg of the underlying economic activity that includes the entire complex of SCM.

As the fragmentation of production progresses and, therefore, the proportion of the intangible part of transaction costs – in this book referred to as the 'soft transaction costs' – in total transaction costs increases, more of that iceberg disappears under water. Elaborating on this metaphor somewhat further: the density of SCM is increasing, which implies an increase in the value of the non-material part of the production. In this way, the fragmentation of production and the shift towards the orchestrating function contributes to a further dematerialization of production and trade. Given the environmental damage caused by the physical part of the distribution function, this is a positive development.

This is not to say that the environmental impact of the physical distribution function is also declining in absolute terms. To return to the metaphor of the iceberg: the increasing fragmentation of production may indeed cause soft transaction costs to become more important, but because of an overall growth in transactions, the iceberg of SCM becomes so much larger that the visible part may also increase. That would imply a larger burden for the environment. This aspect needs further investigation, especially the answer to the question of whether a growing importance of transactions in economic activity can be associated with a decrease or increase in the use of the environmental space because of the physical distribution of goods.

This latter aspect is related to the degree of dematerialization of production. This means that the value of a unit of volume of production increases. Consequently the dematerialization of production, which seems an obvious trend in a transaction economy, will, *ceteris paribus*, lead to a relative reduction in environmental pressure. Yet, this does not imply that this pressure will also decline in absolute value. Possibly, the adverse effects of the increase in global economic activity that good transaction management brings about through more demand for transport may outweigh the positive effects of dematerialization of production on the environment. That is why the negative externalities that the physical distribution function brings about deserve the constant attention of the public authorities. Technological innovation, triggered by strict regulations but through creative solutions in distribution methods, can set an example. In its function of 'first-mover advantage', it might even be beneficial to economic activity. This is the so-called 'Porter hypothesis' on the benefits of environmental innovation.

3. Empirics of the hub function of transaction economies

This chapter provides data on the influence of globalization on trade flows, and more specifically on how some European transaction economies fulfil their function as a hub in the trade flows between Europe and the rest of the world. The focus is on the transaction function of the Netherlands, which has a special role as a gateway to Europe, with large trade surpluses to the EU and trade deficits to Asia and the Middle East. To a lesser extent, this is also true for Belgium. The reverse holds for the hub function of Switzerland. That country buys in Europe and sells to the rest of the world. The chapter also looks at Singapore, which has a specific role as a trade hub in South East Asia. Attention is paid to transit trade and re-exports.

3.1 WORLD TRADE IN THE ERA OF GLOBALIZATION

A characteristic of globalization with ongoing specialization and fragmentation of production is that trade is growing faster than production. This is illustrated in Tables 3.1 and 3.2, which present the average yearly real GDP and trade growth in various countries and parts of the world during the last decades.

Table 3.1 shows that GDP growth has been relatively moderate in the G7 between 1981 and 2007. Japan, especially, witnessed low growth rates between 1996 and 2007. The moderate GDP growth in these countries is linked to productivity increases. A major development is the rapid growth of the BRIC countries in the last decades. Table 3.1 shows that these countries not only witnessed a catch-up with the western world and experienced relatively high GDP growth rates, but that the trade growth of these countries was even higher. Especially in the period 1996–2007 trade growth has far exceeded GDP growth in Brazil, China and India, indicating that GDP growth in the BRIC countries has been boosted for a considerable part by trade growth. In other emerging markets such as Indonesia, Singapore and South Africa trade growth seems to be more in line with GDP growth

Table 3.1   Difference between trade growth and GDP growth for G7 and emerging markets (in real terms)

Economy	Growth in trade volume (annually; in %) (1)[c]		Real GDP growth (annually; in %) (2)		Difference between trade and GDP growth (1 minus 2)	
	'81–'95	'96–'07	'81–'95	'96–'07	'81–'95	'96–'07
G7[a]	4.74	5.33	2.70	2.46	2.04	2.86
Canada	6.30	4.92	2.48	3.25	3.82	1.68
Japan	4.81	3.59	3.23	1.31	1.58	2.28
United States	5.07	5.68	3.02	3.18	2.05	2.50
Emerging markets						
BRIC[a,b]	–	12.53	–	7.07	–	5.46
Brazil	6.63	6.54	2.16	2.75	4.47	3.79
India	–	11.54	–	6.74	–	4.80
China	12.59	15.91	10.33	9.50	2.27	6.41
Other						
Indonesia	6.33	4.78	6.89	3.38	−0.56	1.40
Singapore	11.03	7.28	7.92	5.47	3.11	1.81
South Africa	2.22	4.91	1.32	3.46	0.90	1.45

Notes:
a.   Real GDP-weighted average.
b.   BRIC excluding Russian Federation.
c.   Trade volume is based on an average of the import and export volume index. These indices are derived as the ratio of the import (export) value indices to the corresponding unit value indices.

Sources: World Bank for trade statistics; USDA for real GDP statistics.

with the exception of Singapore between 1981 and 1995. On the whole it seems that the gap between trade growth and GDP growth has widened over time.

Table 3.2 presents the growth rates for some European countries. It shows unambiguously that trade growth has consistently outpaced real GDP growth rates in the period 1981–2007. The table also provides evidence in favour of a widening of the gap between trade and GDP growth over time. Trade has taken up a more prominent role in Western Europe. Not only traditional trading nations such as the Netherlands and Switzerland experienced a growing reliance on trade between 1996 and 2007, also the more production-orientated countries such as France and Germany seem to have increasingly focused on trade. The next chapter discusses the new trade theory, which gives an explanation and

Table 3.2   Difference between trade growth and GDP growth for Europe (in real terms)

Economy	Growth in trade volume (annually; in %) (1)[d]		Real GDP growth (annually; in %) (2)		Difference between trade and GDP growth (1 minus 2)	
	'81–'95	'96–'07	'81–'95	'96–'07	'81–'95	'96–'07
EU-15[a,b]	–	5.85	–	2.30	–	3.55
Belgium	–	5.05	–	2.22	–	2.83
Denmark	4.24	4.65	1.54	2.27	2.70	2.38
France	3.44	7.56	2.07	2.21	1.37	5.35
Germany	3.93	7.21	2.01	1.55	1.92	5.66
Italy	4.64	2.61	1.93	1.39	2.71	1.22
Netherlands	4.61	6.76	2.20	2.45	2.40	4.31
Spain	4.53	7.28	2.41	3.83	2.12	3.45
United Kingdom	4.67	4.83	2.36	2.80	2.32	2.03
Europe (n.e.s.)						
Switzerland	2.73[c]	4.51	1.31	1.80	1.43	2.71

Notes:
a.   Real GDP-weighted average.
b.   EU-15 excluding Finland and Luxembourg; Greece is excluded as of 2001.
c.   Average is calculated over the 1989 through 1995 period.
d.   Trade volume is based on an average of the import and export volume index. These indices are derived as the ratio of the import (export) value indices to the corresponding unit value indices.

Sources: World Bank for trade statistics; USDA for real GDP statistics.

focuses on opening the black box of the production function. This new theory may also provide an explanation of why the character of trade flows has changed in this era of globalization.

This section zooms in on a number of relatively small modern European economies, where trade plays a prominent role in economic activity. These can, therefore, be regarded as transaction economies. A closer look at the sizes of trade flows from and to these countries illustrates their position in international trade.

3.1.1   The Netherlands

The Netherlands has, as a commercial nation, a special position because of its location as a gateway to Europe. Because of this hub function it is, in the branding of the country, referred to as 'Hub Holland' ('hup Holland hup' being the supporting yell for the national football team). Figure 3.1

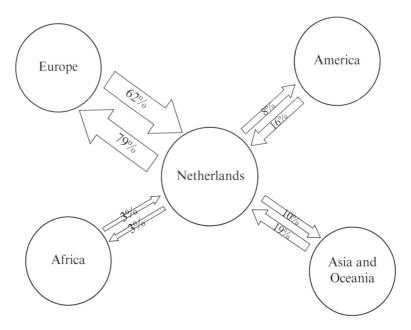

Source: International Trade Center (ITC).

Figure 3.1   Share of continents in imports and exports to and from the Netherlands (2008)

illustrates this hub function in a chart with the relative sizes of trade flows between various continents and the Netherlands. The chart clearly shows that this position as a gateway to Europe leads to a huge trade surplus with the rest of Europe. The reverse is true for trade with America, Asia and Oceania. With these continents, the Netherlands has a trade deficit, which means that the country buys more from these continents than it sells to them. This implies that this country acts as Europe's purchaser: it buys traded goods from the rest of the world and sells them on to the European hinterland. The figure shows that trade with Africa is relatively small. Yet, the position of the Netherlands as purchaser from the rest of the world to Europe should not be exaggerated. The largest proportion of imports originates from other European countries.

Figure 3.2 gives a further breakdown of import and export shares with respect to other European countries (with exports adding up to 79 per cent and imports to 62 per cent). This chart shows the importance of trade between the Netherlands and Germany. No less than 22 per cent of Dutch exports go to Germany and 18 per cent of imports come from Germany.

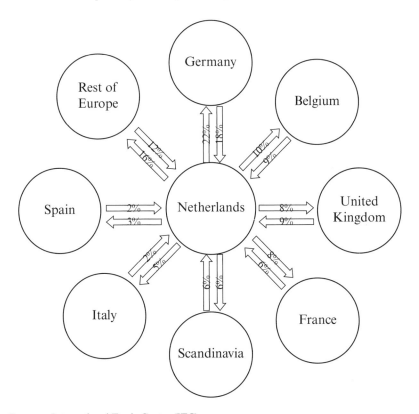

Source: International Trade Center (ITC).

Figure 3.2   *Share of European countries in imports and exports to and from the Netherlands (2008)*

But the Netherlands also has a substantial trade surplus with France (2 per cent), Italy (3 per cent) and the combined group of other European countries (4 per cent).

Table 3.3 gives the composition of trade in goods and services with respect to different categories. It shows that the Netherlands has a considerable export surplus in the agricultural sector (food and animal products), in the petroleum and chemicals sectors, in machinery and in transport services. By contrast, minerals and manufactures are imported to a considerable extent. Noteworthy and somewhat unexpectedly, given the relative size of the financial sector in the Netherlands, this sector shows a relatively small surplus in the trade balance. Finally the trade balance with respect to tourism is negative.

Table 3.3   Composition of trade in the Netherlands (in € bn, 2009)

	Imports	Exports	Balance (exports– imports)	Balance (in % of total imports)
Total goods	**274.0**	**309.4**	**35.4**	**12.9%**
Animal and animal products	6.5	13.4	6.9	2.5%
Vegetable products	12.7	19.1	6.4	2.3%
Foodstuffs	13.2	21.0	7.9	2.9%
Mineral products	44.6	39.0	−5.6	−2.1%
Chemicals and allied industries	36.8	47.4	10.6	3.9%
Plastics / rubbers	8.7	14.7	6.0	2.2%
Raw hides, skins, leather and furs	0.8	0.8	0.1	0.0%
Wood and wood products	6.9	5.9	−1.0	−0.4%
Textiles	8.1	7.3	−0.7	−0.3%
Footwear / headgear	2.0	1.7	−0.2	−0.1%
Stone / glass	3.2	2.7	−0.5	−0.2%
Metals	15.3	16.2	1.0	0.4%
Machinery / electrical	62.4	71.4	9.1	3.3%
Transportation	14.7	11.2	−3.5	−1.3%
Miscellaneous	16.8	16.0	−0.8	−0.3%
Service	21.5	21.5	−0.1	0.0%
Total services	**61.4**	**66.9**	**5.5**	**9.0%**
Transportation services	13.2	18.2	5.0	8.1%
Travel services	14.9	8.9	−6.0	−9.8%
Financial and business services	32.0	37.5	5.5	9.0%
Other services	1.3	2.3	1.1	1.7%
Total goods and services	**335.5**	**376.4**	**40.9**	**12.2%**

Notes: Trade in goods is specified along HS-2 digit level. Trade in service is specified along Balance of Payments (BPM5) level.

Source: International Trade Center (ITC).

In addition to the data on the distribution function of the Netherlands presented above, it is also of interest to consider some illustrative data for *changes* in trade flows. Table 3.4 shows that the share of goods and services imports for intermediate use in production has increased sharply over the period illustrated. It suggests that the Dutch economy has become increasingly involved in the process of the international fragmentation of production. Given these developments, it is remarkable that the imports of wholesale services have increased faster than the imports of wholesale goods. According to data from the National Accounts (NA), the ratio of imports of goods and services, which was 2.65 in 1995, fell to 2.02 in 2005.

Table 3.4   *Average share in GNP of imports for intermediate use in the Netherlands*

Period	Average share in per cent
1980–1989	27
1990–1999	30
2000–2007	33

Table 3.5   *Destination and source of the Netherlands' trade in parts and components*

Region	Export share in %		Average yearly increase in export share in % (1996–2006)	Average yearly increase in export value of parts and components in % (1996–2006)	Import share in %		Average yearly increase in import share in % (1996–2006)	Average yearly increase in import value of parts and components in % (1996–2006)
	1996	2006			1996	2006		
All countries	100	100	–	11.8	100	100	–	9.2
EU	69.4	62.4	−1.0	10.6	65.9	46.4	−3.2	5.2
CEECs	1.6	8.1	34.1	21.6	1.0	2.8	12.2	21.7
Asia	12.3	17.2	4.5	17.1	16.5	35.3	8.9	19.8
BRIC countries								
Brazil	0.5	0.3	−1.7	9.8	0.2	0.1	4.2	13.6
Russia	0.4	2.0	17.4	31.3	0.0	0.1	19.8	29.6
India	0.5	0.5	4.2	15.6	0.2	0.2	3.5	11.9
China	1.1	2.0	15.3	29.6	1.3	9.2	30.9	43.1

Within Dutch manufacturing industry, most opportunities to outsource tasks and services abroad can be found in the machinery and transport equipment (MTE) industries. A study by Berenschot Research (2005) shows that in 2001–2004 almost half the jobs in this sector were moved abroad.

In line with the general trends in world trade, the extent to which the Netherlands is playing its role in the fragmentation of production is reflected in the growing importance of trade in parts and components (Table 3.5). In absolute terms, the import of parts and components in the machinery sectors, in the electrical machinery sector and in the transport equipment sector increased during the period 1996–2006 by 130 per cent, amounting to €37.7 billion. In relative terms the import share of parts and components in the total production value of the above sectors is calculated to have risen from 40.9 per cent to 70.1 per cent. These imports increasingly come from non-EU countries, as illustrated by the fact that the share of EU countries in the import of parts and components in the period mentioned above fell by 19 per cent. The share of Asia more than doubled during the same period. Of the BRIC countries, China accounts for by far the largest part of this increase.

The picture for the export of parts and components is different. The share of exports to EU countries seems to have only slightly decreased in the period 1996–2006. This can partly be explained by the large role of re-exports in the Netherlands (see later). It seems that the Netherlands buys parts and components from the rest of the world and sells them to the European hinterland. A second part of the explanation lies in the increased share of exports to Central and Eastern European (CEE) countries that have joined the EU. The export of parts and components to CEE countries exceeds the imports of this category from these countries. This is not the case with Asia, and with China in particular. It suggests that more assembly operations are outsourced from the Netherlands to CEE countries than to India and China. This again illustrates the pivotal role of the Netherlands between Asian countries and the European hinterland. It also illustrates that the location decision with respect to outsourcing depends upon the comparative advantages in skills and performing specific tasks. Apparently, for assembly operations orchestrated from the Netherlands, CEE countries have comparative advantages to India and China.

3.1.2   Belgium

The hub function of Belgium – a country that as a transaction economy seems to be in a similar position to the Netherlands – is illustrated in Figure 3.3. Belgium also fulfils a role as purchaser for Europe, albeit to a lesser extent than the Netherlands. Yet, trade flows between Belgium and the other European countries are even larger than in the case of the Netherlands. Figure 3.4 shows that Germany and France are the main trading partners of Belgium in Europe. It is interesting to note that the balance-of-payments position of Belgium to most other EU countries is positive, as exports to these countries are larger than imports from these countries, with the Netherlands as an obvious exception. It indicates that the Netherlands also fulfils a role as purchaser for Belgium.

Table 3.6 shows that with respect to the trade in goods Belgium has a considerable surplus in the chemical and allied industries. Not only is this sector Belgium's most important export sector, but also the volume of imports of this sector is highest of all sectors distinguished in the

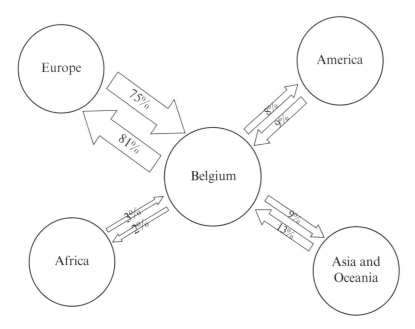

Source: International Trade Center (ITC).

Figure 3.3   Share of continents in imports and exports to and from Belgium (2008)

table. With respect to services, the financial and business services show a large surplus. It seems that, given the way these trade statistics are collected, financial and business services contribute more to the positive trade balance in Belgium than in the Netherlands. Like the Netherlands, Belgium has a sizeable negative balance of travel services.

3.1.3   Denmark

In contrast with Belgium and the Netherlands, Denmark seems to be much more a production-oriented economy than a transaction-oriented economy. Figure 3.5 shows that Denmark is a net exporter to the rest of the world and a net importer from Europe. The other Scandinavian countries are Denmark's largest trading partners within Europe (see Figure 3.6). There seems to be remarkably little trade between Denmark and the large southern European countries, France, Italy and Spain.

Table 3.7 shows that the balance-of-payment surplus of goods trades in Denmark mainly stems from large exports of animals and animal

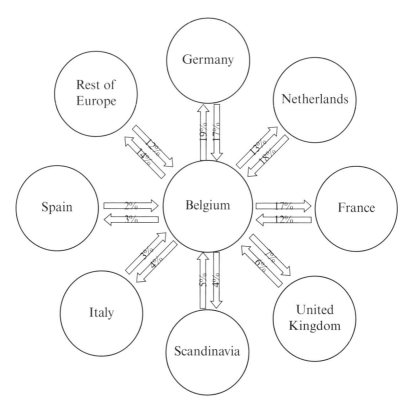

Source: International Trade Center (ITC).

Figure 3.4   Share of European countries in imports and exports to and from Belgium (2008)

products, but chemicals and minerals also contribute to Denmark's export surplus. However, the surplus of the service sectors is considerably bigger in Denmark. These are mainly transportation services – Denmark has a large container shipping company – and other services. On the other hand, travel services and – much in contrast with the Netherlands, Belgium and Switzerland (see later) – financial services contribute negatively to the trade-in-services balance.

3.1.4   Luxembourg

Luxembourg can be considered as a small and somewhat atypical transaction economy. Table 3.8 shows that this country has a huge deficit on its

Table 3.6   Composition of trade in Belgium (in € bn, 2009)

	Imports	Exports	Balance (exports– imports)	Balance (in % of total imports)
Total goods	**252.2**	**265.3**	**13.0**	**5.2%**
Animal and animal products	5.0	6.0	1.0	0.4%
Vegetable products	9.5	8.2	−1.3	−0.5%
Foodstuffs	10.1	12.5	2.4	1.0%
Mineral products	31.8	20.4	−11.5	−4.5%
Chemicals and allied industries	59.9	71.6	11.7	4.6%
Plastics / rubbers	12.9	20.9	8.0	3.2%
Raw hides, skins, leather and furs	0.8	0.9	0.1	0.0%
Wood and wood products	7.3	7.0	−0.3	−0.1%
Textiles	8.9	10.5	1.6	0.6%
Footwear / headgear	2.0	2.7	0.6	0.3%
Stone / glass	10.8	13.0	2.2	0.9%
Metals	17.3	20.3	3.0	1.2%
Machinery / electrical	33.6	30.6	−3.0	−1.2%
Transportation	28.0	26.8	−1.3	−0.5%
Miscellaneous	11.9	10.9	−1.1	−0.4%
Service	2.4	3.2	0.8	0.3%
Total services	**53.0**	**58.3**	**5.3**	**10.0%**
Transportation services	12.8	15.1	2.3	4.3%
Travel services	12.8	7.0	−5.8	−10.9%
Financial and business services	26.7	34.2	7.5	14.2%
Other services	0.7	2.0	1.3	2.5%
Total goods and services	**305.2**	**323.6**	**18.3**	**6.0%**

Notes: Trade in goods is specified along HS-2 digit level. Trade in service is specified along Balance of Payments (BPM5) level.

Source: International Trade Center (ITC).

goods balance, which is more than compensated by an enormous surplus on the balance for services. These are mainly financial and business services, which bring prosperity to this country that is one of the richest in the world. Apart from special financial institutes, such as trust offices, which are located in Luxembourg, much money in this country is also earned by the personnel of international institutions, such as the European Court of Justice, the European Court of Auditors, the Statistical Office of the European Communities (Eurostat) and other vital EU establishments. The Secretariat of the European Parliament is also located in Luxembourg, although the Parliament usually meets elsewhere.

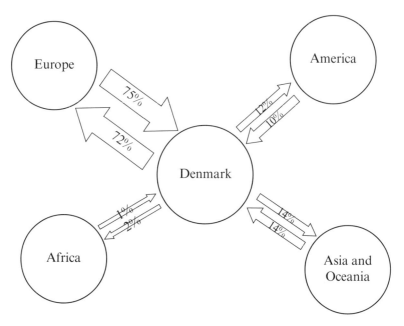

Source: International Trade Center (ITC).

Figure 3.5   Share of continents in imports and exports to and from Denmark (2008)

3.1.5   Switzerland

Switzerland, a country surrounded by EU members but not an EU member itself, can also be regarded as a transaction economy. Yet, Figure 3.7 illustrates that the character of the hub function of Switzerland differs considerably from that of Belgium and the Netherlands. Whereas these trading nations on the North Sea are purchasers in the world and sell to the European hinterland, Switzerland buys in Europe and sells these goods and services to the rest of the world. Figure 3.8 shows that Switzerland purchases much from its large neighbour Germany and also, somewhat surprisingly, from Belgium. Trade with its other big neighbours, France and Italy, is relatively modest.

From Table 3.9 it appears that the surplus on the goods balance of Switzerland mainly stems from large exports of chemicals and allied industries, whereas there is also ample trade in machinery and electrical equipment. The reason is that some large multinationals in these industries, but also in the pharmaceutical industry, have their headquarters

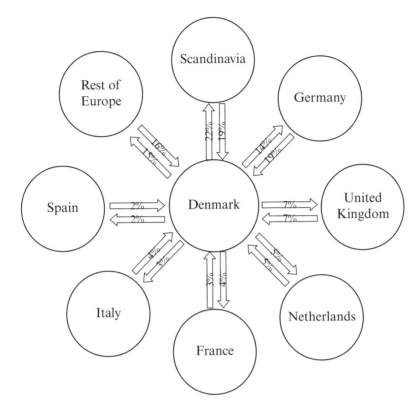

Source: International Trade Center (ITC).

Figure 3.6 *Share of European countries in imports and exports to and from Denmark (2008)*

in Switzerland. With respect to services, financial and business services are dominant. Obviously this has to do with the specific regulations and the size of the Swiss banks. Also the tourist industry in mountainous Switzerland adds to its large surplus on the trade balance of services.

3.2 THE HUB FUNCTION OF SINGAPORE

It is interesting to compare the hub function in trade of the transaction economies in Europe, discussed in the previous subsection, with Singapore, which fulfils a similar role in Southeast Asia. Singapore was colonized in 1819 by the British East India Company. During World War II, the island

Table 3.7   Composition of trade in Denmark (in € bn, 2008)

	Imports	Exports	Balance (exports– imports)	Balance (in % of total imports)
Total goods	**74.6**	**78.6**	**4.0**	**5.4%**
Animal and animal products	2.5	7.6	5.1	6.8%
Vegetable products	2.9	2.0	−0.9	−1.2%
Foodstuffs	4.2	4.9	0.7	1.0%
Mineral products	6.5	9.5	3.1	4.1%
Chemicals and allied industries	6.0	9.4	3.4	4.5%
Plastics / rubbers	3.8	2.3	−1.5	−2.1%
Raw hides, skins, leather and furs	0.5	0.9	0.4	0.5%
Wood and wood products	3.6	1.9	−1.7	−2.3%
Textiles	4.1	3.7	−0.4	−0.5%
Footwear / headgear	0.8	0.5	−0.3	−0.4%
Stone / glass	1.5	1.7	0.2	0.3%
Metals	7.3	5.4	−1.9	−2.5%
Machinery / electrical	17.2	17.7	0.5	0.6%
Transportation	8.3	3.4	−4.9	−6.6%
Miscellaneous	4.8	6.1	1.3	1.8%
Service	0.7	1.7	1.0	1.3%
Total services	**42.6**	**49.5**	**6.9**	**16.3%**
Transportation services	22.7	32.1	9.4	22.1%
Travel services	6.7	4.6	−2.1	−4.9%
Financial and business services	11.4	1.8	−9.6	−22.6%
Other services	1.8	11.0	9.2	21.7%
Total goods and services	**117.2**	**128.1**	**10.9**	**9.3%**

Notes: Trade in goods is specified along HS-2 digit level. Trade in service is specified along Balance of Payments (BPM5) level.

Source: International Trade Center (ITC).

became occupied by the Japanese empire, but reverted to British rule in 1945. In 1959, it achieved internal self-government. The country was poor and politically unstable. However, under the prime ministership of Lee Kuan Yew from 1959 until 1990, an interesting mix of authoritarianism in politics and liberalism in economics was created. In that period the country's economic performance was spectacular. Singapore welcomed many international businesses to invest directly in the country and it is an excellent example of how to take profit from ongoing globalization. A reason for the successful growth of Singapore is that it is very effective and able to change and adapt easily. The government managed to mobilize

Table 3.8   Composition of trade in Luxembourg (in € bn, 2009)

	Imports	Exports	Balance (exports–imports)	Balance (in % of total imports)
Total goods	**13.4**	**9.2**	**−4.2**	**−31.4%**
Total services	**25.9**	**43.9**	**18**	**69.6%**
Transportation services	1.1	2.3	1.1	4.4%
Travel services	2.6	3	0.4	1.4%
Financial and business services	21.4	37.6	16.2	62.7%
Other services	0.7	1	0.3	1.1%
Total goods and services	**39.2**	**53**	**13.8**	**35.2%**

Notes: Trade in goods is specified along HS-2 digit level. Trade in service is specified along Balance of Payments (BPM5) level.

Source: International Trade Center (ITC).

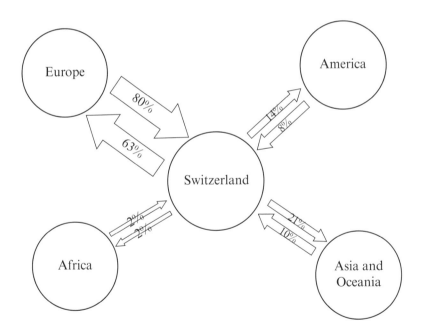

Source: International Trade Center (ITC).

Figure 3.7   Share of continents in imports and exports to and from Switzerland (2008)

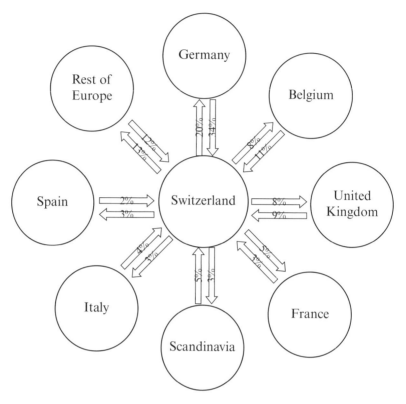

Source: International Trade Center (ITC).

Figure 3.8   *Share of European countries in imports and exports to and
                from Switzerland (2008)*

all production inputs in Singapore, introduced effective policies, and provided many Singaporeans with good education.

Nowadays, Singapore keeps reforming the government, procedures,
legal systems and policies to ensure that it remains a good place to do
business and provide the flexibility these unstable times need. This way
Singapore has reached a unique advantage, namely being flexible and efficient in its governing system. Trading with Singapore is easy; doing business in and with Singapore is easy, which gives a competitive advantage
over other countries. Investors in Singapore are very well protected by
an efficient and responsive judicial system. In Singapore it takes 150 days
on average to enforce a commercial contract in court, the fastest time in
the world. Another example of efficient governing is the tax reforms that

Table 3.9   Composition of trade in Switzerland (in € bn, 2008)

	Imports	Exports	Balance (exports– imports)	Balance (in % of total imports)
Total goods	**124.7**	**136.4**	**11.6**	**9.3%**
Animal and animal products	1.3	0.5	−0.8	−0.6%
Vegetable products	2.6	0.7	−1.9	−1.6%
Foodstuffs	3.8	3.6	−0.2	−0.2%
Mineral products	11.4	4.2	−7.2	−5.8%
Chemicals and allied industries	22.5	44.2	21.7	17.0%
Plastics / rubbers	5.4	4.2	−1.2	−1.0%
Raw hides, skins, leather and furs	0.8	0.4	−0.3	−0.3%
Wood and wood products	4.8	2.9	−1.9	−1.6%
Textiles	5.2	2.5	−2.7	−2.1%
Footwear / headgear	1.0	0.2	−0.8	−0.6%
Stone / glass	10.6	9.7	−0.9	−0.7%
Metals	9.7	7.4	−2.4	−1.9%
Machinery / electrical	24.0	29.2	5.2	4.2%
Transportation	10.6	4.0	−6.6	−5.3%
Miscellaneous	11.2	22.9	11.7	9.4%
Service	–	–	–	–
Total services	**24.8**	**53.1**	**28.3**	**114.1%**
Transportation services	5.7	4.4	−1.3	−5.0%
Travel services	7.5	9.8	2.4	9.6%
Financial and business services	2.8	37.6	34.8	140.6%
Other services	8.9	1.2	−7.7	−31.0%
Total goods and services	**149.5**	**189.4**	**39.9**	**26.7%**

Notes: Trade in goods is specified along HS-2 digit level. Trade in service is specified along Balance of Payments (BPM5) level.

Source: International Trade Center (ITC).

the government introduced during the Asian financial crisis. It lowered business costs through a series of tax cuts, rebates and exemptions. It also removed the stamp duty on almost all documents, making Singapore one of the best places to do business. For exporting and importing, in Singapore only four documents are needed. It seems to be the fastest country in handling export and import documentary: only five and three days respectively are needed.

Some formal institutions and other aspects of the system explain why the Singapore system has worked reasonably well over the past 50 years. There is an important anti-corruption agency, which has unfettered powers of investigation and arrest. Also, public servants have adequate salaries. Lee Kuan Yew wanted a third of the nation's best brains to be working in the public sector.

It seems that Singapore has been designed as a kind of ideal transaction economy. It was able to build up its position from scratch, under the strong leadership of Lee Kuan Yew, who can be regarded as a prototype of a benign dictator, although formally operating in a democratic setting. It is interesting to note that a Dutchman played a prominent role in transforming Singapore to a modern business centre. Albert Winsemius was an economic advisor of the government from 1961 until 1983. A year after his first visit to Singapore, he presented a 10-year economic development plan to the government. He saw Singapore as an entrepot trade country. Trade barriers had to disappear completely, according to Winsemius. This was needed to become the world's financial and industrial centre and an international junction for transporting over land and sea. Winsemius also advised the government about the large-scale housing projects in Singapore. This would make Singapore more attractive to investors. Finally, Winsemius managed to get Philips, Shell and Exxon to Singapore.

Figure 3.9 illustrates that Singapore has a role as purchaser from the world and seller to the nearby regions of Asia and Oceania. In a way it is similar to the role the Netherlands and Belgium fulfil in Europe. China and Malaysia are the biggest trading partners of Singapore in Asia, but the largest trade surpluses are with Hong Kong and Indonesia.

The major surplus on the goods balance of Singapore stems from the exports of machinery and electrical equipment, as reported in Table 3.10. This is by far the most important sector of economic activity in Singapore, as also the imports of this sector are the largest of all the sectors considered. The chemical and allied industries show a substantial balance surplus as well. On the other hand, Singapore appears to be a large net importer of minerals, which is, in terms of total trade (imports plus exports), the second-largest sector of the country. Total service trade in Singapore is also substantial. Financial and business services are the most important here, but the surplus is much smaller than that of Switzerland. It indicates that the activities of the financial sector in Singapore are more in line with those in the Netherlands and Belgium than with those in Switzerland. A reason may be that Singapore is an important seaport and is not land-locked like Switzerland. Transportation services also play an important role in Singapore. There is a negative balance in travel services. Figure 3.10 shows that trade between Asia and Singapore mainly relates to countries in East Asia. China is important in this respect but not dominant.

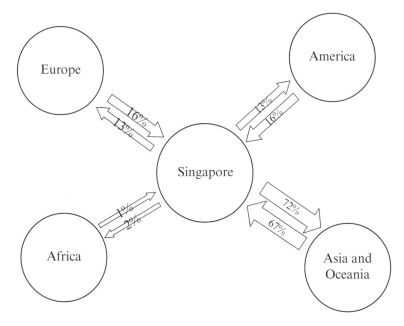

Source: International Trade Center (ITC).

Figure 3.9 *Share of continents in imports and exports to and from Singapore (2009)*

3.3 TRANSIT TRADE AND RE-EXPORTS

In many cases, value added from economic activity in transaction economies stems from processing foreign imported goods, which after processing are resold abroad. If the added value is only limited, these imports and subsequent exports are registered as transit trade or as re-exports. Goods are regarded as transit goods if they pass through a country without the involvement of an owner of that country. Transit trade remains outside the trade statistics of the NA and is, therefore, not included in the previous figures and tables on trade flows. Examples are goods that are transported through a country but which do not change owner or are not further processed. In the case of re-exports, goods are temporarily owned by citizens or firms of the country in which these imports and exports are registered. Examples in the case of the Netherlands include the import of computers from China and adding software to the computers to adapt them to the European market. The important issues here are to what extent

Table 3.10   Composition of trade in Singapore (in € bn, 2009)

	Imports	Exports	Balance (exports– imports)	Balance (in % of total imports)
Total goods	**176.2**	**193.5**	**17.2**	**9.8%**
Animal and animal products	1.6	0.4	−1.2	−0.7%
Vegetable products	1.5	0.7	−0.8	−0.5%
Foodstuffs	2.8	3.1	0.2	0.1%
Mineral products	43.3	29.5	−13.7	−7.8%
Chemicals and allied industries	8.9	17.3	8.4	4.8%
Plastics / rubbers	3.4	5.9	2.5	1.4%
Raw hides, skins, leather and furs	0.5	0.3	−0.2	−0.1%
Wood and wood products	1.5	1.6	0.1	0.0%
Textiles	1.8	1.3	−0.6	−0.3%
Footwear / headgear	0.3	0.1	−0.2	−0.1%
Stone / glass	5.3	4.3	−1.0	−0.6%
Metals	8.7	5.9	−2.8	−1.6%
Machinery / electrical	74.9	95.8	20.9	11.8%
Transportation	9.4	7.1	−2.3	−1.3%
Miscellaneous	7.1	7.1	0.0	0.0%
Service	5.2	13.1	7.9	4.5%
Total services	**59.1**	**65.2**	**6.1**	**10.3%**
Transportation services	19.0	22.0	3.0	5.1%
Travel services	11.3	6.6	−4.7	−8.0%
Financial and business services	28.4	36.3	7.9	13.4%
Other services	0.4	0.3	−0.1	−0.2%
Total goods and services	**235.2**	**258.7**	**23.3**	**9.9%**

Notes: Trade in goods is specified along HS-2 digit level. Trade in service is specified along Balance of Payments (BPM5) level.

Source: International Trade Center (ITC).

high technical knowledge is required with respect to processing, logistics knowledge or knowledge of marketing, and how much added value re-exports bring about. Often the distribution function goes far beyond just the physical distribution. It requires a lot of specialist knowledge (see the discussion on SCM in Section 2.3). Moreover, the distribution function forms an integral part of the much broader-based economic activity in a transaction economy.

Unfortunately, there is not much systematic empirical data on transit trade and re-exports. In the Netherlands there has been a debate about whether the growth of re-exports should be considered a favourable

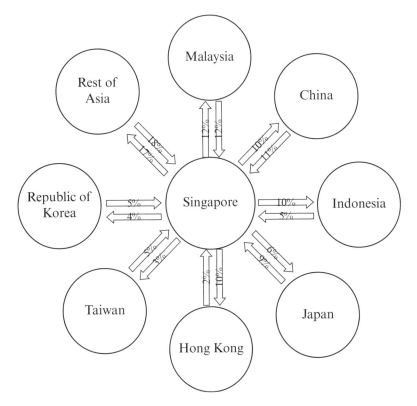

Source: International Trade Center (ITC).

Figure 3.10   *Share of Asian countries in imports and exports to and from Singapore (2009)*

economic development or not. Obviously, added value of re-exports is relatively low so that re-exports contribute less to GDP than exports. A study by Kuypers et al. (2012) uses linked micro-data in order to assess the characteristics of firms which focus on re-exports in their economic activity. It appears that value added per €100 of re-exports is eight times lower than per €100 of exports, respectively €7.5 against €59. Yet it seems that its hub function provides the Netherlands with a comparative advantage for re-exports, as the share of re-exports in total exports has risen from 20 per cent in 1980 to 49 per cent in 2010.

In order to compare developments in the Netherlands with those in other countries, researchers from the Central Planning Bureau (CPB) have collected some scattered data on re-exports in various countries.

Table 3.11   Re-exports as a share of total exports (1995–2000)

	1995	2000
Belgium[a]	28.3%	32.7%
Denmark[a]	14.7%	20.0%
Finland[a]	0.0%	4.1%
France[a]	–	30.6%
Germany	9.9%	13.8%
Hong Kong	64.7%[b]	88.5%
Netherlands[a]	33.1%	42.9%
Singapore	41.2%	42.9%
Sweden[a]	1.8%	2.3%
United Kingdom[a]	5.2%	–

Notes:
a.   The share of re-exports for these countries is calculated on manufactured goods only.
b.   Figure is based on 1990.

Source: Mellens, Noordman and Verbruggen (2007).

Table 3.11, based on a study by Mellens et al. (2007), presents the relative sizes of re-exports in these countries. It is obvious that re-exports have become more important over time. This development is linked with the increasing fragmentation of production and globalization. The table also shows that re-exports are relatively unimportant in countries which are mainly focused on production, such as Denmark, Germany, Sweden and the United Kingdom. On the other hand, the share of re-exports in total exports is sizeable in transaction economies such as Belgium, the Netherlands and Singapore. In Hong Kong almost all exports relate to goods and services which obtained only limited added value after having been imported.

Table 3.12 provides data on the composition of re-exports in the manufacturing sector for some European countries. Computers comprise a relatively large part of re-exports in the Netherlands, the UK and Sweden, whereas Finland seems to have specialised in re-exports of transport equipment.

3.3.1   The Netherlands

Further data on the volumes and values of re-exports and transit trade illustrate the importance of the distribution function in the Netherlands. Since the volume of transit trade is not included in the Dutch trade statistics, other sources for this data are to be used (Kuipers et al., 2003). It has

Table 3.12 Composition of re-exports of manufactures (as percentage of total value, average over 1995–2000)

	Belgium	Denmark	Germany	Finland	France	Netherlands	UK	Sweden
Agriculture and food products; beverages and tobacco	8.0	13.5	4.2	10.6	4.8	8.1	0.0	10.6
Mining and quarrying	13.0	0.1	0.2	0.1	0.2	0.6	18.2	0.0
Textiles and leather products	4.4	15.3	10.9	0.8	6.6	7.0	0.0	17.7
Chemicals and chemical products	17.6	8.8	8.2	0.4	16.5	13.5	0.0	19.1
Basic metals	3.1	3.3	3.2	1.4	6.2	4.3	14.2	3.6
Machinery	8.3	10.0	9.3	5.5	10.9	7.2	0.0	7.4
Computers	4.7	8.8	10.9	8.0	7.1	24.0	29.7	19.3
Radio, television and communication equipment	4.6	9.9	12.7	3.4	9.8	13.6	21.9	3.7
Transport equipment	13.7	11.6	18.3	65.5	19.5	4.7	12.7	10.7
Other products	22.5	18.6	22.2	4.3	18.6	16.9	3.3	7.8
Total	100.0	100.0	100.0	100.0	100.0	100.0	100.0	100.0

Source: Mellens, Noordman and Verbruggen (2007).

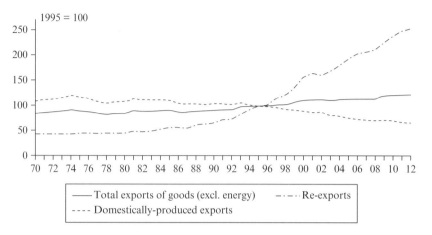

Note: For the period 2008–2010, provisional figures are taken from the National Accounts (Nationale Rekeningen) of Statistics Netherlands (CBS). For 2011 and 2012 figures are based on CPB (Netherlands Bureau for Economic Policy Analysis) estimates.

Source: Mellens, Noordman and Verbruggen (2007).

Figure 3.11   Volumes of domestically-produced exports, re-exports and total exports of manufactures in the Netherlands (1970–2012)

been calculated that transit trade amounted to €150 billion in 2001 with an added value of €2.1 billion (1.5 per cent of turnover). The transit trade also provides employment for 29 700 people. Transit trade witnessed in the period 1987–2001 a 4.2 per cent increase per year. Between 1987 and 1992, this growth averaged 7.4 per cent per year, and after 1992 2.4 per cent per year. The lower growth after 1992 is partly a substitution effect, where a part of the transit trade shifted to re-exports.

For the Netherlands, data on re-exports are available on a more regular basis than for other countries. Re-exports are recorded in the official balance-of-payments statistics. Figure 3.11 illustrates the huge increase in the relative importance of re-exports in this country in the last 40 years. Table 3.13 gives the share of re-exports in total exports for various commodities in the Netherlands. More than half of the exports of machinery and transport equipment consists of re-exports. It is interesting to note that this share increased until the start of the credit crisis in 2007, and decreased thereafter. Re-exports of chemicals and related products have also increased considerably in the last decade, and this increase continued during the credit crisis.

It is obvious that re-exports have become increasingly important in

Table 3.13   *Structure of re-exports of the Netherlands (in € bn, 2002–2009)*

	2002	2003	2004	2005	2006	2007	2008	2009
Food and live animals	6.2	6.4	7.0	7.3	7.9	9.2	10.4	10.0
Beverages and tobacco	0.6	0.5	0.6	0.5	0.6	0.6	0.8	0.7
Crude materials, inedible excl. Fuels	2.9	3.0	4.3	4.7	6.0	6.7	5.7	4.1
Mineral fuels, lubricants, related materials	4.8	4.4	4.7	6.9	10.1	12.3	10.5	9.2
Animal and vegetable oils, fats and waxes	0.5	0.5	0.6	0.7	0.7	0.7	1.1	0.6
Chemicals and related products	11.7	11.7	13.8	15.1	17.2	20.6	24.0	25.4
Manufactured goods	7.6	7.4	8.2	8.7	11.6	13.6	13.3	9.8
Machinery and transport equipment	49.7	49.2	56.0	60.7	66.5	73.0	66.4	56.2
Miscellaneous manufactured articles	13.9	14.7	15.6	17.3	19.2	18.4	22.4	21.1
Commodities not classified elsewhere	0.1	0.1	0.1	0.1	0.2	0.1	0.1	0.4

Source: Statistics Netherlands (CBS statline).

the Netherlands. Yet, in this context, the distribution function of the Netherlands is in the economic policy debate looked upon rather dismissively as 'carrying boxes'. The idea is that this activity yields low profit margins but puts a drain on the environment. Data from Statistics Netherlands (CBS) show that the margins are between 11 per cent and 13 per cent. The assessment of whether re-exports are profitable to the country and contribute to its welfare depend on the way re-exports are defined and on the extent to which production is related to the use of imported raw materials (for example, chemicals and agricultural products). To assess whether the increase in re-exports is good or bad for the economy, one should consider the relationship between added value and labour input. It may be true that a margin of just over 10 per cent is sufficient for a profitable business. The fact that the share of re-exports in the recent period has increased so much is an omen and may indicate that it is profitable indeed.

That is why the negative connotation of this distribution function as just 'carrying boxes' may not be justified. Even in the Golden Age, the Netherlands, and Amsterdam in particular, was already known for its staple market. For the Dutch traders it constituted a major source of income, and the current position of the Netherlands with large transit trade and re-exports can be regarded as a continuation thereof. The qualifications and quantifications of the distribution function of the Netherlands above show how important this function, together with the related services of SCM, are for a transaction economy.

Unfortunately, we still have little insight into the sizes of the transaction costs and, therefore, into the potential competitive advantages that can be obtained by good transaction management in this respect. It is possible to quantify the added value of the logistics and transport sectors, but this concerns only the visible part of the iceberg of SCM (see Chapter 2). An example of the soft transaction costs that have to be taken into account to calculate the costs and benefits of the distribution function are the additional congestion costs of road transport. A part of these costs can be calculated by multiplying the cost of waiting with waiting time in traffic jams (see for example Dewees, 1979). However, these cost calculations do not include the (transaction) costs that arise as people anticipate additional travel time because of road congestion. When this anticipation afterwards proves unnecessary, the additional costs have still been made. It is also possible that other costs are incurred to avoid traffic jams (other, more expensive travel times, for example during the night) so that traffic jams are reduced. In that case, these additional costs bring about positive externalities and the net effect of these additional costs should be included. Moreover, transport that is in principle valuable, or a useful visit, can be abandoned because of long travel times. In other words, if there were no traffic jams, travel would be more profitable. These kinds of costs should be calculated and valued when weighing the societal costs and benefits of the distribution function in combination with SCM, and wishing to make economic activities in this field more profitable and competitive through transaction management.

3.3.2   Singapore and Hong Kong

Mellens et al. (2007) also collected some data on re-exports in Singapore and Hong Kong. Given its share of re-exports within total exports, the phenomenon of re-exports in the transaction economy of Singapore seems to be of similar importance as in the Netherlands. Yet the growth in the share of re-exports, with 4.6 percentage points between 1995 and 2005, is rather modest (Table 3.14). A reason may be that the composition of exports and re-exports in Singapore are more similar than in the Netherlands. The main destination of these re-exports is Malaysia, followed by Hong Kong and China. Less than 10 per cent of the re-exports of Singapore has Europe as its destination, with the UK, Germany and the Netherlands as main importing nations.

Table 3.14   *Re-exports and domestically-produced exports in Singapore (current prices, in Singapore $ bn, 1995–2005)*

	1995	2000	2005	% annual change in value 1996–2005	% annual change in volume 1996–2005
Re-exports	69.0	101.9	175.1	9.8	11.1
Domestically-produced exports	98.5	135.9	207.4	7.7	8.9
Total exports	167.5	237.8	382.5	8.6	9.9
Share of re-exports (in %) [a]	41.2	42.8	45.8		

Note: a.   re-exports divided by total exports. Prior to 2003, data excludes trade with Indonesia.

Source: Mellens, Noordman and Verbruggen (2007).

Table 3.15   *Re-exports and domestically-produced exports in Hong Kong (current prices, in HK $ bn, 1982–2005)*

	1982	1990	2000	2005	% annual change 1983–2005
Re-exports	44.4	414.0	1391.7	2114.1	18.3
Domestically-produced exports	83.0	225.9	181.0	136.0	2.2
Total exports	127.4	639.9	1572.7	2250.2	13.3
Share of re-exports (in %)[a]	34.9	64.7	88.5	94.0	

Note: a.   re-exports divided by total exports.

Source: Mellens, Noordman and Verbruggen (2007).

In contrast to Singapore, trade data for Hong Kong show that re-exports witnessed an enormous growth, especially in the 1980s, and today almost all exports of Hong Kong consist of re-exports (Table 3.15). Hong Kong can be seen as the prototype of a nation which has been completely transformed from a production to a transaction economy. Obviously, China is the main trading partner. In 1995 62 per cent of the re-exports of Hong Kong was 'made in China'. In 2005 about 22 per cent of all trade flows, exclusive of transit trade, of China were shipped via Hong Kong.

3.4 CONCLUSION

The hub function is an important characteristic for trading nations. Whereas the Netherlands and, to a lesser extent, Belgium act as purchasers for Europe, on the other hand Switzerland buys in Europe and sells to the rest of the world. Singapore holds a similar position to the Netherlands and Belgium in Asia: it buys from the rest of the world and sells to the Asian hinterland. Obviously skills to keep specific transaction costs low contribute to these various ways of value creation through the hub function. It appears that re-exports gain importance in these trading nations, albeit that value added in re-exports is much smaller than in production-oriented exports.

4. Transaction cost economics

This chapter discusses a key theme of this book. It explains the theory of transaction cost economics and, from this perspective, looks at the broad significance of transaction costs in the modern economy. It shows what types of transaction costs can be distinguished and how transaction costs affect the working of the economy. Ample attention is paid to the fundamental problem of exchange and to the institutional aspects of solving the game of trust. The role of procurement in the modern strategic management of the firm acts as an example of the importance of transaction costs in industrial organization.

4.1 IMPORTANCE OF TRANSACTION COSTS

The crucial importance of transaction costs in a world with increasing specialization and division of labour has already been amply discussed in the previous chapters. The question now is how transaction costs can be defined and what types of transaction costs can be distinguished and categorized. The fragmentation of production, where the production chains of goods and services are split into a growing number of parts, can be seen as a feature of specialization in the globalizing world. The economic theory of industrial organization partly explains how and to what extent this happens. In an industrial organization with fragmented production, from an analytical perspective, it is essential to distinguish between production costs and transaction costs. Production costs can be defined as all costs that are made within the parts of the production chain, including development costs. Therefore, loosely speaking, transaction costs are all other costs that relate to coordinating and connecting the various parts of the production chain.

From that perspective, *transaction costs* can be defined as *the costs incurred in coordinating and connecting all parts in the production chain.* Hence, a considerable part of transaction costs are in fact coordination costs. As mentioned in Chapter 2, transaction costs relate to both coordination and transfer costs within firms where coordination takes place through the hierarchy (vertical transaction costs), and to costs of outsourcing and trade between firms where coordination takes place via the market mechanism (horizontal transaction costs). Sometimes pseudo-market mechanisms and hybrid forms of governance (for example, through competitive transfer prices, or strategic alliances) are introduced within a firm or between firms to keep these costs low and promote efficiency. Thus, *transaction costs* can also be defined as *all costs of transactions in a broad sense.* These transactions relate to trade transactions between firms and persons, but also to transactions associated with coordination within the firm.

Often these costs relate to the 'hassle' associated with the buying and selling of goods and services and with the relocation of production. A firm that has the ability to create a more attractive market situation for its product or service by reducing the costs of trade can be internationally successful, because this type of cost is important in international trade. Hence, good transaction management is a major quality to enhance the competitive position of a firm.

In the case of 'real' trade through market transactions with horizontal transaction costs, there is a transfer of property rights. In such a situation of market trade, transaction costs relate to finding a suitable trading partner, negotiating, setting up and signing a contract, monitoring compliance with the contract and imposing fines if the agreements are violated. Transaction costs are partly caused by formal trade barriers such as import tariffs, but an important part of these costs stems from informal barriers arising from differences in language and culture, ignorance and lack of trust. This marks the distinction between 'hard' and 'soft' transaction costs.

The section on supply chain management (SCM) already mentioned examples of soft transaction costs. Hard transaction costs include observable costs such as transport costs, import duties and customs tariffs. The soft costs comprise all costs of making and monitoring contracts, information costs, costs due to cultural differences and miscommunication, unwritten laws, trust-building, networking, risk costs, costs due to safety regulations and provisions, and so on. These soft transaction costs are much harder to quantify than the hard transaction costs. It is likely that in this era of globalization these soft transaction costs, where a good business sense is needed to estimate their sizes and to avoid these costs as much as possible, will constitute an increasingly important part of the total costs of doing business. Indeed as the hard costs due to trade liberalization and reducing transport costs decrease, the soft costs gain relative importance. This also follows from the development of SCM where the focus, as stated in Chapter 2, is more and more on lowering soft transaction costs.

Of course, in practice a precise delineation between 'hard' or tangible transaction costs and 'soft' or intangible transaction costs is difficult to make. Yet the distinction is useful from the perspective of transaction management, now that soft transaction costs gain importance over hard transaction costs. It implies that the focus of transaction management should be more and more directed at reduction of soft transaction costs. Such reduction of soft transaction costs at the level of the firm, both in business to business (B2B) relationships and in intrafirm relationships, will enhance the competitive positions of firms and therefore contribute to social welfare. At the national level, a transaction economy may foster its ability to reduce the soft transaction costs and obtain a comparative advantage in that respect.

Hard and soft transaction costs not only play a role in the usual commercial transactions where goods or services change ownership. In the case of hiring personnel, there are also ample transaction costs to take into account: search costs, information costs, application costs, the costs of getting acquainted with the job, learning costs, redundancy costs and all costs of the personnel department, including advertising costs. Indeed, here a contract is a transfer of the ownership of an employee to his or her boss. In addition, the costs of marketing and information costs can partly be regarded as transaction costs (see Box 4.1). Within firms all kinds of departmental meetings, discussions about work routines, regulatory measures and internal compliance bring about transaction costs.

The characterization and history of trading nations shows that traditionally a key competency of these nations has been to foster the (international) division of labour through low transaction costs. Even Adam Smith knew this: to him the Netherlands was the shining example of a trading nation. It is important that the transaction economies are able to maintain that position in the future. Therefore, it is desirable that the challenges offered by the ongoing globalization and fragmentation of production are not only analyzed from the perspective of the theory of international trade, but also from the integration of that theory with the theories of industrial organization and institutional economics. The latter theoretical perspective is also referred to as new institutional economics. This casts a better light on the role that transaction management plays in this respect. The remainder of this chapter elaborates these theoretical perspectives.

4.2   TRANSACTION COST ECONOMICS

The focus of the economic theory of transaction costs is not new. Coase (1937) formulated the first ideas about it more than 75 years ago. The reason for Coase to consider transaction costs was to explain why firms of any size exist in a world where the invisible hand of the market mechanism provides the optimal allocation of goods and resources. In other words, the question is why sometimes the visible hand of the hierarchy is preferred to the invisible hand of the market. The answer has already been given: the allocation of goods through market trade is not free but brings about all kinds of transaction costs. According to this theory of Coase, firm size depends directly on the nature of the transaction. In the case that the (marginal) transactions costs are higher for exchange within the hierarchy than for exchange through the market, it is obvious that parts of the firm are to be split and thereby can benefit from lower transaction costs of trade through the market. The firm size then decreases. The opposite – transaction costs are lower in the hierarchy than through the market – provides an argument for expanding the firm. It is also a reason why a takeover of a firm, or a merger between firms, may be considered. This argument is of current interest now that activist shareholders (private equity, hedge funds) interfere more and more with the strategic policies of firms in this respect. The perils surrounding the credit crisis of 2007–2010 and of the subsequent debt crisis in the euro zone also show that when such strategic calculations with respect to marginal transaction costs subsequently prove to be wrong, it will bring about huge societal transaction costs.

The further development and application of the economic theory of transaction costs to exchange transactions in the (international) trade, for example by Greif (1993, 1994, 2000) and Rauch (2001), is more recent. This trade-oriented theory of transaction costs is based on a central notion in the work of Douglass North (1990), namely that the ongoing interaction between rules and players, or between institutions and organizations, underlies the success or failure of an economy. That is why trade theory is linked with the theory of institutional economics. Institutions in the sense of North do not only include formal institutions, such as legal rules and regulations. Informal institutions are very important as well, if not more so. These include socio-cultural phenomena such as the prevailing values and norms, mutual trust and the commercial or mercantile skills of a nation. This is where soft transaction costs come into the picture. Greif has shown that institutions play a crucial role in satisfying the basic condition for exchange, namely to be able to commit to a trade contract. In a way institutions are a solution to the game of trust (see the next sections). In the early Middle Ages, Jewish merchants – the 'Maghribi traders' – were bound to keep their promises on trade agreements through family ties and other social networks, even though their deeds could only be controlled much later because of the large distances and travel times. Later, this institutional system of using family ties was replaced by more formal institutions such as legal systems.

Recent work by Helpman (2006) illustrates the importance of transaction costs for the success of firms in internationalization. The argument is that doing international business brings about considerably higher costs in the start-up of and during international operations. The consequence is that internationalization is only feasible for a firm of a sufficient size. This scale or specialization – being knowledgeable of doing international business – makes it achievable to recover the investment costs of knowledge on transaction costs in international trade over several transactions. Such a scale and specialized knowledge of international issues is a prerequisite for firms to be able and continue to be able to operate successfully in the current status quo of 'open borders'. In terms of the Edgeworth box (see Figure 2.1), the high transaction costs of international trade should be compensated by the large productivity gains due to economies of scale within the hierarchy of the firm.

4.2.1 Definition of Transaction Costs in the Literature

As mentioned, Coase (1937) was the first to introduce the concept of transaction costs into economic theory. The problem Coase noted with mainstream economic theory was that the firm was treated as a black box. That is extraordinary, given that most resources in a modern economic system are employed within firms. How these resources are used depends on administrative systems and not directly on the operation of a market. Therefore, the definition of transaction costs by Coase is short and compelling: '*The costs of using the pricing mechanism*' (see also Coase, 2005). It has to be discovered what prices are: negotiations are to be undertaken, contracts have to be drawn up, inspections have to be made and arrangements have to be made to settle disputes (see, for example, Box 1.1). These are all transaction costs. Their existence implies that alternatives to the market as a coordination mechanism, such as hierarchical coordination, may be preferable to relying on the price mechanism. If as yet the market is selected as a mechanism to find out about prices, transaction costs are all costs which the market mechanism and the functioning of the market bring about.

The economic theory of transaction costs was subsequently elaborated by Oliver Williamson, who, in 2009, joined Coase and North as winners of the Nobel Prize in economics. Williamson defines transaction costs as '*the costs of running the economic system*' (see, for example, Williamson, 1975, who followed Arrow, 1969). Like Coase, Williamson is concerned with the question of why the hierarchy is sometimes preferred over the market as a coordination method. The answer of transaction cost economics is that it postulates two processes which uncover and explicate the incentives and bureaucratic cost consequences that attend the move from market to hierarchy. These processes are *replication and selective intervention*. If a firm could replicate the market in all circumstances where the market works well, and could intervene selectively in those circumstances where markets break down (in case net gains are to be expected), then the firm could never do worse than the market (through replication) and would sometimes do better (through selective intervention). But a firm will in practice never be in such an ideal situation. Therefore, the move from the market to the hierarchy, or the move back from hierarchy to the market, is always a question of trade-offs. Transaction cost economics, and for that matter, transaction management, aims at making these trade-offs explicit so that a choice can be made for the 'best' governance structure with lowest net costs.

Nowadays, the term 'transaction costs' mainly relates to the transaction itself: it covers *all costs involved in entering into, implementing and complying with a transaction.* From that perspective, Cheung (1987) defines transaction costs '*as all costs that do not occur in a "Robinson Crusoe" economy of direct exchange*'. In other words, all costs that in the traditional description of welfare gains from exchange in the Edgeworth box are not taken into account (see Section 2.1).

North and Wallis (1994) distinguish between transformation and transaction costs. Transformation costs relate to the genuine processing of goods or services, which is to be regarded as the actual production. By contrast, transaction costs occur when goods or services change ownership. North (1990) observes that the neoclassical paradigm as the primary basis for traditional mainstream economic theory only holds true when there are no transaction costs. In other words, neoclassical theory assumes a frictionless economy. By contrast, when transaction costs are involved, they bring about allocative distortions. In that case, the economy reaches a different equilibrium than when there would be no transaction costs. From the viewpoint of allocative efficiency, this new equilibrium is less than optimal. This is another way to indicate that the lower the transaction costs are, the better it is for social welfare. In that case, more welfare-enhancing transactions can be made.

In transaction cost economics, two main sources of transaction costs can be distinguished which result from the relational behaviour of the economic agents engaged in the transaction. These are:

1. Bounded rationality; and
2. Opportunistic behaviour.

Bounded rationality has two reasons: (i) informational complexity and (ii) informational uncertainty. Informational complexity refers to the fact that individuals have limited abilities to process all available information. Hence, an individual is unable to process all relevant aspects of a transaction. Informational uncertainty, by contrast, refers to the fact that it is impossible to perfectly foresee all future states of the world. Individuals engaged in a transaction cannot perfectly foresee all the contingencies involved in a transaction and, therefore, suffer from incomplete information. When individuals are not globally rational, but behave according to bounded rationality, it is impossible to specify complete contracts without costs. Hence, bounded rationality may lead to transaction costs. However, it is not a sufficient condition for such costs to occur. Bounded rationality is also cost-rational if the marginal benefits gained from additional information-gathering no longer justify the additional transaction costs because of incomplete information and the related incomplete contracts.

Opportunistic behaviour refers to the 'self-interest seeking behaviour' of individuals (Williamson, 1985). Without opportunistic behaviour it would not be necessary to fully specify complete contracts. Therefore, the transaction costs that arise through bounded rationality do not exist per se, in case individuals do not want to gain advantage over the loss of another individual. However, when individuals exhibit opportunistic behaviour the opposite is true. Individuals may use the incompleteness in contracts, which exist through bounded rationality, for their own gains. This opens up opportunities for strategic behaviour and executive hazards. This in turn causes the necessity for trading partners to monitor each other and to enforce contracts legally. The next sections discuss how mutual trust may reduce opportunistic behaviour and thereby imply lower transaction costs.

A third major source of transaction costs stems from the characteristics of the good s or services that are object of the transaction. This relates to:

3.   Asset specificity

Here, *asset specificity* is defined as the extent to which an investment supporting a transaction has more value in that specific transaction than in any other purpose. Besides these opportunity costs of the specific transaction, asset specificity also relates to what it would cost to 'redeploy' – in Williamson's terminology – on other activities (for example, sunk costs). In other words, asset specificity determines the scope of the continuing interest of both contracting parties in each other (Williamson, 1985). When there is no asset specificity, markets are perfectly contestable, and individuals will not want to invest in continuing economic relationships.

Asset specificity relates to goods or services that are bound to certain specifications. When the first transaction has been defined and approved with respect to these specifications, the following transactions can take advantage of the fact that the specifications are known and, thereby, fewer transaction costs need to be made. By contrast, the more goods or services are tailored to the individual requirements of the buyer, the higher the asset specificity. In the remainder of this book, the degree of asset specificity repeatedly emerges as an important determinant of transaction costs and of how transaction management can create value. It is obvious that there is a relationship between asset specificity and standardization (see Chapter 7), as standardization will make the specifications transparent and, therefore, reduce asset specificity. Uniform standards ensure that traders need to spend less time defining the specifications of the goods or services so that they will encounter fewer transaction costs. By contrast, the demands of buyers to suppliers can be so specific that standards have to be developed that can only be used in that particular situation. This enlarges the mutual interest that buyers and suppliers have in maintaining their trade relationships.

Apart from asset specificity, Williamson (1985, Chapter 3) distinguishes two other aspects which are determinants of transaction costs and which stem from the characteristics of the transaction, namely *uncertainties* and *frequency*. Uncertainties surrounding the organization of a transaction may also involve significant costs, whether they are linked with the behaviour of agents or are the result of organizational deficiencies or inadequate institutions. Of course, uncertainties can be drivers of both opportunistic behaviour and bounded rationality. The influence of 'frequency' on transaction costs is more difficult to determine. The idea is that the frequency of a transaction matters because the more often transactions take place, the more widely-spread are the fixed costs establishing a non-market governance system. It implies that the more frequent transactions take place, the lower the costs per transaction, given fixed costs over all transactions. There is, however, not much empirical evidence of this relationship.

4.2.2   New Institutional Economics

The linking of transaction costs economics to the theory of institutions gives rise to the *new institutional economics*. The term was first coined by Olivier Williamson in 1975. Williamson (1996) distinguishes two approaches, namely the earlier property rights approach and the more recent comparative contractual approach. The two approaches first appeared to be rival theories of organization, but in new institutional economics they became two complementary parts. One of these parts deals predominantly with background conditions (expanded beyond property rights to include contract laws, norms, customs, conventions, etc.), while the second part deals with the mechanisms of governance.

In their introductory chapter of the *Handbook of New Institutional Economics*, Ménard and Shirley (2005) note, in line with previous arguments in this chapter, that new institutional economics abandons the standard neoclassical assumption that individuals have perfect information and unbounded rationality, and that transactions are costless. New institutional economics assumes instead that individuals have incomplete information and limited capacity to collect information. Therefore, they face uncertainty about unforeseen events and outcomes, and incur transaction costs to acquire information. To reduce risks and transaction costs formal and informal institutions are created – formal institutions such as constitutions, laws, contracts and regulations, and informal institutions such as structuring and inculcating norms of conduct, beliefs and habits of thought and behaviour. Because new institutional economics focuses on making choices to be embedded in such institutions, it has a much broader reach than neo-classical economics, which is traditionally largely concerned with prices and outcomes. Yet new institutional economics does not abandon neoclassical economic theory. The orthodox assumptions of scarcity and competition are accepted by new institutional economists. Moreover, it seems that modern mainstream economic theory is directed more and more at combining elements of neo-classical economics with transaction cost theory.

From this perspective Ménard (2005) considers new institutional economics as the theory that encapsulates two branches identified by Williamson: one dealing with institutions (in the way discussed by North) and how these institutions frame transaction costs; the other dealing with arrangements which Coase grouped under the expression 'institutional structure of production' and which Williamson labels 'mechanisms of governance'. These arrangements comprise alternative ways of organising relationships among economic units in order to take advantage of the division of labour while economizing on bounded rationality and safeguarding parties against contractual hazards. According to Ménard, the golden triangle defining new institutional economics consists of transaction costs, contracts and property rights. In his view transaction costs provide an explanation to the existence of alternative modes of organization as well as tools for understanding the characteristics of these arrangements. Contracts represent a focal point in new institutional economics because of their role in relaxing the role of bounded rationality, fixing schemes of reference for future actions and checking on opportunistic behaviour. Well-defined property rights, and institutions for implementing them, form a prerequisite for making the transfers of rights possible, and the trade-off among arrangements meaningful. In this way property rights affect contractual hazards and embed transactions into specific institutional environments.

4.2.3   Modern Theories on Transaction Costs and the Organization of Production

Chapter 2 stated that, with the fragmentation of production and much international outsourcing, comparative advantages no longer, in the Ricardian sense, relate to finished products and services, but rather to a trade in tasks. From that perspective, Grossmann and Rossi-Hansberg (2008) present a model for the determinants of international trade which makes an explicit distinction between trade in goods (which is the traditional approach to modelling international trade) and trade in tasks. Here, production involves conducting a continuum of 'tasks'. Different economies are now not trading in finished goods, but rather these tasks, or subsets of the production process, are tradable. Some tasks may require high-skilled labour input, whereas other tasks require low-skilled labour, another factor input such as capital or different categories of labour.

Tasks can be performed abroad when it is less costly for a firm to perform a task offshore than domestically. Offshoring tasks incurs transaction costs. The crucial assumption is that some tasks are moved abroad more easily than others. This implies that moving some tasks abroad may incur more transaction costs than other tasks do. So when will firms choose to move tasks abroad? This will only be the case when the joint costs of foreign factor input and transaction costs are less than the domestic costs of factor input. Hence, in this framework, some tasks will still be performed at home, whereas others can be performed abroad.

What are the relevant implications of this distinction between trade in goods and trade in tasks for the management of transaction costs and for its consequences for the labour market? Assume, for the sake of expositional purposes, that only low-skilled tasks can be moved abroad. By lowering transaction costs it becomes profitable to move more low-skill tasks abroad. Grossmann and Rossi-Hansberg distinguish three effects of the reduction in transaction costs:

1.   Productivity effect;
2.   Relative-price effect; and
3.   Labour-supply effect.

The *productivity effect* occurs through a decline in the costs of tasks being moved abroad. Firms incur lower costs, since more tasks can be performed offshore less expensively, which drives up the demand for domestic factor inputs, thereby increasing the return to domestic factors. The *relative-price effect* occurs through a change in the terms of trade of a country. This effect is likely to influence the return on low-skilled labour adversely. An improvement in the terms of trade, defined by the price of exports in terms of imports, will put downward pressure on low-skilled wages since the exporting, high-skilled industry becomes more profitable and will draw resources from the import-competing sector. Finally the *labour-supply effect* occurs through the release of domestic labour, which is freed by moving labour abroad. This effect is also likely to depress low-skilled wages.

Meanwhile, a decrease in the costs of offshoring affects high-skilled labour and other factor inputs as well. According to the model of Grossmann and Rossi-Hansberg, offshoring low-skilled tasks has no productivity effect for other factor inputs, since it has no direct effect on the wage bill of these other factors. However, the relative-price effect and the labour-supply effect do have such a direct effect. The relative-price effect, causing an increase in the terms of trade, boosts the high-skilled-intensive exporting industry and thereby the return on high-skilled labour. The labour-supply effect drives down the relative prices of low-skilled labour, which is equivalent to an increase in the relative prices of high-skilled labour.

Overall the conclusion from this theory on trade in tasks is that a decrease in the costs of offshoring can affect the returns on low- and high-skilled labour in different ways. When, for low-skilled labour, the positive productivity effect outweighs the negative relative-price and labour-supply effects, low-skilled labour will benefit. Otherwise, the return on low-skilled labour decreases. The return on high-skilled labour will increase in all cases, since both the relative-price effect and the labour-supply effect are positive. Therefore, from the perspective of distribution the important issue is whether the positive effects for low-skilled labour outweigh the adverse effects. This seems to be different for small and large economies. In the first case, domestic low-skilled labour benefits from the increased offshoring, whereas domestic high-skilled labour and other factors are unaffected. In the case of a large economy such as the United States, which may influence world prices, the situation is different. The question here is whether the productivity effect outweighs the relative-price effect. This depends, for example, on the elasticity of demand of the traded goods, which determines the relative strength of price movements. The conclusion is that it is equally possible for low-skilled labour to benefit than it is to lose out from the reduction in the costs of offshoring. As before, the return on high-skilled labour is only affected by the relative-price effect

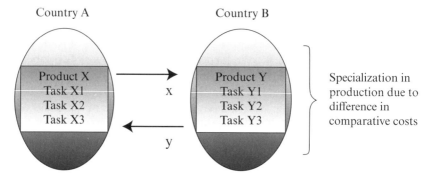

Figure 4.1a   Traditional Ricardian explanation of international trade

and thereby benefits from reducing the costs of offshoring. These effects differ little when the model allows for other tasks next to low-skilled tasks to become tradable as well.

However, the effect that domestic factors can gain from offshoring tasks could also be predicted by Ricardian determinants such as comparative advantage. Therefore, the question is whether the trade-in-tasks model really makes a difference in explaining trade flows. Baldwin and Robert-Nicaud (2010) argue that it does. The special feature of the trade-in-tasks model is that when certain tasks are moved abroad, this is done in all industries. For example, when low-skilled tasks are moved abroad, this occurs in both low- and high-skilled labour-intensive industries. Therefore, trade in tasks will even occur when there are no differences in relative endowments. This kind of trade is not explained by the traditional Heckscher–Ohlin framework. Thus, the trade in tasks model successfully links trade and transaction costs to Trefler's (1995) 'missing trade puzzle' (Baldwin and Robert-Nicaud, 2010).

Figures 4.1a and 4.1b illustrate the transition from trade in finished products and services to a trade in tasks. Trade induced by comparative cost differences implies that a country will specialize in producing goods or services where its comparative cost advantage is larger than its trading partner's. Figure 4.1a illustrates this traditional Ricardian trade theory for two countries, A and B. Country A produces product X and the whole production process with tasks X1, X2 and X3 is executed at home. A similar situation applies for country B with product Y. Here, the tasks Y1, Y2 and Y3 are conducted in the home country. In this traditional trade situation, comparative advantages in production lead country A to export product X to B and country B to export product Y to A.

However, when the potential for the increased fragmentation of

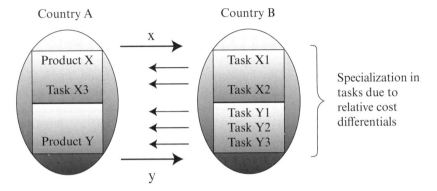

Figure 4.1b   International trade resulting from fragmentation of production and trade in tasks

production becomes exploited, specialization will take place at a more detailed level, namely at the level of tasks. Now the international division of labour no longer covers the different products but the tasks in production. The higher the degree of standardization and the lower the customer contact – thereby the lower the asset specificity – the easier it is to separate the tasks that can be outsourced. Figure 4.1b assumes that the organization of the production of both product X and product Y takes place in country A. This country has an apparent comparative advantage in orchestrating production. All tasks with respect to product Y are outsourced to country B, whereas for product X only task X3 is conducted at home, for instance because that task requires specific skills that cannot yet be outsourced or because the transaction costs of outsourcing are higher than the reduction of the costs of executing the task abroad. It is clear that a major change in trade flows between the countries results from this new organization of production. Country A is exporting both products X and Y, whereas it is importing tasks. For country B, which has a comparative advantage in the execution of tasks, the opposite is true.

This trade in tasks can imply that trade within industries, so-called intra-industry trade, increases. But that is not necessary. After all, the tasks that are outsourced can equally well be executed as services that are attributed to other sectors. Think of the production of microchips that are used in products from different sectors, or think of outsourcing the administration and parts of the ICT. Whatever the case, the increased focus on trade in tasks shows that a productivity increase does not solely have to be the consequence of a technological innovation in production, but that a transaction innovation, which reduces transaction costs through better exploiting trade in tasks, can also lead to an increase in productivity.

4.2.4   Opening up the Black Box of the Production Function

The obvious result of these changes in the way international trade depends on comparative advantages is that a new economic theory is needed for a good understanding of the impact of the globalization and fragmentation of production. The traditional theory of economic growth has to be thoroughly revised to really understand what is happening. In their review article on these new theoretical developments, Antràs and Rossi-Hansberg (2009) argue that the traditional theory of the production function sees the way production factors are transformed into a final product as a black box. The new theory seeks to open this black box. Not only the input volume of the production factors and the possibilities for substitution are important for the description of the production process, but also the organization of production should be made endogenous. This creates a theory where elements of the theory of industrial organization are integrated into trade and growth theories. Obviously this new theory on the organization of production is much related to the notion of Coase on the institutional structure of production and the new institutional economics, discussed before, which also aims at opening the black box of production.

Transaction costs play a major role in this combination of theories. An important aspect of this theory is that the heterogeneity of production factors should be taken into account. In this context, Grossman and Maggi (2000) describe how the choice of the organization of production may depend on the available qualities of the workforce and, hence, on the warranted characteristics of labour input as a production factor. On the one hand, there can be a production process where the knowledge of brilliant and creative people is needed but, on the other hand, there can also be a production process that is based on established procedures using reliable workers complying with a hierarchical working environment. Firms may internally exploit these differences in talents for the organization of production, but they can also give rise to an international trade in tasks where one country is gifted with one type of talent and another country with the other type.

4.3   THE FUNDAMENTAL PROBLEM OF EXCHANGE AND TRANSACTION COST ECONOMICS

Transaction costs are associated with what Greif (2000) labels the fundamental problem of exchange. This fundamental problem is whether *'one can ex ante commit to being able and willing to fulfil contractual obligations ex post.*' In other words, a necessary condition for exchange is that for each partner in the exchange transaction there must be certainty that the other partner will keep their promise and deliver what has been agreed upon. Greif approaches this issue by stating that '*one will not enter into a profitable exchange relationship until the other party can ex ante commit to fulfil his or her contractual obligations ex post.*' Only under that condition can the exchange be mutually beneficial for both parties. This required security is often difficult to obtain because of a feature typical of many exchange transactions: it is *sequential.* This means that contracts and promises about delivery are made in advance of actual delivery and payment. This gives the party that is last to fulfil his or her obligations the opportunity to behave opportunistically and to benefit at the expense of the other party. This is a major cause of opportunistic behaviour, which, as explained before, is regarded as one of the sources of transaction costs.

This problem becomes even worse when specific investments are required in a particular exchange relationship. In this situation, there is the threat of a 'hold-up'. Such hold-ups – which are named after raids in the Wild West where people had to hold up their hands in order to prevent them grasping their pistols and firing back – imply that the last party to meet the obligations misuses the opportunity to change the conditions of the exchange to his or her advantage. In the case of a labour contract, a hold-up may happen where a worker, who has had high learning costs to become acquainted with the work and become productive, demands a higher wage at the moment he or she becomes really productive. It implies that his or her boss is unable to recover these learning costs. The threat of a hold-up constitutes an obstacle to entering into an exchange contract and should be avoided. However, such a hold-up can only be avoided when for both parties the associated transaction costs and gains with keeping the contract are lower than the net costs of breaking the contract.

The fundamental problem of exchange essentially boils down to avoiding the opportunistic behaviour associated with the sequential characteristic of the exchange. In game theoretic terms, the fundamental exchange problem can be understood as a form of the prisoner's dilemma. The optimal solution in terms of welfare for both parties ('the Pareto-optimal solution', see Box 2.1) implies that both sides behave cooperatively. However, for each party separately it is rational not to do so, which in principle results in a non-Pareto-optimal outcome. That is why trade institutions are needed to ensure that there is an optimal solution in the prisoner's dilemma, for example through the enforcement of costly penalties if a party does not comply with the contract. In more general terms, a solution to *the game of trust* is required. The next section elaborates on how institutions can contribute to this solution to the game of trust.

From the perspective of new institutional economics Greif (2005) posits that two complementary types of institutions are needed for market-based exchange. These are *'contract-enforcement institutions'* and *'coercion-constraining institutions'*. The contract-enforcement institutions determine the transactions in which one can credibly commit to fulfil contractual obligations and, therefore, the exchange relationships into which economic agents will enter. Better contract-enforcement institutions will bring about lower transaction costs for solving the problem of the sequential character of transactions and they will, therefore, enhance the use of the market mechanism for coordination. Yet, the feasible extent of markets depends on protection from coercive power. Displaying one's goods in the market facilitates their confiscation by those with coercive power. That is why for contract-enforcement institutions to be effective, there need to be coercion-constraining institutions. The upshot of these institutions is that they influence decisions at the social level regarding the acquisition and use of coercive power. Political institutions, which limit the power of rulers, can be seen as such institutions. However, there are examples, for example in imperial China, of extensive market economies without such strict political institutions. According to Greif, a more general way to characterize coercion-constraining institutions is that they are effective by making violence economically productive as it is used to protect property rights from abuses. They secure property rights by discouraging those who can use coercive power to abuse rights from doing so, and by motivating those who have coercive power, such as rulers, the elite or states, to protect rights. That is how, for making the market mechanism work efficiently, an adequate combination of contract-enforcement institutions and coercion-constraining institutions is needed. However, markets are not always the most efficient forms of organization. Ouchi (1980) has shown, in a study about the efficiency of markets, bureaucracies and clans, that under certain conditions bureaucracies and clans are more efficient as a form of organization than markets due to the conditions which give rise to the costs of mediating exchanges between individuals.

4.3.1 Stages in Market Transactions

In a commercial exchange transaction, three stages can be distinguished from the perspective of transaction costs, namely:

1. The contact stage;
2. The contract stage; and
3. The control stage.

In the *contact* stage of a potential transaction, the buyer is looking for information about his or her preferred product (price and quality), potential suppliers or, when the product does not yet exist, which producer could invent and/or produce it for him or her. The seller is trying to find a buyer for his or her product through marketing activities. Transaction costs come forth out of the fact that information is not free, not complete and not easily accessible. Traders have to invest in searching. Evidently this search for information is more difficult when, in an international context, communication is blurred by differences in language, ways of information distribution and culture-based business norms. The reduction of the transaction costs of contact involves a mechanism with two essential characteristics. First, information about business opportunities must be spread to all members of the business community who might be interested in being informed. Second, it must be guaranteed that this information is of high quality – that is, the information can be trusted to be relevant and true. The distribution of reliable information is a characteristic function of networks. Mutual trust among the members of the network increases the quality of the information. Some empirical backing for this claim can be found in the studies of Rauch (2001) and Rauch and Trindade (2002), which point out the role of co-ethnic business networks in solving this problem of missing information on business opportunities. Ethnic (Chinese) networks seem to be more influential in bilateral trade on differentiated than homogeneous goods. Portes and Rey (1999) note the importance of the 'geography of information', measured by, for example, telephone call traffic and multinational bank branches, in a study on bilateral cross-border equity flows. Combes et al. (2002) present empirical support for their claim that business and social networks help reduce informational trade barriers in France.

The *contract* stage starts directly at the moment the potential trading partners have found each other and are inclined to make a deal. Here, transaction costs are made in negotiating the terms of the contract. Parties have to decide how to reasonably split up the expected rents of the transaction and what to write down in the contract. They should not aim to put all eventualities in the contract. It is costly to write out all details, it is useless because some arrangements cannot be verified by third parties (verification problems), it is impossible because many eventualities cannot be foreseen (fundamental uncertainty) and it may have unwarranted side effects in the form of growing distrust between the parties if one takes explicit account of everything that might go wrong. Contracting becomes even harder in an international context. Parties have to learn the particularities of the legal system of the other country. In addition, cultural problems appear when one is contemplating what to write down (and what not to) in the contract. Appropriate business norms vary between cultures. For example, in the United Kingdom it is common to write down every detail, while in other cultures, such as the Netherlands, it is customary to just write down the rough outline of the agreement and to fill in the details during the fulfilment of the agreement. These differences can lead to misunderstandings. Writing down all details creates a sphere of security in one case (the contract provides a solution for every problem that might occur), but it can also signal distrust (why does the other party want to write down all these eventualities; does he foresee problems; doesn't he trust me?).

Cooray and Ratnatunga (2001) illustrate the problem in an interesting account of the troublesome cooperation between a Japanese customer and an Australian producer. They show how cultural differences can lead to completely different perceptions about how to build a cooperative relationship. The Japanese buyer was focused on developing a long-term close relationship with his Australian partner, because it is customary in Japan to stay with a producer as long as the producer sells the product. It is a strategic decision with long-term consequences for a Japanese firm to choose a supplier. The Japanese, therefore, asked for much information about the quality and price of the product, and installed their own personnel in the Australian firm because they are also accustomed to cooperating with their producers to improve the product. The Australian firm, however, was not used to providing such detailed information about their production process and costs. A second problem arose because the Australians wanted to develop the relationship along personal lines, whereas the Japanese counted on strict formal control and evaluation procedures. In the end, an intermediary, with knowledge of both cultures and firms, was hired to solve the mutual adjustment problems. In general, striving for low contract transaction costs implies quick negotiations that result in a fair distribution of the rents.

The stage of *control* consists of the monitoring and enforcement of the contract. Both involve high transaction costs, especially at long distances. Monitoring means that business partners check whether the other party is doing what he or she promised to do. If the check turns out that this is not the case, the next step is the enforcement of the contract. The most common solution for enforcement is to start a legal procedure. Especially in international trading relationships, this is often a troublesome affair. It takes time and money in large quantities, and foreigners often feel mistreated by prejudiced national courts when they file a claim against a national firm. The outcome of the process can be uncertain. In general, there is the verification problem, which means that it is often difficult or even impossible for third parties, such as judges, to value the quality of the goods or services delivered. Country-specific cultural values and norms also penetrate national legal systems. In the United Kingdom, the law is commonly regarded as a device to protect people from the government. The basic thought is that the government should not interfere in private matters. British judges, therefore, base their decisions in legal disputes extensively on what parties have voluntarily agreed on, even when power asymmetries might have influenced the voluntary element. By contrast, the German and Dutch legal systems take the idea that contracts should be 'reasonable' for both parties. The government is seen as a mechanism to correct injustices. German and Dutch judges, therefore, have and use the right to reinterpret and reconstruct contracts until their outcomes can be considered 'reasonable' for both parties. This means that two contracts with the same wording can lead to different legal decisions depending on the kind of legal system in the country in which the file is claimed. In such cases, the control transaction costs can be held low in instances where the transaction partners comply with the terms of the agreement, so that there is no need for intensive monitoring or legal enforcement.

Table 4.1 summarizes the various types of transaction costs encountered in the three stages. It also indicates the sources for these costs. It should be noted that the costs in the first stage, the contact stage, are so-called sunk costs, which means that these costs are also made when the contract and ensuing trade exchange do not ultimately take place.

This aspect of sunk costs, and more generally the question of whether the transaction costs are recurrent with each transaction or whether they are once-and-for-all costs, gives rise to an alternative typology of transaction costs. From this perspective, transaction costs can be divided into *ex ante transaction costs*, which make a transaction possible, and *ex post transaction costs*, which are the follow-up to a transaction agreed upon.

The first type comprises costs associated with search and signalling, negotiations, the 'ink costs' of writing the contract, etc. These costs relate to the contact and contract stages and can be considered sunk, once-and-for-all costs. The second type, the ex post transaction costs, consist of the monitoring costs, the costs of maladaption and deliveries which are not in accordance with warranted specifications, the costs associated with renegotiations, the legal costs to settle disputes, the costs of adjustments or of termination of the contract. These costs mainly relate to the control stage of the trade relationship and are partly recurrent and partly once-and-for-all costs.

Table 4.1   Types of transaction costs at different stages of trade transactions

Stage	Type of transaction	Sources of costs	International complications	Due to:
Contact stage	Investment in information about cus-tomer/supplier or potential producer	Information is costly	Hindered communication	Differences in language
	Investing in the relationship	Information is incomplete		Differences in culture
		Information is unavailable		Differences in means of communication
Contract stage	Investment in costs of preparing contract	Distribution of profits	Divergent expectations between the parties, verification problems and uncertainty	Differences in culture
		Formulation of agreement		Differences in legal system
Control stage	Costs of compliance of agreement	Monitoring costs	Greater uncertainty	Exchange of information by larger distance
	Investing in continuing/improving the relationship	Enforcement of contract provisions		Problem of interpretation in verification
				Ignorance of law and system of values and norms

4.4   SOLUTIONS TO THE GAME OF TRUST

The previous section mentioned Greif's argument that finding a solution to the fundamental problem of exchange is akin to finding a solution to the game of trust. Here, trust may be a substitute for extensive negotiations and the drafting of contracts, which can bring about many transaction costs and which are, from an economic perspective, never 'complete'. Trust can be seen as an expectation about the future behaviour of the trading partner, where a false expectation may bring about considerable costs. When both parties trust each other, it implies that both parties expect cooperative behaviour from the other party and explicit or implicit compliance with the agreements.

In fact in many circumstances trust between trading parties can be seen as a cooperative solution of a prisoner's dilemma where the trigger mechanism built into the repeated game does not completely exclude cheating. Therefore, placing trust is not a free lunch; there is also risk involved. This makes agents cautious about gathering reliable information about potential business partners (contact), carefully formulating the agreement (contract) and adequately monitoring and enforcing it (control). What do people indulge to accept these risks and to trust the other, or how can this risk be contaminated so that trust can develop? To answer this question, two main types of trust-generating mechanisms can be distinguished with a *formal* and an *informal* basis.

In the case of formal trust, we can, for instance, think of legal protection with respect to agreements between parties, where fines, or even the prospect of going to jail, can prevent opportunistic behaviour. In general, however, institutions constitute a major device in solving the game of trust. This formal trust is related to the rational choice concepts of trust and extrinsic motivation. Formal trust is closely linked to what is known by other authors as instrumental trust, rational trust, calculative trust (Williamson, 1993), self-interested trust, synthetic trust (Putnam, 2000), fragile trust, narrow trust or egoistic trust and, to some extent, system trust. All these notions of trust are related to each other in the sense that they identify this type of trust as being about the calculation of selfish interests in pecuniary terms. It is expected that people take into account all the financial incentives involved, use a 'rational way of thinking' and are not 'hindered' by emotions. Therefore, if it is profitable to cheat, one will cheat without remorse. People will act trustworthily when it pays to act trustworthily. The main idea of this approach is that the trust problem can be understood as a social coordination problem. To prevent both players ending up in the Nash equilibrium outcome of the prisoner's dilemma (both players playing the uncooperative or untrustworthy strategy), there are two solutions.

The first is to play the game an indefinite number of times. In other words, a repeated game is needed to solve the game of trust. This allows reputation effects to emerge. Prior trustworthy behaviour forms a valuable asset because it enhances the chance of finding future business partners. The reputation mechanism works best when the time horizon of the players is large, when there are many potential partners and when information about past behaviour is easily accessible to all players. This forms an important reason why trading networks exist, since they fulfil these requirements. The second solution is to change the outcomes of the game in such a way that it becomes favourable for the players to act in line with the agreement. On a bilateral level, this can be organized by promising bonuses for good compliance or by taking 'hostages' that are returned when the agreement has been fulfilled. Another way to invoke trustworthiness is by using intermediaries, for example banks that issue letters of credit. The most important way of solving the trust problem is by relying on judicial power to enforce legal contracts. Threats of fines and imprisonment scare agents away from untrustworthy behaviour. Therefore, according to this second solution, a kind of contract that is hopefully self-enforcing and prevents cheating should preclude traders ending up in the non-cooperative prisoner's dilemma solution of no trade.

It should be noted that these trust mechanisms on a formal basis cannot remove all risk. In the first place, bounded rationality and incomplete information make it impossible to make all the necessary calculations. Moreover, the behaviour of other people is guided by a fundamental uncertainty called free will. Good prior intentions can always change when unforeseen circumstances occur. It has already been noted that legal contracts can be expensive, inherently incomplete, possibly unverifiable and subject to the particularities of the addressed legal system. On top of this, too much emphasis on formal trust might hurt informal trust. When relationships are guided by too much formal trust, based on extrinsic motivations, this can 'crowd out' informal trust, which relies on intrinsic motivation.

Trust mechanisms with an informal basis cover the relational and social-cultural mechanisms that build trust. Informal trust is based on intrinsic motivations. This type of trust is closely related to the concepts of social trust, moral trust, personal or blind trust (Williamson, 1993), socially-oriented trust, resilient trust, broad or altruistic trust, generalized trust (Putnam, 1993) and social capital (Fukuyama, 1995). Both at the individual and the institutional level, there are a number of different mechanisms that generate informal trust.

At the individual level, the way in which people deal with uncertainty varies from person to person. Responsible for this is the extent of 'ontological security' a person experiences (Giddens, 1991). This has a direct influence on the individual's 'natural' level of trust in others, called 'basic trust' (Giddens, 1991) or 'trusting impulse' (Stztompka, 1999). In (bilateral) relationships, the problem of incomplete information is countered by the psychological mechanism of satisficing (Simon, 1983). Agents collect and process information up to a certain aspiration level. When cooperation goes on for a while, a personal relationship develops between the contracting partners, and custom and routine slip in.

This is a rational way to deal with bounded rationality because the limited processing capacity of the human brain is not distracted by operations that go well. When the relationship proceeds within certain 'tolerance boundaries', attention can be given to other problems. When these boundaries are crossed, the routine aspect of the trust relationship disappears and agents will pay close attention again to the relationship, collect information and possibly narrow the tolerance boundaries. When the relationship gains a durable character, agents might reach the stage when they start to identify with each other and each other's interests. This will first lead to making the relationship informal. Ethical and moral considerations start to rule the relationship. This can even lead to a distortion of the perception of the trustworthiness of the other party. An example of this is cognitive dissonance. Contradictions between facts (about the behaviour of the other party) and beliefs (about the trustworthiness of the other party) give an uneasy feeling, which is solved by reinterpreting the facts in such a way that the beliefs can hold. Then, the relationship can be called one of blind trust (Williamson, 1985).

Informal trust mechanisms are also active at a collective level, namely in organizations, villages, cities, ethnic groups, networks and countries. In these groups, a trust culture might develop among its members. This is '*a system of rules – norms and values – regulating granting trust and meeting, returning, and reciprocating trust; in short, rules about trust and trustworthiness*' (Sztompka, 1999). If social control is effective, breaking such rules is followed by serious social sanctions.

The advantage of informal trust mechanisms above formal trust mechanisms is that one does not have to pay to keep afloat an entire legal system with its lawmakers, lawyers, judges and police. However, building informal trust can be a difficult and lengthy process, especially when one wants to enter a group or network of which the membership ties are based on kinship, ethnicity, religiosity or place of birth. Examples of such closed trade networks date from the Maghribi traders in the 11th century (Greif, 1989, 1993), the Jewish diamond merchants in the 1960s (Wechsberg, 1966) to modern ethnic Chinese networks (Rauch and Trindade, 2002).

Microeconomic game experiments suggest that these informal forms of trust are relevant to explain human behaviour in some economic situations. A common conclusion of those experiments – often shaped as social coordination problems – is that people are indeed inclined to behave trustingly and trustworthily (guided by norms such as reciprocity and fairness), instead of playing the 'rational' strategy of non-cooperation. This result even holds true when high sums of money are at stake, when the participants are not students and when no reputation effects can be built up (one-shot interaction with anonymous strangers).

A related informal form of trust is based on common values and norms. Being a member of the same cultural or religious society may induce people to trust and be trusted without any formal guarantee. This form of trust can primarily be found in homogeneous communities with common values and norms where the 'institutional setting' assures that the community will provide a costly punishment for cheating. These communities can consist of family, close friends, colleagues or members of the same profession, as well as citizens from the same village, region or country.

It is difficult to judge which one of these different types of trust has most practical relevance. First, there will be a substitution effect: when the legal system is better developed, the effects of corporate reputation and social networks are less important. Furthermore, there is complementarity: without a reasonably functioning legal system, reliance on an informal form of trust may also become more costly. In most practical situations, there is generally a combination of these two types of trust and their relevance may differ from situation to situation. In this respect, the question also arises as to what extent each type of trust relies on rational behaviour. Here, the distinction can be made between *calculative trust* and *moral trust*. Formal trust can be associated with calculative trust and rational behaviour. But it may be true that reliance on informal trust can also be regarded as rational. Rationality, in this case, refers to a balancing of the benefits and costs of cheating. For instance, when it is costly to build up a reputation of trustworthiness, and when by cheating this reputation gets lost (whereas keeping the reputation will considerably reduce future transaction costs), it becomes rational not to cheat. This is exactly the repeated game character of the institutions for informal trust where a high price has to be paid for being expelled from the family or community, or for a loss of face. This may even explain why altruism has been detected in laboratory experiments with one-shot games: the rationality to be altruistic may be found in an intrinsic drive to conform to social habits, or even a fear of 'God'.

Trust is related to various forms of transaction costs. These transaction costs both comprise the costs to establish trust based on formal institutions (contract drafting costs, investment costs in knowledge of foreign law, costs of monitoring arrangements, costs of legal proceedings for non-compliance) and those associated with the informal or relational aspects of trust (building common bonds and friendships, learning foreign languages and foreign cultures). In terms of calculative trust, all of these costs incurred to establish trust should be recovered by the lower transaction costs that the reputation of being trustworthy brings about. It should already be mentioned that this building-up of trust for trade relationships brings about positive externalities. Not only the traders themselves benefit from it in the negotiation of a transaction: social welfare will also increase because of the benefits of specialization and scale effects that result from the additional transactions. This emphasizes that the provision of an efficient working (international) legal system and education in foreign languages and cultures has the character of a public good and should be considered a reason for the involvement of the government (see also Chapter 9). Problems of trust between countries will impede trade. Increased trust among countries will remove these informal barriers to trade and will foster trade.

Overall the literature on trust provides insights into the general mechanisms that govern the relationship among trade, transaction costs and trust. This gives rise to the following points:

1. Trust problems are a source of trade barriers and transaction costs. More trust means fewer trade barriers and fewer transaction costs. Thus, more trust leads to more trade.
2. Two types of trust can be distinguished: formal trust and informal trust. Both types are important in international trade.
3. Another distinction is between calculative trust and moral trust. Although at first sight, calculative trust, which is considered to stem from rational behaviour, seems to be linked to formal trust, whereas informal trust can be identified with moral trust, this may not be true. In fact many types of informal trust also stem from rational behaviour in the sense that cheating brings about fewer gains than the costs of the loss of reputation. Here, the solution to the game of trust is institutionalized as a repeated game.

4.5 CATEGORIZATION AND MEASUREMENT OF TRANSACTION COSTS

To be able to quantify the relative importance of transaction costs, a considerable amount of research must still be performed. A first step is to come to a clear and operational classification of the various forms of transaction costs. This will allow a distinction between direct production costs and transaction costs to be made. This is necessary to show how important business transactions are for individual firms and, aggregated to the macro level, for the country as a whole. It should be realized that transaction costs do not only relate to trade and activities that are directly connected with the organization of production. Various business services that support these activities also bring about transaction costs. Consider the financial and legal services, and the book-keeping and control services of accountants. The latter ensure that the official reporting of firms is correct so that stakeholders (suppliers, customers, financiers, shareholders, government) are not obliged to endure costs valuing such reporting. A calculation of total transaction costs at the macro level will probably show that they increase in proportion to production costs. This seems paradoxical when the strength of a transaction economy is considered the ability to reduce transaction costs. Such a result would mean that lower transaction costs foster transactions more than proportionally, so that a higher volume of transactions more than compensates for the lower unit price of transactions. This would corroborate the potential of the transaction economy. The lower transaction costs may involve an increase in the fragmentation of production so that more tasks of the production process are outsourced. This will reduce the actual production costs so that transaction costs constitute a larger proportion of the total added value. Thus, the value creation in the transaction economy becomes more transaction-intensive.

Clearly dividing transaction costs and production costs is unfeasible (see the case of marketing in Box 4.1). In spite of these problems of definition and measurement, some attempts have been made to estimate the sizes of transaction costs at the macro level. Following the methodology of North and Wallis (1986), De Vor (1994) asserted that in 1990 total transaction costs in the Netherlands economy amounted to almost 53 per cent of GNP. This implies that more than half of the value added in production in the Netherlands relates to conducting transactions. In the period 1960–1990, total transaction costs increased by about 9 percentage points. This can be ascribed completely to an increase in the private sector. According to De Vor's measurements, transaction costs in the private sector in 1990 were over five times higher than those in the public sector. Van Dalen and Van Vuuren (2005) use occupational data to demonstrate that in the Netherlands approximately 25 per cent of workers are employed in transaction jobs, 29 per cent if one includes transport tasks. However, these occupational data do not take into account time spent on coordination by production workers. Klamer and McCloskey (1995) note that one-quarter of the GDP is related to persuasion – that is, talks to make 'real production' possible. In their survey on 'trade costs', Anderson and Van Wincoop (2004) illustrate the size of these trade costs by highlighting the tax equivalent of these costs. For example, what would be the tax tariff on direct production costs if all trade costs where regarded

---

BOX 4.1   TRANSACTION MANAGEMENT AND MARKETING

Marketing can be considered a form of transaction management as far as it intends to provide information about the nature and quality of products or services. In principle, these forms of providing information through marketing reduce the information costs to buyers so that they will decide more often to purchase and make a transaction. The example of marketing shows that the line between what can be considered real production costs and what can be considered transaction costs is often difficult to draw. After all, marketing can also contribute to the image of a product and thereby increase the emotional value of the product. Think of all branded products and of the fact that some people are prepared to pay additional money if they can play on the same brand of basketball shoes as Michael Jordan did. That part of the marketing costs can, as development costs and direct production costs, be considered part of the actual production costs. The same holds true for television commercials. In principle, their intention is to provide information on products and services, albeit biased. Therefore, the costs of these commercials can be considered part of transaction costs. However, for some, a television commercial is simply a fun movie, and thereby a consumer good. The costs of making such commercials would in that case be categorized as production costs.

---

as taxes? From a theoretical point of view, trade costs have the same distortional effects on production as taxes do. Anderson and Van Wincoop have a rather broad definition of trade costs so that it comprises most of the transaction costs discussed earlier in this chapter. Their main finding is that trade costs are large and variable. The example of the Barbie doll illustrates these large costs. The direct production costs of the doll are $1, but they are sold in the US for about $10 (Feenstra, 1998). Therefore, the costs of transportation, marketing, wholesaling and retailing have an *ad valorem* tax equivalent of 900 per cent. In their own (rough) calculations, Anderson and Van Wincoop arrive at an estimate of the tax equivalent of 'representative' trade costs for industrialized countries of 170 per cent. The number breaks down as follows: 21 per cent transportation costs, 44 per cent border-related trade barriers and 55 per cent retail and wholesale distribution costs ($2.7 = 1.21*1.44*1.55$). Anderson and Van Wincoop argue that more and better empirical data on the volume of trade costs can be obtained through microeconomically-founded gravity equations (see Chapter 6).

4.6   PROCUREMENT[1]

Procurement provides an exemplary aspect of running a business where transaction costs play a major role. Over the past 25 years, the role of procurement within firms has changed dramatically from that of simply buying goods and services to overseeing an integrated set of management functions. Procurement has crept into every aspect of management, from category management to managing supplier relationships, to contracts and payments, to strategy. As firms look beyond short-term costs and the scope of procurement-related issues has grown, managers responsible for procurement are paying more attention not just to what they spend on goods and services but to the broader costs of operating, maintaining and replacing the items and resources they purchase over time.

Procurement professionals play an essential role in managing the complex interface between firms and stakeholders in order to maximize value. In today's global economy, procurement managers have to identify and manage the different sources of transaction costs. They will need to do this in areas where they have varying degrees of control or influence. To assist management in understanding its cost exposure, it is helpful to consider transaction costs along two dimensions: i) in terms of objective and subjective issues; and ii) in terms of internal and external influences.

Objective and subjective issues. Objective issues are tied to measurable factors and are of a technical or professional nature. They are usually linked to financial issues such as direct costs, improved quality, on-time delivery, transportation costs and lifecycle costs. These costs can primarily be seen as hard transaction costs. Subjective factors, by contrast, are related to emotional, religious or intuitive views about the world and how these views connect to the organization. Although not overtly related to finance, such issues (for example, unethical business behaviour, diminished confidence in a brand or adversarial labour relations) can result in significant transaction costs and have major financial implications. These are mainly soft transaction costs. Partly these soft transaction costs relate to the issues of trust discussed earlier in this chapter.

Internal and external factors. By internal factors, we mean factors related to the specific business: its market position and its reputation and brand. These are distinct from external factors, which are tied to developments outside the firm in areas such as regulation, labour costs and currencies.

The combinations of internal, external, objective and subjective factors create a complex spectrum of exposures that can affect the financial health of a firm, if not its very existence. In a global economy, knowing the risks and opportunities of the different exposures is a critical management competence. Although management decisions will originate in many different parts of the firm, procurement managers will need to keep a close eye on the various cost exposures and flag concerns as they arise. Procurement, therefore, will need to become more closely connected with strategic decisions throughout the firm.

Table 4.2 lists the various types of costs that need to be considered in today's procurement decisions. The table distinguishes between the objective and subjective factors that bring about procurement costs, the internal factors that can be influenced by the procurement or strategic policy of the firm and the external factors that are exogenous to the firms decisions. It emphasizes the role of transaction costs, especially soft transaction costs. As mentioned, these costs are becoming increasingly important and have made procurement an essential part of strategic decision-making in global companies.

It is interesting to address the elements of the two dimensions of Table 4.2 against the conventional definition of the total cost of ownership (TCO) and the total cost of acquisition (TCA). In conventional jargon, TCO addresses the cost of goods or services at the moment of acquisition plus all the costs that will follow during its lifetime, including the cost of disposal (recurring cost, RC). TCA refers to the direct cost of acquisition (DCA) plus the transaction costs (TC):

$$TCO = TCA + RC \qquad (4.1)$$

$$TCA = DCA + TC \qquad (4.2)$$

So that:

$$TCO = DCA + RC + TC \qquad (4.3)$$

This illustrates the dilemma that the procurement profession has been facing for a long time. Transaction costs have generally been seen as a smaller, one-time component of the TCO and, therefore, the focus has been on the DCA and RC. The DCA is a subject that has the keen interest of both the internal stakeholder and the procurement department. The RC, while being addressed by the procurement department at the time of the acquisition of goods or services, is generally seen by the internal stakeholders as their exclusive responsibility and managed accordingly.

Table 4.2   Classification of procurement costs

Objective (hard) factors	Internal factors (decisions within a firm's control)	• Search and information costs connected with identifying suppliers • Direct costs of acquisition • Transport costs • Quality assurance • Installation and maintenance costs • Intellectual property costs • Training
	External factors (decisions controlled by others)	• Legislation in relation to trade • Currency effects • Import/export permits, levies • Labour costs and safety standards • Government rules and regulations
Subjective (soft) factors	Internal factors (decisions within a firm's control)	• The effect of sourcing decisions on existing jobs • The effects on reputation and brand value • Corporate culture: will staff members support new suppliers? • Sustainability trade-offs inside the firm • Risk aversion: will staff be able to deal with the risks associated with new supply options? • Internal people planet profit (ppp) considerations
	External factors (decisions controlled by others)	• Sustainability considerations in relation to local and global economic environments • Cultural differences connected with doing business • Political differences concerning democratic rights, distribution of wealth, unions and political stability • Customer views on desirable sources/suppliers • Labour circumstances • Environment • Social responsibility

Consequently, procurement finds itself in a position of sharing responsibility and benefit claims with others in the firm.

The above split of TCO into different components illustrates the various roles and responsibilities of procurement. Traditionally procurement has three roles:

1. The commercial strategy towards external stakeholders, aiming at minimizing the DCA;
2. Internal stakeholder management, aiming at optimizing the RC; and
3. Execution (Requisition to Pay, RtP).

These three strategic roles can be conducted rather independently, where minimizing the DCA and optimizing the RC cost elements from the first two cells of the table may be relevant for decision-making and where a flawless execution through the RtP process should be provided. However, these three strategic roles may bring about transaction costs, so that they are dependent on a fourth strategy, namely the *sourcing strategy*. As indicated above, this strategy becomes more and more important in the era of globalization, both from the perspective of procurement and from the perspective of the general management of the firm. The 'make or buy' and location decisions are major elements of this sourcing strategy. The sourcing strategy is to try to minimize TC or, to be more precise, divide the DCA, RC and TC in such a way that the broad measure of TCO, with all TC included, is minimized.

The DCA and the further cost are the two factors that typically drive purchase decisions. They are largely related to objective costs (as noted in Table 4.2). The first step in extending the purchaser's decision framework is to identify transaction costs as a cost category that needs to be managed separately. The second step is to give subjective costs the same level of attention as objective costs. Finally, purchasers must acknowledge that many of the soft issues do not just operate within the decision framework of procurement but are integral to the strategic position of the firm; hence, they need to be addressed by a wider management group.

4.6.1 Managing the Soft Side of Procurement

The importance of detailing and managing hard costs on a category-by-category basis is obvious. These costs are listed in the two upper cells of Table 4.2. However, a major part of the globalization challenge is figuring out how to conduct business both profitably and ethically, which requires a more comprehensive understanding of how to manage the soft issues (for example, the trade-offs between the environment and profits). Decisions to source products offshore – for example, outsourcing production parts and services – often lead to higher transaction costs than originally expected. This has implications for regional employment and economic growth because these transaction costs may affect the profitability of outsourcing and reduce economic activity. Moreover, it may lead to social unrest at home and a loss of trust in the firm, which can give rise to a *new* set of transaction costs.

As an example, the external considerations in ppp (people: social aspects; planet: environmental aspects; profit: shareholder's interests) can be mentioned. These different elements of what constitutes a sustainable business policy require careful consideration by the management of the firm. Decisions on this may entail risks that, if they indeed materialize, yield high transaction costs. The extent to which a firm is inclined to run these risks can be considered an internal factor and is, therefore, in the third cell of Table 4.2. Another example is that decisions to outsource work and jobs abroad may imply the dismissal of employees in the establishment at home, which can lead to social unrest and in turn entails many transaction costs.

'Social responsibility' is an important element in the last cell of the table. In this respect, social responsibility can even be seen as a rational business strategy rather than one dictated by social commitment and the generosity of businesses. Indeed, it is in the interests of the firm to foster long-term sustainability when it is expected that the additional costs of such a strategy in the short run will more than fully be compensated by lower costs in the long run. When a firm respects the environment and provides a good social policy for its employees, it signals its intentions to be socially responsible. This may affect consumer preferences, such that the risk of losing a buyer or an unwilling workers strike is avoided. Of course, these risks and their costs are difficult to estimate. Therefore, in practice firms make different choices with respect to caring about sustainability and corporate social responsibility.

However, from the perspective of reducing total transaction costs in a trade-off between more transaction costs in the short run but less costs in the long run, it is difficult to separate this ethical business behaviour from rational behaviour for the interest of the firm. Reckoning with environmental issues of sustainability, or creating a good social climate and working conditions for the workforce, may bring about additional transaction costs in the short run, but in the long run such behaviour may considerably reduce transaction costs. Through such seemingly correct socially responsible business conduct, costs stemming from adverse public opinion or shirking of workers can be avoided. Judgments on the sizes and relative importance of these transaction costs are difficult to make, as shown by different corporate policies between, for example, Shell and Exxon with respect to environmental issues.

Given the postulate of rationality in economics, it is an intriguing question why firms should engage in genuine altruistic behaviour towards society. Assuming rational behaviour, Graafland et al. (2007) conducted a survey of 20 Dutch business executives about the influence of their eschatological beliefs on socially responsible business conduct. By extending the personal utility functions of business executives by three elements, namely the probability to enter heaven (rather than hell), utility in the heavenly state and utility in the hellish state, they tried to measure to what extent their decisions and ethical behaviour were driven by these motives. Their results from the empirical analysis were somewhat mixed. They found no relationship between socially responsible business conduct and the belief that good works influence the eternal destination. Yet, in a partial correlation a significant positive result was obtained for those executives who believe that good works influence the heavenly utility and their socially responsible business conduct. Overall, it seems that the extension of rational behaviour to include eschatological beliefs provides some further explanation of the ethical conduct of businesses, but that the additional explanatory power is limited.

Trust constitutes a major element in the relationship between globalization and procurement. On the one hand, trust formation and building up the reputation of a reliable partner in trade can involve transaction costs but, on the other hand, when trust between suppliers and clients is established, it can considerably reduce the transaction costs of procurement. These arguments are extensively elaborated in this chapter. In addition to these arguments, Hunt (2004) describes how a bond of trust may permit an implicit 'quid pro quo' to substitute for a bribe. From a societal point of view, this reduces corruption, but bribes may also be costly in procurement, not so much because of the direct amounts of money to be paid, but more so because of the negative consequences that bribing may have on public opinion. Building the trust and trustworthy behaviour of firms can also be beneficial to society as a whole. In other words, trustworthy behaviour brings about positive externalities. By contrast, a loss of trust and reputation will not only involve high transaction costs for the firm itself but also for society as a whole. An example is the case of Enron, which, according to McAfee (2004), was considered a market-maker. Its largest business was in natural gas contracts, where it created a long-term natural gas market by offering to buy or sell long-term natural gas contracts. Trust is a major asset of such market-makers. When Enron revealed $1.2 billion in hidden debt, which represented the visible portion of something like more than $8 billion of hidden debt, in a matter of months Enron's revenues went from over $100 billion per year to nearly zero. Enron collapsed while other firms with questionable accounting survived because Enron's operations were completely dependent on being trusted by its clients. Obviously this loss of trust was not only harmful to Enron itself, but caused a loss of trust and, therefore, higher transaction costs in the whole business community. In this respect the rational behaviour of a firm to be and remain trustworthy can also be seen as socially responsible business behaviour.

4.7   CONCLUSION

Transaction cost economics, and in a more general sense new institutional economics, constitute the theoretical background for transaction management. Transaction costs are frictions which cause the economy to deviate in practice from the neoclassical model of a frictionless economy. Transaction costs occur in all kinds of transactions associated with specialisation in the production of goods and services. They relate both to horizontal transactions between firms and economic agents, and to vertical transactions within the hierarchy of the firm. A reduction of transaction costs, for instance due to good transaction management, allows for more transactions to be conducted, and hence for a more effective use of the advantages of specialisation resulting from comparative advantages and positive returns to scale. Such a reduction of transaction costs may lead to less costs per transaction, but in the end transaction costs may constitute a larger part of total costs when the lower transaction costs induce a new organisation of production where the production chain is split up further to take advantage of specialization.

It is difficult to make a clear-cut empirical distinction between direct costs of production and transaction costs. Yet at the macro-level transaction costs are estimated to constitute 30 per cent to 50 per cent of total production costs. It is conceivable that this share will become larger when globalization progresses.

Transaction costs have various sources. They may stem from the behaviour of the agents involved in the transactions due to incomplete information and opportunism, or they may stem from the characteristics of the assets in the transaction. In this latter case, sources of transaction costs are specificity and uncertainty, and also the frequency of the transactions is determinant for the costs associated with these transactions. A major way to reduce transaction costs is to establish a credible and reliable institution which sets rules for the transaction and prevents cheating and opportunistic behaviour. These can be the formal rules of a legal system, but informal rules based on trust and reputation may be even more important.

Procurement provides a good example of how these theoretical arguments of transaction cost economics work out in practice. Here a trade-off may exist between cost reduction in the short run and in the long run. When procurement managers are strongly focused on purchasing goods or services at the lowest costs in the short run, in the long run it can be harmful to the firm, when the purchase is considered as unethical, or when it damages the relationship between the seller and buyer.

NOTE

1. Based on Den Butter and Linse (2008). See also Den Butter (2012).

5. The transition from production to orchestration

This chapter pays attention to how economic activity in transaction economies gradually shifts towards a situation where the orchestration of production becomes a major economic activity. Parts of the production process are outsourced to subcontractors and suppliers in the home country, but also to subcontractors abroad (outsourcing, offshoring). Three examples of this transition from production to orchestrating production are discussed.

5.1   ORCHESTRATING THE PRODUCTION CHAIN

As noted previously, the global fragmentation of production implies that the production chain is split up into more and more parts and that outsourcing the parts of the chain that are produced abroad becomes increasingly important. To know how to do this is precisely what creates value in the era of globalization. This decoupling of the production chain and creating value by outsourcing requires a good level of skill to organize and coordinate the whole production process. This is what the orchestrating function is all about. Transaction economies focus increasingly on this orchestrating function, presumably because of their comparative advantages in specific knowledge and infrastructure, and because of their ability to create adequate institutions for fostering exchange, as discussed in the previous chapter. This induces a shift of economic activity from production itself to organizing production. The orchestration of production based on the appropriate cost considerations of what, where and by whom to produce is a vital issue for transaction management.

Figure 5.1 pictures the transition from a manufacturing-oriented firm to one focused on trade and orchestration. Part A of the figure shows the traditional way of organizing a firm, which executes most of the production at home at one plant. Direct production costs constitute the major part of the total costs. This figure mimics a case where two of the inputs of production are purchased elsewhere. Only, here (horizontal) transaction costs are to be made. The sales to the product market are executed by the

A. Traditional production-oriented firm

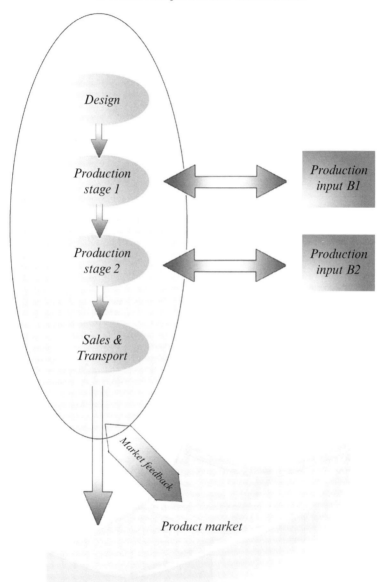

*Figure 5.1   The growing importance of transaction costs with the
fragmentation of production*

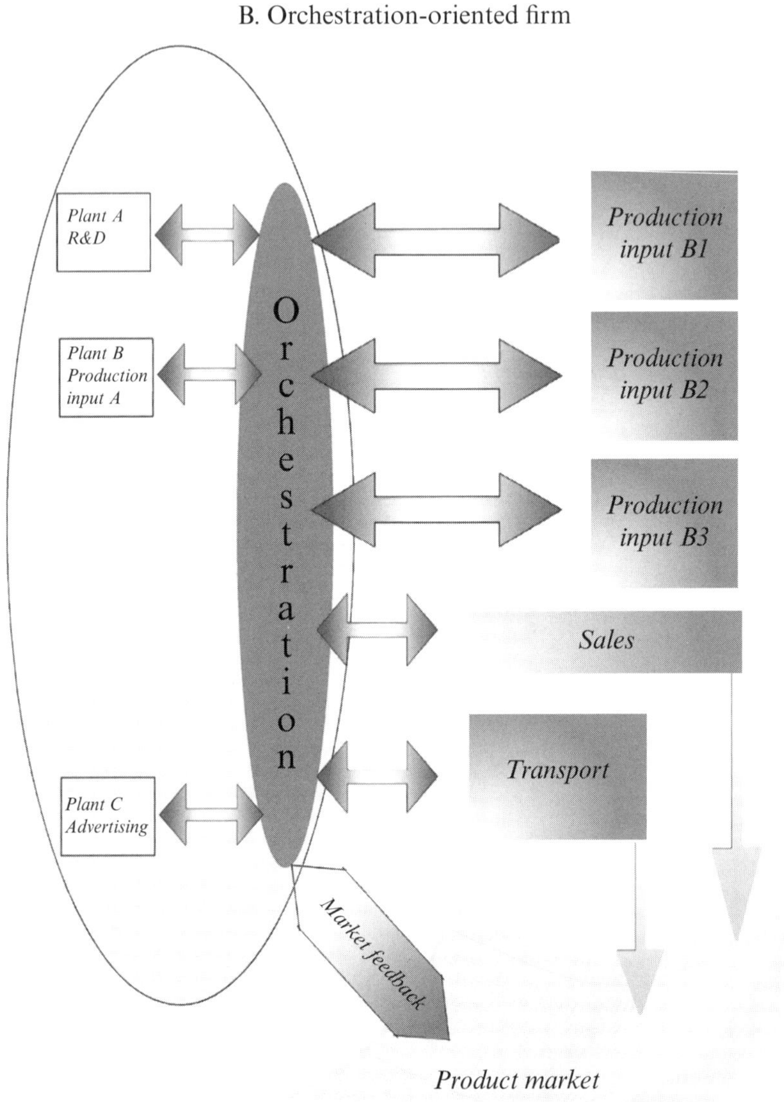

B. Orchestration-oriented firm

| Plant A R&D | Plant B Production input A | Plant C Advertising |

Orchestration

Production input B1
Production input B2
Production input B3
Sales
Transport
Market feedback

Product market

Figure 5.1 (continued)

sales department within the firm. The same holds true for transport. In this organization of the firm, transaction costs play a relatively minor role, because the production process comprises only a few links in the chain and, therefore, there is relatively little need for coordination. It is assumed that the management of the firm knows how to coordinate the different stages of production and how to connect the parts of the chain so that (vertical) transaction costs are low.

Part B of Figure 5.1 represents a firm where production is much more fragmented, and is outsourced partly through the market to other firms (outsourcing, subcontracting) and partly takes place either in separate plants of the firm (at home or abroad) or in independent subsidiaries. By way of an example, this orchestrating firm has also outsourced its sales and transport. However, in both types of organizing production it is necessary that the firm itself gains feedback from the market: it is essential that the management is aware of the changing conditions in the product market. These are aspects that cannot be outsourced.

In the industrial organization with a fragmented production in part B of Figure 5.1, direct production costs are assumed to be much lower than these costs in the traditional organization of the firm in the upper part of the figure. The way of organizing production in part B takes much better advantage of the relative costs and benefits of scale effects and comparative advantages for making the individual components of the product. In this way, the fragmentation of production makes the most of the benefits of global specialization: the production takes place where costs are lowest.

5.1.1 Orchestration Gains Importance with the Fragmentation of Production

Figure 5.1 distinguishes between comparative advantages *within* the various stages of production and comparative advantages *among* different parts of the chain. Large-scale production, technological progress and process and product innovation within a part of the chain provide an advantage in terms of direct production costs. This will bring about an increase in productivity within the specific stage of the production process and cause a competitive advantage for making that specific part of the product.

Organizational innovations and innovations that improve the coordination among the parts of the production chain reduce transaction costs and thereby create value by increasing productivity in the orchestrating function. This implies a competitive advantage in orchestration. In a transaction economy with a tradition of trading, the focus is primarily on these kinds of innovations that reduce transaction costs. Hence, in such a transaction economy, economic activities are more and more directed towards the orchestration function.

The increasing orientation of the industry sectors in transaction economies towards the orchestration function is inevitable in this era of globalization and the fragmentation of production. Only those parts of the production chain where these economies have a real comparative advantage are preserved for production at home. These are the parts of the chain that require specific knowledge and where the coordination costs of outsourcing or subcontracting are higher than the benefits of specialization (for example, task X3 in Figure 4.1b). The trend, however, is that the benefits of outsourcing or subcontracting increasingly outweigh the coordination costs. That is precisely why much of the actual industrial production and even production of services is no longer located within the borders of the transaction economies. It is a trend that is present within many traditional industries. At the same time the boundaries between the sectors of industries have increasingly become blurred. The required knowledge for orchestration has a general and a firm-specific component, but it can be expected that the importance of sector-specific knowledge will diminish.

It is most probable that in a transaction economy, a significant part of the added value, which is in the classification of the National Accounts (NA) attributed to the industry sector, in fact stems from the orchestrating function of the international firms (including multinationals). Therefore, a SWOT (Strengths, Weaknesses, Opportunities, Threats) analysis of the economy that relies on this classification of sectors in the NA, which is still frequently used to determine the competitiveness of a country, seems to be losing meaning. This is linked to the discussion on picking or backing winners in targeted industrial and innovation policies (see Section 9.5). Instead of looking for *key sectors* in the economy that are most promising to enhance the structural strength of a country, it is better to focus on *key competences* (see Box 5.1). Moreover, even within the traditional NA classification of sectors there are many differences among individual firms, so that benchmarking and identifying best practices provide more information on strengths and weaknesses than a SWOT analysis at the sector level.

5.2   OUTSOURCING: LOCATION AND 'MAKE OR BUY' DECISIONS

The above arguments make clear that the fragmentation of production can take place in various ways. The previous chapters indicate that a

---

BOX 5.1   WHAT DOES AN ORCHESTRATING FIRM LOOK LIKE?

An orchestrating firm is a firm that earns a considerable part of its added value directly or indirectly by the intermediation and orchestration of transactions. Knowledge of the production process and of the position in the network of related firms provides an orchestrating firm with the ability to generate revenue in addition to (or instead of) the physical production. For such a firm, the provision of services (rather than goods) in the context of keeping transaction costs low becomes more and more important. The more a firm focuses on the orchestration of production, the more innovations that reduce transaction costs will be valuable for that firm. The transition of production to the orchestration of production also has a major impact on the staffing of a firm. Knowledge of and experience in manufacturing remain vital, but the staff of the firm must also have good skills in resolving coordination problems in production, for example those caused by cultural differences. This is why good transaction management increasingly becomes a key competence of internationally-operating firms.

---

first important choice to be made for the organization of production is whether to coordinate through the hierarchy or through the market: the '*make or buy*' *decision.* This choice depends, conforming with the theory of Coase (1937), on the size of the transaction costs at the margin: when these marginal transaction costs are higher for production within a plant owned by the firm than for purchasing products from outside suppliers in the market, then production should be outsourced to the market. The opposite is true when purchasing at the market brings about more transaction costs – that is, when vertical transaction costs are lower at the margin than are horizontal transaction costs. In that sense, the transaction costs at the margin determine the size of a firm. A decrease in transaction costs through the market will lead to the firm becoming smaller or to a division of the firm into various autonomous parts. If the relative reduction of transaction costs through the hierarchy is largest, the firm size will increase. In that case mergers and acquisitions will create value.

The second important choice is between foreign and domestic production. In general, the strategic decision is to determine where the individual parts of the production chain will be carried out. This is the *location decision* (see Box 5.2). Again, the transaction costs at the margin will determine the

BOX 5.2   KRUGMAN, WINNER OF THE NOBEL
PRIZE IN ECONOMICS IN 2008, AND
THE THEORY OF THE NEW ECONOMIC
GEOGRAPHY

The location decision also plays an important role in the theory of
the New Economic Geography by Paul Krugman, winner of the
Nobel Prize in economics in 2008. This theory integrates with his
ideas about international trade. Like in the theories of transaction costs and new institutional economics in this book, the focus
of Krugman's theory is on the falling costs of transportation and
exchanges. As a result, economies of scale in production can be
better exploited. This promotes global specialization and induces
a greater product variety, and thereby results in higher real
wages. Moreover, such a reduction in transaction costs causes
migration to the cities, which leads to a larger population in urban
areas. The reason is that transactions can be made at lower costs
in cities because of lower search costs and higher probabilities of
good matches between supply and demand. This phenomenon
is especially apparent in developing countries. However, in the
industrialized world this migration to the cities also has a self-
reinforcing effect that creates a highly developed urban centre
with a periphery lagging behind in development. Krugman's
ideas have been influential in policy analysis. An example is the
regional policy of the European Union. Krugman has also shown
that fears of a 'race to the bottom' are unfounded in a world where
scale effects of agglomeration economies are strong enough.

decision. The relocation of production activities abroad – in general terms
labelled as outsourcing and offshoring – where the transaction costs of
moving production abroad are smaller than the gains through the decline in
production costs, is now subject of much research. In the case of outsourcing
through the market, it is labelled and registered as *outsourcing*. In the case
of foreign production in a plant owned by the firm, for example through a
subsidiary, it is labelled and registered as foreign direct investments (FDI).
Gains from moving production abroad, either through outsourcing or
through FDI, will eventually stem from those parts of the production chain
where production abroad is much cheaper because, for instance, of low
wages. However, specific skills in a foreign country may also be a reason to
move parts of the production chain abroad. In the case of FDI, this is the

Table 5.1 '*Make or buy' and location decisions*

Ownership Location	Make	Buy
Home	Domestic integration	Domestic outsourcing (subcontracting)
Abroad (offshoring)	FDI	International outsourcing

vertical FDI. The resulting intracompany trade can be directly explained from the theory of comparative advantage. However, much of the FDI has a *horizontal* nature: the same goods and services are produced both abroad and at home. A major reason is that access to the local market is often seen as an opportunity, where the benefits of direct access outweigh the transaction costs of relocation and potential diseconomies of scale. Moreover, proximity to local markets can be advantageous because it enables flexibility with respect to local preferences and changes in local tastes. This argument is related to the asset specificity of products for the local market. It should be noted that the gains in terms of direct market access could be seen as a reduction of transaction costs, so that both vertical and horizontal FDI can be explained by comparative advantages in transaction costs.

In this respect, Helpman (2006) argues that the distinction between horizontal and vertical FDI gradually disappears because of the development of more complex integration strategies. In the same vein Ménard (2005) discusses various types of hybrid arrangements which can be regarded as modes of organization in-between markets and hierarchies. Hybrids include all forms of inter-firm cooperation in which property rights remain distinct while joint decisions are made, requiring specific modes of coordination. Table 5.1 summarizes the various choices to be made in the location and 'make or buy' decisions.

The role of transaction costs and productivity gains in outsourcing can be illustrated in the stylized numerical example of Box 5.3. This numerical example shows a number of strategic issues that should be taken into account in the decision to move production abroad:

1. The size of the transaction costs of relocation; here, also long-term effects and risks should be considered.
2. The price elasticity of demand – that is, the ability to sell more products and the room it gives to reduce the product price as a consequence of the productivity gain. In other words, the issue is the distribution of productivity gains between consumers and producers (including shareholders).

BOX 5.3   NUMERICAL ILLUSTRATION OF
          PRODUCTIVITY GAINS FROM
          OUTSOURCING

This box provides a simple and stylized numerical example of how outsourcing may change productivity and may cause shifts in labour demand. The main aim of this numerical exercise is to show which conditions and assumptions are relevant in the modelling of the economics of outsourcing from the perspective of transaction management.

Suppose a firm has 10 employees that produce 100 units of a product. There is no capital involved. At a wage level of 10, the labour costs are 100. Now the firm decides to outsource production to a country where production costs are half those at home. In this new situation, the 10 employees are transferred from production at home to the orchestration of production in the low-wage country where they are able to achieve an output of 400 units. Production costs are now 200 (400 × 0.5) and the transaction costs of outsourcing 100 (pay for employees in the orchestrating function). Total costs are therefore 300, so that productivity rises by 100 per cent (from 100 to 200). These profits can be distributed among the employees so that their wages increase to 20, or they can be used for reducing the price of the product (it can also be reinvested or paid to shareholders). Whatever the case, in the current compilation method of the NA, the productivity gains are observed as an increase in the productivity of the industry, whereas in reality they should be attributed to trade and transaction innovations and not to process or product innovations, as is usually the case with productivity growth in industry. This is the productivity effect described by Grossman and Rossi-Hansberg (2008) in their theory on the trade in tasks (see Section 4.2). This supports the argument in the previous chapter that an analysis of productivity increases at the sector level, in conformity with the set-up of the NA, and is not informative. Instead, a functional set-up of the NA should be looked at.

For reasons of simplicity, the numerical example assumes that employment at home does not change. The 10 employees who originally were production workers are now engaged in organizing and coordinating the production in the low-wage country. In this example, the outsourcing of production and the resulting increase in production will create new employment abroad. How many new jobs are created in the low-wage country depends on the relative productivity and wages in that country. If productivity in the low-wage country is half of that at home (5), the wages in the low-wage country are assumed to be one-quarter of the wages at home (2.5). This implies that the additional employment in the low-wage country is 80 (400/5). The wage sum amounts to 2.5 × 80 = 200, as assumed.

3. The future development of wages in the country where the production has been outsourced; maybe at the time of the decision, wages are still low, but for the foreseeable future a significant increase is expected to take place.
4. The development of wages at home, including the transition costs of training employees for their new jobs as orchestrators and coordinators; these transition costs can be considered a non-recurrent part of transaction costs. In the example of Box 5.3 these training costs are not taken into account. Furthermore, it is assumed that the wages of employees with an orchestrating function are equal to the wages of those with a production function.

It is clear that the strategic decision of firms to move production abroad is a difficult one and requires a lot of good information and intuition (which can be characterized as good business skills and an entrepreneurial spirit). Underestimating all the transaction costs associated with such outsourcing may mean that it does not ultimately prove to be beneficial after all. In that case outsourcing is reversed. Another reason to regret the strategic decision to outsource may be that too much weight is given to labour costs and that the cultural differences in countries with low wages (for example, in Asia) are not properly taken into account. These additional and unforeseen transaction costs may even be so large that it is ultimately better and more profitable to outsource to countries with higher wages (for example, Eastern Europe), but where cultural barriers are lower. Moreover, the numerical example assumes that the quality of the outsourced production is equal to the quality of production at home. Maintaining such quality in outsourced production may also entail unexpectedly high transaction costs, or it may lead to a poorer-quality product so that the sales revenues decrease. This will again make outsourcing less profitable than originally expected.

Recent academic literature explains the strategic decisions to outsource or offshore and the determinants of the different choices using model-based analyses. Gattai (2006) offers a survey of these models of the 'make or buy' and location decisions. In principle there are four alternatives from which to choose:

1.   Continuing the domestic production of the firm;
2.   Moving production abroad through FDI;
3.   Outsourcing to the domestic market (for example, using local subcontractors); or
4.   Outsourcing via the market through foreign suppliers.

Remarkably, according to Gattai, few models discuss all options simultaneously: most models cover at most two of the four alternatives mentioned above. However, in an empirical study using micro data from a sample of Italian manufacturing firms, Federico (2010) analyses the determinants of the location decision (at home or abroad) and the mode of organization (outsourcing versus production through FDI or local plant). He finds that foreign integration through FDI is chosen by the most productive firms and domestic outsourcing by the least productive firms. Yet, in many cases there is no clear dividing line between 'make or buy'. In that respect Oxley (1997, 1999) undertakes an examination of the governance properties of different types of strategic alliances between firms. When a choice between these different forms of alliances – as in-betweens between markets and hierarchies – have to be made, the logic of transaction-cost economics suggests that more 'hierarchical' alliances will be chosen for transactions where contracting hazards are more severe. It relates to cases where there is more asset specificity, or to cases where firms operate in an environment with weak institutions, for instance with respect to protection of property rights.

The relationship between trade and outsourcing entails a number of conceptually interesting questions. An important component of the transaction costs is the costs that must be made to familiarize yourself with your partner. These costs are partly sunk investment costs, which must be made to establish an outsourcing or offshoring relationship, and can only be earned back over time during the relationship. This creates several problems (see also Sections 4.3 and 4.4 on trust):

1.   It can lead to potential hold-up problems when the bargaining power of the partners is unequal; the result can be that the partners do not trust each other so that the business relationship will not be established.
2.   Building a reputation of trustworthiness takes time and must be built step-by-step; one misstep can eradicate trust completely.

3. Trust in an individual producer or trader may be influenced by the collective reputation of its industry or country. This means that the behaviour of the individual entails externalities, which can cause free-ridership and thereby sub-optimal investment behaviour in a reduction of transaction costs. The consequence is that individual suppliers may be tempted to provide inferior quality goods or services in an attempt to profit from the reputations of their colleagues in the home country or industry. If customers notice, they will be less inclined to rely on the general reputation, which leads to increased transaction costs. These reputation externalities associate with the *branding of a country*.

The problem of outsourcing is equally relevant for small and medium-sized enterprises (SMEs). In particular the splitting-up of the production chain into evermore component parts where productivity gains obtained through specialization takes place via (innovative) SMEs. These SMEs either create value by focusing on the production of specific components that can be sold worldwide or deliver specific, knowledge-intensive services that are needed for a good and low-cost execution of the orchestrating function. In both cases value creation refers to products and services with a high 'asset specificity'. These developments are apparent in the construction industry, where an increasing part of the projects is carried out by specialist subcontractors (see Section 5.4).

The arguments of this section suggest that a reduction of transaction costs through innovations in the orchestrating function can significantly contribute to the competitiveness of a country, which moves more and more in the direction of a transaction economy. In that sense, there is a clear analogy with the social innovation that Volberda et al. (2007) see as an important aspect of globalization meeting the challenges of the organization of the industry. Both for transaction management and for social innovation, knowledge of the structure of demand and supply in the production chain is essential. This knowledge is about the functioning and dynamics in the respective networks.

5.3   THE DUTCH COMPANY IHC HOLLAND MERWEDE AS AN EXAMPLE OF THE TRANSITION TOWARDS THE ORCHESTRATION FUNCTION[1]

IHC Holland Merwede (IHC) is a good example in the manufacturing industry of how a company that was oriented to sheer production is

transforming to an orchestration function with a significant technological component. The company has its customers in the dredging, specialized shipbuilding and offshore industries and offers them advanced and
efficient technological solutions. IHC specializes in designing, building
and installing dredging equipment. Moreover, IHC supports the use of
this equipment for end-users throughout the whole product lifecycle.
This means that IHC also provides the maintenance, repair and supply of
parts for its customers in the worldwide operating dredging industry. In
that respect, the company plays a major role in the risks that its customers take in their dredging contracts. The dredgers strongly benefit from
the reliability of their equipment and want these capital goods to be in
use continuously. Because of the high specialization in a specific product
segment IHC takes a special position in the Dutch shipbuilding industry.
As the prospects are favourable for the dredging industry – think of the
growing need for ports and waterways and the increasing extraction of
minerals from the seabed – IHC may in the future expand its position as
the orchestrator of supply and maintenance of this dredging equipment.

5.3.1   The Need for Orchestration

That is why the need arises for IHC to act more on a worldwide scale as
orchestrator because in the future it will be less able to rely on today's
clustered location of the sector in the Netherlands and Flanders with four
big dredging companies (Boskalis, Van Oord, Jan de Nul and DEMA).
Nowadays the relationships between these firms in the cluster are strong
and trust is high. The common language, culture and physical proximity
so far favoured the design and implementation of innovations. Given the
low likelihood of free-ridership and of a hold-up, there was a good understanding of the mutual needs without leading to duplication. So in that
sense the cluster has been instrumental in reducing transaction costs. In
the case of IHC it is also related to the technological advantage obtained
on direct competitors.

5.3.2   Focus on the Two Functions of the Company

The shipbuilding industry and, more generally, the total metal-using
sector, however, are under increasing pressure. The dredgers were already
executing projects all over the world, but nowadays, and in the future, they
are and will be increasingly dependent on innovative projects in Asia and
South America at the expense of more mundane European projects. Given
this pressure and views about the future, it is necessary but also a challenge
for IHC to respond to the new positioning in the market and industry. In

order to meet this challenge the company could in the future specialize through two business units, namely:

1. Control of transaction costs for suppliers; and
2. Control of transaction costs for customers.

The first function for IHC to focus on, the control of transaction costs for *suppliers,* implies providing assistance to providers who are considering moving their production elsewhere at home or abroad. IHC itself has several times completed this step successfully and availed itself of sufficient specialized knowledge to judge these kinds of transactions on their ability to create value. Such operations bring about large, specific risks. First, there is the risk that contractors, when contracts are signed, will have fewer incentives to deliver at unchanging prices and comply with the contract (moral hazard). Second, there is the risk that production parts are outsourced to subcontractors for the wrong reasons (adverse selection). A good risk assessment, and reduction of risks is only possible in a situation with such dilemmas when there is a sufficient scale in terms of internationalization and knowledge of local conditions. Those companies who have this knowledge and scale, in this case IHC, can grasp the surplus through the internalization of the risks, while at the same time serving the other firms (customer and local contractor). This will then further establish the role of IHC as orchestrator by being trusted in the sector and by enhancing its reputation as a trading partner.

The second function for IHC to focus on, the control of transaction costs for its *customers,* implies that the company should, in a smart way, be responsive to the needs of the dredgers. The essence of this function is similar to that of the transaction cost control function for the suppliers. The person or firm that has the most knowledge of the risks should become the owner of the risks. In this way value can be created through this knowledge on how to reduce risks. IHC may, in the future, further exploit this knowledge by financing the supply of equipment. For example, risks can be managed by IHC through leasing contracts. This form of transaction management reduces transaction costs throughout the sector and, hence, will again contribute to the trust and reputation of IHC.

5.3.3   What do we Learn from the IHC Case for other Branches of Industry?

The case teaches us that there are two prerequisites for firms within the manufacturing industry to become worldwide leaders in the orchestration function. It also provides a feel for how to further implement the concept of business orchestration.

Prerequisite 1: the position of the company within the sector

The example of IHC shows that the company has a relatively strong starting position in the dredging industry. Within the sector there are no other major suppliers of dredging equipment and entry is not easy. In addition, with respect to its own suppliers, IHC has a strong position as a customer. This position of IHC in the cluster structure, as it still exists, provides the opportunity to gain knowledge about the needs of customers.

Prerequisite 2: knowledge intensity (specificity and risks/uncertainty)

The future demand for IHC's goods and services not only shows an upward trend in volume, but also a geographical relocation and a change in the nature of the demand. These are favourable conditions for the transition to orchestration. This new type and location of demand suggests that risks become larger and more difficult to assess for the dredgers, which are buyers of IHC's products. At the same time it causes the market for dredgers to become more competitive so that profits will be lower. That is why dredging firms will have a strong interest in sharing risks with their providers. They want a dredging ship to be continuously operational. It is noteworthy that it is not so much labour costs but rather capital costs that form the greater part of total costs. If dredging activities are stopped, for example, because of equipment failure, it soon gives rise to a huge loss on the contract sum. This implies that the dredgers are increasingly asking IHC for reliable products and services, and that they will also involve IHC in the development of new technologies and in the making of new contracts. This means that asset specificity becomes more and more important for the services of IHC.

This specificity of the required equipment and the possible role of IHC in the management of operational risks before, during and after the dredging activities involve IHC further developing itself into a knowledge-intensive company. IHC already has an advantage with respect to this type of knowledge and is able to extend it further. Furthermore this knowledge cannot easily be copied by competitors or new entrants. This is typical of such specific knowledge and gives rise to long-term relationships between IHC and its customers and suppliers. Knowledge-intensive industries and firms have, compared with knowledge-extensive industries and firms, a significantly better prospect of obtaining positive future returns from the transition to orchestrator in the sector.

In general, the knowledge intensity within a firm or sector is often the result of the degree of asset specificity of the demand for goods and services. A more or less homogeneous demand does not provide incentives for the development of knowledge. Here, new knowledge is soon common knowledge and the competitive advantage quickly fades away. This is the type of knowledge in production sectors where competition leads to efficiency, but where the actual profit margins are very small. By contrast, new risks that are difficult to assess because of a lack of previous experience will enhance the degree of asset specificity. A more sophisticated and targeted technology is a response to such risks. This specificity of demand enhances the knowledge intensity of the producer much more than that of the customer. The new knowledge is to be used in a more efficient production of the traditional core product, but it can also be sold or rented to customers in controlling their risks. This is typical for the second prerequisite of the transition to the orchestration function: the specificity of knowledge and technology that is used to control the risks (see Box 5.4).

The case of IHC can serve as a good example that may apply to many other firms within the manufacturing industry. In fact, in this sector many more firms are in the transition process towards the orchestration function. They are aiming to exploit their trading skills, their knowledge of and prospects for the product markets, and their education levels and high quality (business) institutions to develop and become worldwide orchestrators. No doubt many 'industrial' or 'manufacturing' firms are already largely those that trade in tasks rather than being focused on the physical production of goods. As mentioned previously, the productivity growth of these firms mainly stems from innovations in transaction management and less so from innovations in production. The problem in interpreting this productivity growth is that, according to the registration guidelines of the NA, they still count as firms in the manufacturing industry, so that their productivity growth is commonly ascribed to industrial innovation. As was remarked earlier, a functional classification of these activities in the NA would be helpful for a better interpretation of where these productivity increases stem from.

A certain degree of trust between firms in a sector is necessary before the process of transition towards orchestration can take place. When a firm starts up the transition process, it must be confident that the proceeds of the transition and innovation can be fully grasped. This is more easily achieved when the starting position is in a clustered sector – that is, a sector where firms are close to each other. Moreover, the future orchestrator is bound to fulfil a certain pivotal role in the sector. The position of the firm should, therefore, be stronger than that of its immediate competitors, customers and suppliers.

Finally, it is necessary that production in the industry be of a knowledge-intensive nature. This does not only apply to the production in a narrow sense, but may also be true for the sale or logistics of the product. In any case, transaction costs will play a major role in the sector or market. As a matter

BOX 5.4   TRANSACTION MANAGEMENT AND RISK MANAGEMENT

A good assessment of risks constitutes an important part of the skill of managing transaction costs. Central to the existence of a risk is that there is a situation of uncertainty with the probability of a negative outcome. Sometimes risk is just a synonym for uncertainty, but that interpretation is not obvious given the generally negative connotation of the word risk in everyday language. In the case of an investment in a share of a firm, the average investor would qualify the possibility of a price decline as a risk, but not a price rise of the share. Here, the word risk only relates to one part of uncertainty, namely the chance of a negative impact. To determine the extent of risk, two dimensions are relevant, namely:

1.   The magnitude of the consequences of negative events; and
2.   The probability of the occurrences of those events.

For the assessment of risks in strategic decisions, knowledge about these two important dimensions is essential. When adverse events are supposed to occur more or less independently of each other, one can insure against the risks. This is a matter of *risk diversification.* To calculate the insurance premium, insurance companies should have good empirical knowledge on the two dimensions of risk described above, or at least should have a good intuition to estimate the order of magnitude of both dimensions. If not, the risk is still uninsurable. Because the insurance company will incur insurance costs, it is a necessary condition that the person who wants to be insured is *risk averse,* otherwise insurance does not make sense. The extent of risk aversion is a matter of individual preferences and is reflected in the individual welfare function. However, from a social welfare perspective, there may also be specific preferences for risk aversion (or for risk solidarity). In that case, the state will make insurance compulsory.

Risks and uncertainties bring about various transaction costs. First, there are insurance costs, or alternatively, the costs to avoid risks. The insurance company will always include clauses in the insurance contract that encourages the insured to make his or her best efforts to reduce the risk – that is, to reduce the probability of the occurrence of the negative event. An example is a deduction of the payment in the case of damage (the extent of 'own risk') and/or a bonus malus system in the premium. This is to avoid moral hazard, which is inherent to insurance. Second, there are the often high costs if the negative event takes place in spite of the avoidance costs. Risks can never be eliminated. This implies that there should always be a balance between the expected costs of the negative event and the avoidance costs. The strategic decision that forms part of transaction management relates to the choice between avoidance costs and insurance costs. Obviously there is a trade-off between these two types of costs. When a firm makes high avoidance costs, insurance premiums will be lower. Here, the sum of the avoidance costs, the insurance costs and the expected additional costs in the case of a negative event should be as low as possible. In this risk assessment, knowledge of the two dimensions of risk, given the appropriate level of risk prevention, is essential. Economic theory teaches that, given the asymmetric information about risks, the 'ownership' of the risk should be with the party that has the best knowledge about the risk. Additionally, fairness in allotting the risks plays a major role in the negotiations about who will be responsible for the risks (see Ménard and Oudot, 2010). In a more general sense an appeal to fairness will lower the costs of negations and of contract enforcement (Den Butter and Ten Wolde, 2011). In the IHC case, it is IHC that has the best knowledge of the risks and of a fair split of risks when using the dredging equipment. More generally, the knowledge of risks is often a reason for outsourcing to specialist suppliers, contractors or service providers.

of fact, the skill to keep transaction costs low is an essential condition for the orchestrator to become competitive. This exemplifies the importance of good transaction management for the successful completion of the transition from a production-oriented firm to a worldwide orchestrator of production.

5.4 TRANSACTION MANAGEMENT IN THE CONSTRUCTION INDUSTRY[2]

The previous sections mainly relate to outsourcing and to the transition from a production-oriented business to an orchestration-oriented business with respect to firms that operate on a global scale. However, at the national level a similar shift in the focus of business activities also takes place. From this perspective, this section illustrates the importance of the transaction costs and orchestration function for the construction industry, which is part of the traditional manufacturing industry. The major question here is to what extent the orchestration function gains importance in the construction industry and to what extent the growing importance of this function is recognized by the management of the main contractors. With respect to this last question, it seems that the perception of the management does not catch up with actual market developments. Too much emphasis is still placed on technical knowledge and the knowledge of construction itself instead of on the knowledge of how to coordinate and subcontract various tasks in the production chain of the construction industry.

5.4.1   Industrial Organization in the Construction Industry

The construction industry is a good example of a chain economy. The bulk of the companies are local or regional SMEs. In the production chain, procurement, sales and actual production activities are split up into various parts, where each part adds value to the end product. Therefore, the industrial organization is much in accordance with panel B of Figure 5.1. The strategic question for companies in the construction industry is how and where to position itself in this chain. In the complex processes of construction work, such as design, realization and management and demolition, it is impossible to personally retain the production in each part of the chain. Therefore, the construction industry has a long tradition of working in cooperation with specialists who handle their own parts of the chain. The way in which this cooperation is organized is continuously prone to change because of market developments.

The key question is how the coordination, targeted at the control of costs, time, quality and risks, takes place in linking the various parts and specialists' tasks of the production chain. One possibility is a consortium of cooperating firms – strategic alliance – whereas another possibility is one firm that produces parts of the production chain itself and coordinates the entire chain. An extreme situation is that such a firm exercises complete control over the whole production chain with respect to design, finance, purchase, production, sales and after-sales, but commits the actual work on all parts of the chain to specialized subcontractors. In that case orchestration is the only role of the firm.

Actually, there is a tendency towards more and more subcontracting in construction. Eccles (1981) discusses this tendency from the perspective of transaction costs. A major reason for subcontracting is the larger complexity of the construction process, with specialization as a direct consequence. The main contractor increasingly plays the role of orchestrator, while the actual activities are carried out by specialized subcontractors or have been outsourced to the prefab industry. This subcontracting, outsourcing and ensuing coordination problems bring about transaction costs. Here, subcontracting implies that the main contractor buys products and services from suppliers and specialized firms. This tendency is in line with the overall pattern in the manufacturing sectors of industry. In this way, contractors in the construction industry transform from mere executors of work to information- and communication-intensive orchestrating companies. It can be argued that the skills in keeping transaction costs low and thereby exploiting the possibilities for advanced specialization determines to a large extent the innovative capacity of construction firms. This makes transaction management relevant for the construction industry.

5.4.2   Subcontracting in the Construction Industry

Empirical data for the Netherlands provide ample evidence for the trend in the construction industry that a growing amount of work and activities are executed by subcontractors. Data collected by the Economic Institute for the Building Industry (EIB) show that the number of specialized firms increased over the past 25 years by approximately 13 per cent, whereas the number of general construction companies has decreased by approximately the same percentage (see Sijpersma, 2004). Although the division of the data between general and specialized construction firms does not entirely correspond to the distinction between main contractors and subcontractors (for example, a specialized firm sometimes acts as a main contractor and a general construction company can sometimes be involved in subcontracts), the information is generally indicative of the increasing importance of subcontracting. A trend also becomes clear when looking at the average share of value added in the gross turnover of general firms in the building sector. This share decreased from approximately 25 per cent in the period 1987–1991 to almost 21 per cent in the period 1997–2001. This implies a reduction in own production of 16 per cent. In the infrastructure construction sector, the fall of the share is still larger, namely from 35 per cent to 28 per cent. This means a reduction in own production of 20 per cent.

According to evidence from surveys with the main contractors conducted by the EIB, the major reason for subcontracting is the increasingly specialized character of the activities and the knowledge and risks connected with it. Another important argument is that by subcontracting variations in the availability of production, capacity can be smoothed. In principle, construction companies prefer to make use of an established network of specialized subcontractors. These preferences are also reflected in the most important selection criteria when choosing a subcontractor. The selection is in the first place made on the basis of the requested quality of the work and the (insured and/or trusted) guarantees that the subcontractor can offer. Earlier experiences with the subcontractor and its proven reliability play an important role in the selection process. This shows that trust formation and establishing a reliable network are important elements for the reduction of transaction costs, including failure risk and communication errors.

These data emphasize the importance of the transaction costs for subcontracting. Specialized firms can deliver a quality product that the main contractor cannot, or only at very high costs. The gains of specialized firms delivering quality products more and more outweigh the transaction costs so that subcontracting increasingly becomes profitable. A steady relationship with subcontractors and suppliers that have already acquired a reputation for reliability also strongly contributes to keeping transaction costs low. Another reason for subcontracting can be that a specialized subcontractor has more knowledge of the risks of the part of the work or tasks outsourced. In that case, it is most efficient to make the subcontractor the owner of the risk (see Box 5.4).

In addition to the results of the EIB surveys, the practice of the construction industry indicates that at present there is, at least in the Netherlands, a tendency towards a reduction of trust and a hardening of mutual relations because of stricter regulation with respect to collusion and the commissioning of contracts. The result is harsher competition on price and less attention on cooperation and quality. This tendency is a consequence of the shrinking construction market and the increasing distrust between principal commissioners and contractors, following a parliamentary enquiry on collusion and the illegal actions of construction companies in the Netherlands. The result is that the number of contractors applying for work in open tenders has increased. This may lead to an increase in transaction costs and also has direct consequences for the relationships among construction companies, their principal commissioners and the subcontractors and specialized firms. This development can be considered a possible illustration of the U-shaped relationship between the degree of competition and the innovative strength in construction. On the one hand, the tightened rules for open tenders in (government) contracts may contribute to the fact that by means of subcontracting and specialization the fixed production capacity available for construction can be used in a more flexible manner. On the other hand, the strict tender rules might mean that production capacity cannot rapidly be extended or scrapped so that production demand should be matched to available productive capacity in an efficient manner. Therefore, the design of an adequate tender system for the construction industry is still much needed. This would be an institutional innovation that reduces transaction costs.

The tendency of increased subcontracting and specialization is also reflected in the composition of the staff of the construction industry (see Box 5.5). In general, this shift from sheer production to executive and coordinating functions or, to put it in another way, from 'making' to 'coordinating and trading' can be observed all over the industrial sector. For instance, De Beer (2001) shows how changes in the professional structure are related only partly to shifts between sectors from agriculture and industry to the service sector. Major shifts between production workers and managerial and coordinating staff in administration, accountancy, policy support and so on can also be observed within a great variety of sectors of the economy. This shows that the increasing importance of the trade and orchestrating function is underestimated when one only looks at shifts in types of employment between sectors.

5.4.3 The Gap between the Perceptions and the Facts about the Way of Operating

In construction companies that carry out a large part of construction production by themselves, the management has other core activities than when the actual activities are mainly outsourced to subcontractors. In the latter case, the activities of the firm focus on orchestration and coordination. In the case of much 'do it yourself' production, the management will mainly be reactive. The focus of the firm is on techniques, and most of the tasks are sheer production tasks. By contrast, when the firm finds (and considers) itself on the other side of the spectrum, and when most of the activities are outsourced to others, proactive management is required that focuses on the orchestration of the building process.

To make the transition from a production-oriented to an orchestration-oriented way of management profitable for the construction company, it is essential that the CEOs, directors and managers are aware of this transformation. It requires a major change in the emphasis, attitude and philosophy of the management. The management has to focus more and more on the customer and on the orchestrating function. To examine the extent to which this change in attitude has taken place in practice, ten Dutch companies, which have been made anonymous here, were asked

---

BOX 5.5   SUBCONTRACTING IN THE CON-
STRUCTION INDUSTRY LEADS TO
CHANGES IN THE COMPOSITION OF
PERSONNEL

Kok (2004) uses labour market data from the EIB to calculate that in the Netherlands the personnel in executive, technical and administrative staff functions (so-called UTA personnel) in construction has increased in the period 1990–2001 by more than 20 per cent. In the same period, the increase in the number of personnel directly involved in production at the construction sites rose by only 10 per cent. This relatively large increase in UTA personnel can be attributed mainly to one category: the coordinating staff functions. Here, the increase amounted to 80 per cent. This is a direct consequence of the extension in the number of tasks with respect to acquisition, calculus, project preparation, organization, coordination and administration and accounting. In that sense, the increase in UTA-personnel is a sign of an increase in transaction costs relative to direct production costs in the construction industry. Obviously the gains from organising production through subcontracting more than compensate for these higher staff expenses.

This increase in UTA personnel continued after 2004. In the period 2005–2009 the increase amounted to about 25 per cent. On the other hand, from 2005 onwards, there was a decline in the number of personnel directly involved in production. This decline in construction-site personnel can partly be attributed to an outflow of employees to self-employed. Nowadays the UTA staff comprises almost one third of the total number of construction workers, compared to less than a quarter in 1990. The construction management staff remains the fastest growing category of personnel in the construction industry. In 2009 the number of staff members has doubled as compared to 1990. All in all, it seems that the transition from production to transaction jobs, associated with outsourcing and specialization, remains an important phenomenon in the construction industry.

---

where they would place themselves on the scale between 'do it yourself' and full outsourcing and subcontracting. Using actual financial data from these companies, it was then calculated which position they actually occupied on the scale. Table 5.2 gives the results of this exercise.

Table 5.2 Perceptions and actual positions of a sample of ten building companies in the Netherlands on the scale between 'do it ourselves' and 'orchestrated outsourcing'

Company	Extent of orchestration		
	Perception	Actual	Gap
A	21	38	17
B	27	62	35
C	32	60	28
D	31	73	42
E	33	58	25
F	47	73	27
G	36	75	39
H	55	63	8
I	26	51	25
J	21	55	34

Notes: Explanation data on extent of orchestration:
● 0–20 focus on own production without a feeling for or understanding of orchestration;
● 20–50 focus on own production with a feeling for or understanding of orchestration; and
● 50–100 focus on orchestration with a feeling for and understanding of own production.

Source: Measurement of performance on purchases and market analysis of ten building companies (Van Megchelen, 2005, offers an elaborate report – in Dutch).

The outcomes show that in many construction companies there exists a considerable discrepancy between the position on the scale where a firm places itself and the actual position of the firm. The perception clearly lags the actual development. This implies, for instance, that construction companies still place too little emphasis on their coordinating and orchestrating functions and too much emphasis on the technical and production sides of construction.

Comparing the actual data with the perceptions can contribute to more awareness for the construction firms of their positions in the production chain. It may induce their management to place more emphasis on the orchestrating function of the firm. Therefore, this is an important tool for the management of (construction) companies and can effectively inspire them into a strategic repositioning of the management functions. In this way, a better perception of the actual position of the firm between production and orchestrating may reduce transaction costs for the firm, for instance by reducing 'failure costs'.

5.4.4   The Importance of Transaction Management in the Construction Industry

Both the macroeconomic analysis and the study of perceptions of individual firms reported in this section show that the role of outsourcing/subcontracting and, consequently, the role of transaction management is becoming more and more important in the construction industry. However, management is slow to catch up with these developments. This implies that, in construction, considerable productivity gains can still be realized by saving on transaction costs in coordinated subcontracting. To integrate this 'awareness of transaction management' better into the management of construction companies, more attention to the following aspects would be warranted:

1. *Procurement:* The procurement policy must be upgraded to play a major instead of a minor role in management. The construction company should hold a central position as a principal commissioner to obtain realistic and innovative offers from suppliers and specialists. This involves a larger awareness of the importance of procurement policy, where offers should be negotiated in a more proactive way and where there should be ample communication with potential suppliers. This communication reduces the transaction costs (including failure costs). Furthermore, in the relationship with the subcontractor, the price of the materials and sheer production costs should not be decisive for commissioning, but rather the total costs, including all transaction costs to be made by the company itself, should be.
2. *Product policy:* More focus on consumers' wishes and innovative products is possible, because the technological legacy and functional risks will also be outsourced to subcontractors (and manufacturers).
3. *Personnel policy:* The competences/abilities of the staff should gradually change from knowledge and skills in routine production and technical aspects towards supervision and coordination skills. Here, a proactive instead of a reactive approach is warranted. Of course, for the matching and coordinating of activities, good insight into the technical possibilities and pitfalls remains essential.
4. *ICT policy:* Good exploitation of the possibilities of ICT may contribute to a further reduction of transaction costs. More effort should be made to efficiently use ICT, using it to focus on external instead of internal relationships (directed at cooperation and proactive steering).
5. *Strategic policy:* The transition to the orchestrating function should be well planned and targeted, with realistic time schedules to avoid high transition costs (also a part of transaction costs). These investments in 'trade capital' (intangible capital), which keep transaction costs low

---

BOX 5.6   TRANSACTION MANAGEMENT BY THE
ROMANS BY USING A TRADEMARK AS
AN INDICATOR OF QUALITY IN THE
CONSTRUCTION INDUSTRY

The example of the Syndics in Chapter 1 shows that in the Golden Age traders were already aware that, by setting standards, the quality of 'laken' transaction costs could be reduced. However, managing transaction costs in the construction industry is even older, and goes back to the era of the Roman empire (or even before). Figure 5.2 shows a stamp on a brick from a Roman building, which acts as a proof of quality for the brick factory. Therefore, this brick factory, by using a scorpion as a trademark, tried to establish its reputation for making bricks of good quality. In that respect it can be seen as a form of branding. The stone with its trademark is now exhibited in a little room next to the Santa Prudenziana, one of the oldest Christian churches in Rome. Today trademarks, especially in the form of logos, are still important indicators of quality. An example is the symbol of the Saint Jacob's shell used by a large Anglo–Dutch oil company, which, by the way, started as a trader in Japanese ornamental shells. This logo is so well known by the public that the last change was to skip the company name Shell below the logo (Figure 5.3).

---

in the long run, partly bring about positive externalities. Therefore, it is important that such investments be made with (regional) colleague firms. One can think of benchmark firms for best practices, education, ICT, keeping up the reputation of the industry, standards for quality and legal standards with respect to purchase and sales conditions. As Chapter 7 elaborates, standards will bring about a considerable reduction of transaction costs. Moreover, investments should be made to establish a reputation of reliability for the firm, for instance through a trademark which signals quality (see also Box 5.6).

A further recommendation is to share experience and know-how with colleague companies by means of a common database. With all these suggestions enabling movement towards the creative orchestration function and thereby reducing transaction costs, it remains important to keep a full understanding of technical matters and to maintain know-how on new developments.

Figure 5.2   Transaction management in Roman times

5.4.5   Conclusion

The construction industry is predominantly considered a traditional part of the manufacturing industry. Moreover, it has been a part of the sheltered sector of the economy, as it has not been exposed much to international competition. As yet, in the construction industry, the possibilities of a productivity improvement by means of innovation and specialization can be found particularly in reducing transaction costs in the production chain. This emphasis on the orchestration function enables the implementation of technological innovations in the construction process at relatively low costs and at larger scales. In this way the productivity gains from a further division of labour can be exploited as well.

5.5   TRANSACTION MANAGEMENT BY TRUST OFFICES[3]

The previous sections provided case-study examples to highlight the importance of transaction management in the transition from a production-oriented to an orchestration-oriented firm. By tradition most transaction

Source: Shell Trade Marks reproduced by permission of Shell Brands International AG.

Figure 5.3   Changes in the logo of Shell as a trademark

economies have a strong financial sector (see Chapter 3). In a general sense, all activities of financial institutions can be considered transaction management. It is an important (and traditional) function of banks to ensure that owners of capital come into contact with those investors who can offer, given the associated risks, the highest return. In this context banks play a role as intermediates: through their knowledge and expertise they can achieve lower transaction costs in financial transactions than in the case of direct transactions between lenders and borrowers of money and capital. Another major role of banks is that they can adapt the terms for the supply and demand of money and capital, for example by attracting money for the short-term (against relatively low interest rates) and lending it for the long-term (at higher interest rates), such as in the form of mortgages and other long-term credit. The payment system can also be considered a form of transaction management because it allows transactions in two steps (goods and services for money, and money for goods and services). The transaction costs of barter are considerably higher. This section focuses on the quality of the transaction management of a small and rather unknown part of financial services, namely the trust offices. Such trust offices which conduct administrative and fiduciary services are located in a number of countries and places with specific tax rules for multinational corporations. Trust offices are, for instance, operating from the Bahamas, Curacao, the American state of Delaware, and Luxembourg. This section is about the transaction management of trust offices in the Netherlands.

5.5.1   Position of Trust Offices

A result of the long tradition in international banking and finance in the Netherlands is that there is an internationally-oriented regulatory environment and a sophisticated network of trade-supporting industries. From a fiscal point of view, the Netherlands is attractive for multinational operating corporations (MNCs) because of an extensive network of bilateral tax agreements, the participation exemption and, most importantly, a stable and reliable fiscal climate and adequate supervision. The feasibility of advanced tax rulings between MNCs and the tax authority reduces the risk for MNCs on the fiscal consequences of tax planning structures.

Taxes, like all transaction costs, have a distortional effect on production. The decision about where to locate their legal headquarters has a large financial impact for MNCs. These companies use *offshore finance* to reduce international tax liabilities and to structure financial transactions in an efficient way. In this way they try to minimize the total transaction costs associated with tax payments and the consequent financial transactions. These costs do not only consist of the amount of taxes to be paid, but also of additional transaction costs, such as reporting costs, information costs and the costs of compliance to (local) rules and regulations. Trust offices (also known as fiduciary offices) act as local representatives on behalf of foreign clients. They provide advisory and management services in the field of corporate financial planning. Therefore, trust offices play an important role in reducing transaction costs for their clients (see also Chapter 6).

The transaction cost perspective on globalization provides some insights into two major questions with respect to the position of trust offices, namely: (i) what factors can be determinants for the location decision of trust offices in the Netherlands, and more particularly in Amsterdam; and (ii) what role do these trust offices play in the Dutch economy?

Regarding the first question, the location decision, it is obvious that the decision to locate the offices in Amsterdam is dictated by the fact that transaction costs are relatively low at that location. Here, as indicated above, various types of transaction costs can be distinguished. The major activity of trust offices is the management of firms, of which the special financial institutions (SFIs) form an important part (see De Nederlandsche Bank, 2007). This usually means that a trust office acts as the managing director, providing SFIs with a registered office and with administrative and legal services. SFIs are finance, royalty and holding companies established in the Netherlands, but controlled by foreign owners. They receive and lend financial assets across international borders and constitute important links in the financing chains of large multinational groups of firms as well as playing a role in the context of mergers, takeovers, restructuring and refinancing. Total transactions by these SFIs amount to over €4500 billion a year, which is over seven times Dutch GDP.

One of the main tasks of trust offices is to help clients structure their corporate holdings to optimize their tax situations. Favourable tax arrangements for these financial institutions can be seen as a main determinant of the ability to keep transaction costs low because tax payments are part of hard transaction costs. Therefore, the prevailing tax regime is an important criterion for the location decision.

However, there are other reasons from the perspective of transaction costs for such a location decision. These refer to soft transaction costs. The services of trust offices require skilled and specialized personnel. They should be able to guide the clients of the trust offices through all kinds of necessary procedures. Therefore, excellent contacts with local authorities and a solid knowledge of rules and regulations are needed. Trust offices take care of registration with the local chamber of commerce, the central bank, the social security and the tax authorities. This implies that there is much 'relationship specificity' or 'asset specificity' in the services of the trust offices. This means that the services do not have a routine character but that each service should be tailored to the special situation and wishes of the client (see Nunn, 2007). Such relationship specificity makes the services knowledge-intensive, which can be a rationale to outsource these services to specialized offices. For that reason, the multinational commercial banks, which have their head offices in Amsterdam, may have decided not to provide these services themselves to their clients – some did and some still do – but to delegate them to trust offices. The clustering of these headquarters and trust offices reduces transaction costs through the good network facilities. Moreover, trained personnel is (and should remain) available in Amsterdam. Another reason for the location decision is related to path dependency. The Netherlands pioneered offering 'trust' services.

A final argument is that Dutch trust offices have strict codes of conduct and they are rigorously supervised by the Dutch central bank. Trust offices must have a license under the Act on the Supervision of Trust Offices ('Wet toezicht trustkantoren') of 2004. The licensing process includes a trustworthy test of managers of the managing and supervisory boards, and of shareholders. Furthermore, a trust office's administrative organization and system of internal control measures must meet certain requirements to safeguard the adequate control of potential integrity risks attached to their services (De Nederlandsche Bank, 2007). In this way, as much as possible, reputation losses for clients because of integrity accidents or fraud are prevented. Therefore, the 'trust' that can be given to trust offices through these codes of conduct and strict supervision may considerably contribute to the relatively low transaction costs of trust offices in Amsterdam. Supervision can never be so strict (it would enhance transaction costs too much) as to completely prevent integrity risks, fraud and the consequent loss of reputation for clients. Yet, the efforts of the Dutch authorities to intensify the supervision of the trust offices shows the importance of the institutional embeddedness of these offices. The legal framework and reliable supervision reinforce their credibility as being trustworthy.

The arguments with respect to path dependency and network facilities also provide a clue to the answer to the second question, namely the role of trust offices in the Dutch economy. On the one hand, the clustering of international financial and legal offices and headquarters in Amsterdam facilitates network formation and knowledge transfers, which reduce transaction costs for the trust offices. On the other hand, the presence of trust offices and short communication lines will also reduce the transaction costs for the clients of the trust offices. Therefore, the presence of well-equipped and trustworthy trust offices makes Amsterdam more attractive for the establishment of internationally-operating financial and legal institutions.

These basic services of trust offices do not always require a high degree of sophistication. The value added by trust offices is to be found in additional, client-specific consulting services, such as tax declarations, complex (administrative and financial) restructurings, auditing services, maintaining contacts with banks and regulators or supporting the closure of contracts.

Besides supplying trust services to their clients, trust offices frequently call in other specialized advisors on behalf of their clients. Most important in this respect are the financial and legal industries. Legal and tax advisory firms are frequently consulted for tax planning structures. Notary firms deliver the foundation of legal entities for clients. Here, part of the asset specificity of the activities of trust offices is using the knowledge of these specialized advisors and communicating with them. This indicates the importance of the trust industry being embedded in the network of specialized financial services in Amsterdam and the geographical proximity of these services.

In recent years a restructuring of the trust industry has taken place because of regulatory measures in the industry. Many banks that used to provide trust services have since outsourced those activities because of the risk of conflicts of interest and bankruptcy. Moreover, outsourcing such services to trust offices brings about scale effects that reduce costs for stakeholders. This provides another example of trade in tasks.

5.5.2 The Importance of Integrity and Reliability of Business Operations ('Trust')

The trust industry has been accused of a lack of transparency, and some even consider trust activities harmful to the international reputation of the Netherlands. To surmount this negative image, it has been essential for the trust industry to build a reputation of trustworthy behaviour in its niche market and to continue to do so. This reputation is to be maintained through a commitment that no illegal transactions will be conducted, possibly at some additional transaction costs in the short run. However, such (credible) commitment prevents huge transaction costs from reputation losses in the long run, when clients of the trust offices would be associated with illegal activities. For that reason, DNB (the Dutch Central Bank) emphasized in its 2008 annual report the importance of good supervision, where trust offices are required to have the complete knowledge of the origin and character of the transactions they administer. This credible commitment through adequate supervision, combined with a stable fiscal climate, network externalities and specific expertise, is the major reason for prospects of growth for the trust industry.

It is remarkable but not without significance that the term *trust* in the trust office has received such a negative connotation. Indeed, as Greif's discussion on the fundamental problem of exchange shows, trust plays an important role in bringing down transaction costs. Their relationships with their clients give specialized trust offices huge informational advantages. Therefore, a credible reputation of being trustworthy, based on an excellent and impeccable track record, is instrumental in reducing transaction costs. This is an essential prerequisite for the proper functioning of trust offices in the financial infrastructure. The screening of clients and transactions in the short-term can lead to higher transaction costs, but these are small compared with the potential costs from the loss of reputation. Experience teaches us that well-respected customers do not wish to be associated with trust offices whose integrity – rightly or not – has been called into question.

NOTES

1.   Based on Den Butter and Leliefeld (2007).
2.   Based on Den Butter and Van Megchelen (2005).
3.   Based on Van den Berg et al. (2008).

6. Transaction costs as determinants of trade flows

This chapter outlines how an empirical analysis of international trade flows using gravity equations can provide information for transaction management at the macro-level. Bilateral trade between countries is explained in these equations by the sizes of the countries and the distances between them, as in Newton's explanation of gravity. In these analyses distances do not only relate to physical distances between these countries, and hence to transport costs, but also to other transaction costs, including soft transaction costs such as cultural differences. The sizes of the coefficient values with respect to various distance indicators in these equations show how bilateral trade can be enhanced by reducing the specific transaction costs associated with these distance indicators. Two examples of such calculations are summarized, namely the role of trust as a determinant of trade and the determinants of trade between China and the Netherlands. China–Dutch trade witnessed a relatively large increase in recent decades.

6.1 GRAVITY EQUATIONS

Trade flows and the role of transaction costs as a determinant of such flows can be empirically explained by a gravity equation. The gravity model of trade, already mentioned by Tinbergen (1962), is commonly used for quantitative analysis of trade in contemporary economic research. The dependent variables in such a gravity equation are the bilateral trade flows, namely imports from country A to B, exports from country A to B, imports from country B to A, and exports from country B to A. The distance between countries is an important explanatory variable in these equations. In addition, like the analog of mass in Newton's law of gravity in physics, the volumes of trade are explained by the volumes of production in these countries. Moreover, in this equation additional explanatory variables are included that are indicators of the various types of transaction costs. In fact, these additional explanatory variables can also be regarded to represent the distance between countries, although here there is a different interpretation of being 'remote' than in the case of physical distance. In other words, these indicators of transaction costs can also be regarded as control variables in the regressions, which 'correct' physical distance for other aspects of distance. In this way the importance of the various types of transaction costs for international trade can be determined empirically.

The gravity model has often been criticized for lacking a solid theoretical foundation, since its classic form is only based on an intuitive analogy between spatial interaction in physics and economics. However, literature has found the model to work well empirically, producing sensible parameter estimates (Rose, 2005). In addition, nowadays the gravity model has obtained a rigorous theoretical underpinning by deriving it from models of imperfect competition and product differentiation (for example, Helpman and Krugman, 1985; Anderson and Van Wincoop, 2004). Deardorff (1995) shows that the gravity equation is also consistent with Heckscher Ohlin theory under perfect competition. Thus, the gravity equation can be justified from both neo-classical and new trade models (Wang et al., 2010).

6.1.1   Institutions and Trade

There is an extensive literature on the impact of informal barriers on the level of trade. This literature stresses the importance of soft transaction costs in international trade. De Groot et al. (2004) show by means of a gravity equation that similarity between institutions in countries, and the quality of institutions, offers an additional explanation for trade flows between countries. It illustrates how a good and transparent institutional infrastructure can help maintain low transaction costs. A major argument of this study is that international transactions involve several governance organizations. That is why the quality of these institutions and their capability to protect property rights are important for trade. These hypotheses are tested by adding dummy variables in the usual specification of the gravity equations, indicating whether countries share a border, language, religion or preferential trade agreement and if countries were part of the same colonial empire. It is found that institutional quality has a significant, positive and substantial effect on bilateral trade. Countries with a similar institutional system trade more with one another. A similar institutional system increases bilateral trade by 13 per cent.

De Groot et al. (2005) extend and re-estimate this model by using two additional indicators: (i) if both countries are members of the OECD; and (ii) if only one country is a member of the OECD. The estimations show that OECD membership has a significant positive effect on trade.

However, when including other institutional indicators in the model, the dummies for OECD membership are not statistically significant and the effect on trade becomes negative for both dummies. Institutional quality takes priority over OECD membership. De Groot et al. (2005) conclude that OECD countries trade more with each other, but not because they are both OECD countries, simply because of the effectiveness and the high quality of their institutions. Linders et al. (2005a, 2005b) also examine the effect of institutions and their effect on bilateral trade using the same model as De Groot et al. (2004). They analyse the effects of institutions for various types of traded goods, namely organized exchange products, organized exchange products excluding petroleum, reference priced commodities and differentiated products. The estimations again show that similarity and quality of institutions increase bilateral trade, but institutions matter the most for differentiated products.

Kimura and Lee (2006) compare the influence of various explanatory variables on bilateral trade in services with that on bilateral trade in goods for OECD and some non-OECD countries. Their main results are that the gravity model performs better in explaining trade in services than trade in goods. Geographical distance is more important for trade in services. The dummy for sharing a land border is far more important for trade in goods than for trade in services. The effect of economic freedom has a positive effect on both trade in goods and services but is much more important for trade in services. Regional trade agreements have a positive effect on trade in both goods and services. Finally, they find that trade in factor services may increase the exports of goods.

6.1.2 Institutions and the Ease of Doing Business

An additional way to consider the influence of institutions on bilateral trade flows, as an indicator of the 'non-physical' distance between trading nations, is to look at the ease of doing business. There are many ways in which the ease of doing business can influence the costs of trade. For instance, the costs of setting up a plant, outsourcing production, the ease of exporting or importing products, the ease of hiring or firing personnel, the ease of registering property and the ease of starting up a business are all costs that affect bilateral trade flows. If it becomes easier for businesses in both countries to start a business, register property or export or import their products, the amount of trade between the two countries is likely to increase. Chapter 3 reports how enhancing the ease of doing business has been key to the success of Singapore as a trade hub. The World Bank (2008) constructs an index for the ease of doing business that consists of ten individual indicators relating to: (i) starting a business; (ii) dealing with construction permits; (iii) employing workers; (iv) registering property rights; (v) getting credit; (vi) protecting investors; (vii) paying taxes; (viii) trading across borders; (ix) enforcing contracts; and (x) closing a business. The costs associated with the ease of doing business can again be seen as transaction costs of the soft type. The World Bank provides a ranking of all countries in the world with respect to these indicators and with respect to the composite indicator of the ease of doing business.

In order to investigate whether the ease of doing business as an indicator of soft transaction costs contributes to the explanation of bilateral trade flows, Bakker (2010) includes the rankings and differences in the rankings according to this indicator as explanatory variables in a gravity equation. Because the research mentioned above found that the quality of institutions has a substantial effect on bilateral trade flows, indicators of the quality of institutions are also included in the gravity equation. Here, the study of Kaufmann et al. (2009), which identifies six dimensions for the institutional quality of a country, is followed:

1. Voice and accountability: this captures the influence a country's citizens have in electing government officials and to what extent those officials can be held accountable by the citizens. This also includes freedom of the media.
2. Political stability and absence of violence: this measures the likelihood that a government will be destabilized or overthrown by unconstitutional means or violence.
3. Government effectiveness: this reflects the quality of the policies implemented by the government, the independence of civil services from political pressures and the commitment to these policies. It further captures the quality of the public goods.
4. Regulatory quality: this captures the quality of the government's way of formulating and implementing policies and regulations for private sector development.
5. Rule of law: this indicates the perception of to what degree agents have confidence in, and hold to, the rules of society. It focuses on the quality of contract enforcement, property rights, the police, the law courts and the amount of crime and violence.
6. Control of corruption: this captures the degree to which public power is used for private gain.

In addition to the ten indicators used in the index, these six dimensions also give an indication of how easy it is to do business in a country. Bakker (2010) concludes from his gravity model estimations that the institutional quality indicators are dominant in explaining why countries with good rules and regulations trade more. The addition into the equation of the indicators of the ease of doing business shows that taking this factor into account does not additionally explain bilateral trade flows. This dominance of institutional quality may indicate that businesses find this factor more important than the ease of doing business in a country. Countries with institutions that effectively define and defend property rights, solve disputes efficiently, increase the predictability of economic activity and provide protection against abuse between contractual partners make attractive trading partners. The time and costs wrapped up in procedures to protect property rights, enforce contracts, hire or fire personnel, close or start up a business, get credit, trade across borders, protect investors, deal with construction permits and pay taxes seem to be less important. However, this may not be the full conclusion from this empirical finding: the ease of doing business and institutional quality indicators are highly correlated so that the models that include both indicators suffer from multicollinearity, which might lead to underestimating the effects of the ease-of-doing-business indicators. Therefore, the ease-of-doing-business indicators might be significant when the ease of doing business or the institutional quality is measured differently and the correlation with the other institutional indicators is lower. In this respect, Ménard and Du Marais (2008) note that the construction by the World Bank of the ease-of-doing-business indicators with respect to the ranking of legal systems does not capture much of the real properties and specificities of these legal systems. From that perspective it seems sensible that the six dimensions of institutional quality mentioned above prove to be better determinants of trade flows than the ease-of-doing-business indicators.

In the next sections of this chapter, in line with the preceding discussion of the game of trust in Section 4.3, one specific indicator of soft transaction costs is singled out, namely the degree of mutual trust between countries. This differs from the analyses in Chapter 4 in that it is not trust between individual trading partners, but the role of trust at the macro level of countries that is considered here.

Apart from the focus on this specific determinant of trade flows, Section 6.4 discusses trade between the Netherlands and a rapidly growing trading partner, namely China. This China–Dutch trade can be seen as a topical example of the growing importance of trade in tasks in this era of globalization (see Chapter 4). This discussion also draws from an empirical analysis using gravity equations. The chapter concludes with some lessons for transaction management.

6.2   TRUST AS AN INDICATOR OF TRANSACTION COSTS IN GRAVITY EQUATIONS

A major indicator of the distance between two countries, which is a determinant for bilateral trade flows between two countries and corrects for physical distance, is the extent to which (the inhabitants of) these two countries trust each other. The hypothesis is that the higher the trust, the lower the 'distance' between the countries, which leads, ceteris paribus, to an increase in bilateral trade. A positive influence of 'trust' as an indicator of transaction costs in the gravity equation would imply that efforts to enhance trust between countries would lead to more trade and hence to more value creation. This hypothesis is investigated empirically by Den Butter and Mosch (2003b) by means of a regression analysis where alternative indicators of trust are added as additional explanatory variables in gravity equations explaining international trade flows. The analysis shows the extent to which these measures of trust are able to explain the influence of transaction costs because of problems of trust on (missing) trade.

Figure 6.1 illustrates some characteristics of the indicators of informal trust in this analysis. On average, the most trusted countries are Switzerland and the Scandinavian countries; and the least trusted are Turkey and the Eastern European countries. The trust of a country in other countries goes hand in hand with being trusted by other countries. Only Sweden and Ireland seem to trust other countries somewhat more than that they are trusted themselves, while the opposite is true for Portugal. The data on trust in the Eurobarometer survey further show that there is no clear link between trust in people from the home country and trust in people from another country. This indicates that trust problems are greater internationally than within national borders.

The empirical findings in the analysis of Den Butter and Mosch show that trust has a major impact on trade. When a composite indicator of mutual trust is added to the gravity equation with other relevant explanatory variables, the impact of trust on trade seems to be considerable. A one-point increase in trust will lead to a trade flow that equals about 1.4 times the current volume of trade. Here, trust is measured on a scale from one (no trust) to four (high trust). To clarify the interpretation of this result from the gravity equation: of the countries included in the analysis, the Dutch have the highest trust in the Danes (3.36) and the lowest trust in the Turks (2.20). If Turkey obtained the same level of trust as the Dutch have in the Danes, this would, ceteris paribus, lead to an increase in trade flow between the Netherlands and Turkey of approximately 47 per cent. The empirical analysis also estimates the impact of the trust problem on the 'home bias' in trade. This home bias is the

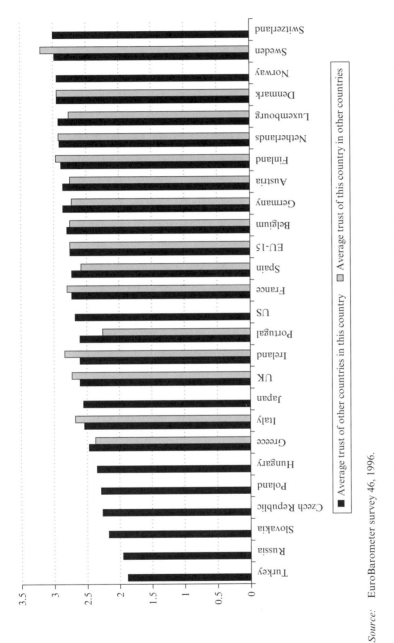

Source: EuroBarometer survey 46, 1996.

Figure 6.1 *Being trusted by others, trust in other countries and trust in the home country according to the Eurobarometer 46 (1996)*

observation that countries that are situated close to each other have more bilateral trade than can be explained by just the distance between them. If the level of trust people have in other countries would be as high as the trust people have in compatriots, international trade would increase by approximately 25 per cent.

Besides indicators of trust from the Eurobarometer survey, the gravity equations used by Den Butter and Mosch include other indicators to represent transaction costs. For example, a negative relationship is found between trade and 'no sea connection'. This indicates that the trading position of a country benefits from being accessible by sea. A decrease in transport costs is probably the underlying cause of this. It is also shown that having the same legal system provides a strong incentive to mutual trade. A similar legal system is thought to lead to lower transaction costs and thereby to more trade because it facilitates the drafting and enforcing of contracts. According to the estimates, the same legal system leads to a trade flow that is 1.5 times larger than the trade flow between countries that have different legal systems. In this analysis, having the same legal system is used as a proxy for formal trust.

According to the empirical analysis, this influence of formal trust on trade flows has decreased over time, whereas the influence of informal trust has increased. There are several possible explanations for this phenomenon. First, there could be a substitution effect between formal and informal trust. One needs a substantial amount of either formal trust or informal trust, but it is not necessary to have both. Possibly, there are even crowding-out effects between them (see the closely-related literature on substitution effects between extrinsic and intrinsic motivations in Frey and Jegen, 2001; Bénabou and Tirole, 2003). Second, it could be that the legal systems of EU countries are converging because of extended harmonization through EU legislation. The effect of differences in national legal systems then disappears and the indicator of formal trust becomes void, in which case informal trust problems become relatively more important. A third explanation could be a change in the inherent characteristics of the traded goods. When the composition of the trade switches from homogeneous to more differentiated goods, the importance of informal trust compared with formal trust increases. Differentiated goods are goods for which, in contrast to homogeneous goods, it is not easy to provide an objective measurement of their quality (for example, experience goods) and/or are goods combined with services (for example, helpdesk services for software packages). These goods have a high degree of asset specificity (see also Section 6.4). Formal trust is less appropriate when dealing with differentiated goods because of contracting and verification problems.

The relative importance of informal trust thereby increases. The empirical analysis does not hint at which of these three explanations is more plausible. It is, of course, also possible that the three effects appear simultaneously.

A division of the observation period in the regression in Den Butter and Mosch's study gives a clue about how causality runs between trust and trade. In general, it can be argued that higher trust leads to more trade, but also that more (successful) trade will lead to higher trust. As it is found that a given level for informal trust is better able to explain future trade than past trade, this strongly suggests that causality runs from trust to trade.

The empirical investigation of Den Butter and Mosch finds a substantial influence of both formal and informal trust on trade flows, considering the fact that the countries in their data set, especially the EU countries, are all more or less highly developed, share many similar cultural characteristics and have many bilateral and multilateral legal agreements. It would not be surprising if the results were even stronger if a data set were used including a greater variety of countries, less developed countries and/or those with a weaker Western orientation. Recent empirical studies conducted from a similar perspective confirm that various cultural and social aspects associated with trust and transaction costs are important determinants of trade flows.

To provide more insight into the order of magnitude of the influence of trust on bilateral trade flows, by way of a concrete, albeit extreme, example, the country pairs Germany–Greece and Denmark–Sweden can be compared. Denmark–Sweden is the country pair with the best trust relationship in the data set, whereas the trust between Germany and Greece is the lowest in the data set. The estimation results indicate that trust problems between Germany and Greece are responsible for 'missing trade' between these countries of the order of 216 per cent of the actual value of bilateral trade. Germany and Greece do not share a legal system like Denmark and Sweden do (accounting for 49 per cent) and their mutual informal trust is much lower than between Denmark and Sweden (accounting for 167 per cent). This does not imply that there are no trust problems between Denmark and Sweden. Although their mutual informal trust is rather high, there is still ample room for a rise that would further enhance bilateral trade between these countries. The similar origin of the legal systems in these two Scandinavian countries does not guarantee the exclusion of all possible legal controversies. Clearly case-study evidence and a detailed analysis of legal and cultural differences are needed to derive more sophisticated indicators of both formal and informal trust. This would provide further evidence of the main empirical finding by Den

Butter and Mosch, namely that a considerable part of missing trade can be attributed to a relative lack of trust. More mutual trust between nations and traders would lead to lower transaction costs and thereby enhanced trade and welfare.

6.2.1 Conclusion for the Influence of Trust on Trade

Trade requires cooperative relationships with trading partners. One has to come to know one's trading partner so that these cooperative relationships will last. Contracts in these relationships are by their very nature incomplete. This implies that the threat of a hold-up is always there. That is why informal forms of trust play an important role in these relationships and allow for low transaction costs, in the sense that the enforcement of delivery at the agreed price, the monitoring of the quality of goods or services to be supplied and determining payment guarantees bring about relatively low costs. These arguments are even stronger in the case of foreign trade partners because more prudence will generally be needed with these partners than with those of the same nationality.

Both formal and informal trust play an important role in trade. Part of Trefler's (1995) mystery of the missing trade – the observation that world trade would be much larger if only comparative advantages in the traditional sense were considered (see Section 2.1) – can be explained by including trust issues. Obviously trust formation in trade relationships brings about positive externalities. Therefore, trust between countries partly has the character of a public good. Although the findings reported above are largely based on a static analysis, they strongly suggest that government agencies for trade promotion should be alert to the mitigating transaction costs that come forth out of trust problems. This implies policies that ease the settlement of international legal disputes, encourage reputation building, increase traders' knowledge of other cultures, strengthen traders' capabilities to speak foreign languages, and promote the formation of international networks, for example by smoothing the regulation on visas for international students and employees. These policy implications require special attention in this era of globalization and developments in ICT. In fact, globalization and the ICT revolution enhance the possibilities to trade with faraway foreign countries by diminishing tariff barriers, transport costs and communication costs, which undoubtedly leads to a surge in trust problems. In particular, reputations become more important since information about past performances will be available to a larger audience through the internet. ICT can, however, never form a true replacement for all personal contacts.

Face-to-face contact will remain essential to develop mutual trust and keep trade going.

6.2.2   The Credit and Debt Crisis, and the Role of Trust

The global credit crisis and great recession of 2007–2010 show that transaction costs can become sky-high in the face of a general loss of trust. The transition from rising to falling housing prices in the US and the financial innovation of securitized asset-backed securities, among which are sub-prime mortgages, had the effect that the equilibrium of mutual trust in the financial markets turned into an equilibrium of mutual distrust. The result was that the mutual lending of financial institutions and provision of liquidities to each other stagnated. This affected the real economy through a cessation of investment credit and because of an enormous decrease in financial wealth. The role for government here is to see that the banking sector moves back to the equilibrium of mutual trust, in the same way as the government has the responsibility to break the prisoner's dilemma in the provision of public goods in the economy and foster an equilibrium of mutual cooperation (see Chapter 9). In the first stage of the credit crisis, governments correctly exploited the trust in government, reflected in (at that time) low interest rates on government loans, when nationalizing and recapitalizing banks that needed support. This trust in government proved valuable in a situation where the mutual trust of banks ebbed away. In the second stage of the credit crisis, financial markets also lost trust in governments, which resulted in high interest rates for government loans for some of the EU countries. Here, the EU tried to guarantee these government loans in order to restore trust in the euro. It must be said that this game of trust was being played in a still-uncharted area. Disagreements between political leaders and uncertainties about the way support has to be given to countries with serious debt problems do not help to re-establish trust and to let the financial markets believe that the large government debts will be fully repaid.

6.3   HISTORY OF TRUST-BASED TRADE IN THE NETHERLANDS

The previous section shows that trust is instrumental in lowering the transaction costs in international trade relationships. The same applies for a feeling for cultural diversity. Both aspects, which are typical for a trading nation, reduce the physical distance between trading partners. A painting by the Dutch painter Hendrik van Schuylenberg, from

Middelburg in the province of Zeeland, offers a wonderful picture of how the Dutch managed to deal with these aspects of trading in the Golden Age (Figure 6.2). This painting is from 1665 and is, like 'The Syndics' by Rembrandt in Chapter 1, part of a collection at the Rijksmuseum in Amsterdam. It shows the activities in and around the headquarters of the United East India Company (VOC) in the city of Houghly in Bengal in the North East of India. The compound is situated on the River Ganges, near the present city of Calcutta. In those days, Bengal was the centre of trade in textiles, opium, hemp and nitrate, a raw material for gunpowder. These products were shipped to various Asian regions and to Europe. By paying taxes and giving gifts to governors and local officials, the VOC was able to obtain the right to trade. Noteworthy is that, as the painting shows, the trading post has an open character and was not defended by military means. A good understanding with the local population and state officials was regarded essential. Moreover, much attention was placed on the local culture, which characterized the Dutch way of trading. Apparently it was realized that this was the way in which trade could best be achieved, namely with the lowest transaction costs. This form of transaction management made the headquarters of the VOC in Bengal one of the world's most profitable trading posts.

The role of trust in trade relationships and the trustworthiness of the Dutch is neatly illustrated by the following quotation from Adam Smith in his *Lectures on Jurisprudence* of 1763:

> Whenever commerce is introduced into any country probity and punctuality always accompany it. These virtues in a rude and barbarous society are almost unknown. Of the nations of Europe, the Dutch, the most commercial, are the most faithful to their word. The English are more so than the Scotch, but much inferior to the Dutch, and in some remote parts of this country they are far less so than in the more commercial parts of it.

In spite of the often blunt and boisterous behaviour of the Dutch, the interest in other cultures and the desire to find friendship and be trusted are important elements of Dutch trading skills. Even today, such skills can be helpful to create a bridge between the Anglo-Saxon, Rhineland, Arab and Asian business models. This intermediation function between various business cultures could be helpful to strengthen the position of the Netherlands as a hub for trade, business and financial services, especially now that a shift in global relations can be observed from the Anglo-Saxon to the Rhineland and Asian models.

Source: Reprinted with permission of Rijksmuseum Amsterdam.

Figure 6.2 Overview by Hendrik van Schuylenberg of trade and local culture in the Bengalese VOC trading post of Houghly in 1665

129

6.4   THE TRADE BETWEEN CHINA AND THE NETHERLANDS: AN EXAMPLE OF TRADE IN TASKS

The trade between China and the Netherlands provides a topical example of the recent trend of globalization and of the role of transaction costs in changing patterns of world trade. China's economy has been growing prodigiously at about 10 per cent per year in recent decades. Its growth has benefited from the worldwide fragmentation of production where parts of the production chain have been moved to low-cost countries. The long tradition of the Netherlands as a trading nation and the fact that it acts as a gateway to Europe (see Chapter 3) has very much influenced trade between the Netherlands and China. Dutch trade with China has been growing even faster than the Chinese economy in the period 1996–2010.

Nowadays China is the Netherlands' fourth biggest trading partner, with 9 per cent of total Dutch imports coming from China. This fast growth and negative trade balance with China, as in most Western economies, has evoked a discussion about the effects on the domestic economy of moving production abroad, especially with respect to employment and economic growth. From that perspective, Suyker and De Groot (2006) and CPB (2006) conclude that Chinese export products are more complements than substitutes for Dutch export products, and that China's growth has had relatively little impact on Dutch employment. In general, these studies indicate that China's growth has mainly had a positive effect on the Dutch economy, for example through lower inflation. Similarly, Gorter et al. (2005) state that the massive reallocation of Dutch economic activities abroad is unlikely and that it will not bring about a rise in Dutch unemployment.

However, little empirical evidence is available on the specific determinants of this growth of trade between China and the Netherlands. The biggest controversy here regards the amount of offshoring in China and its effect on the Dutch economy. Evidence suggests that a considerable number of activities are or will soon be outsourced to countries such as China. The contrasting view is that this type of outsourcing is present but unimportant and has little effect on employment.

Moreover, there is also the view that outsourcing to China, and to other countries with large physical and cultural distances, has been too abundant in the recent past and that some backsourcing will be needed. The latter implies that transaction costs associated with outsourcing have been underestimated and that the gain of lower production costs did, with the benefit of hindsight, not cover the additional transaction costs of outsourcing.

More specifically, the question with respect to moving parts of production abroad is whether this offshoring has occurred through the market (outsourced offshoring) or through hierarchy (in-house offshoring) and whether this decision has been influenced by the asset specificity of the traded goods. As seen in Chapter 4, this 'make or buy' decision and its relationship with asset specificity and transaction costs is a prominent subject in contemporary economic literature. In an empirical study using gravity equations to explain the trade between China and the Netherlands, Den Butter and Hayat (2008) investigate these aspects. Additionally, this empirical analysis provides evidence of the usual determinants of bilateral trade flows, such as GDP growth, tariff reduction and declining transport costs. An important aspect for China–Dutch trade is that, as explained in Chapter 3, a large part of Dutch imports are re-exports – imported goods that are the legal property of the importer and that are exported with no or only very small modifications. For that reason the importance of this function of the Netherlands as a distributor – the gateway to Europe – in explaining the trade growth between China and the Netherlands is part of the analysis. The study of Den Butter and Hayat, which is summarized below, solely considers trade in goods.

6.4.1 Key Statistics

A major argument of this section is that the fast growth of the China–Dutch trade can be neatly explained by the theory of a trade in tasks, given the specific endowments of both countries. First, the differences between the two countries are characterized by a number of economic indicators. Then, developments in their bilateral trade flows are discussed from the perspective of trade in tasks.

Table 6.1 illustrates some important differences between China and the Netherlands. The Netherlands is a medium sized, highly developed and open economy. China on the other hand is much bigger, but clearly less developed and open. The child mortality rate of China, for example, is four times as high as the Netherlands' (2 per cent vs. 0.5 per cent) and (in 2008) less than a quarter of its people have access to the internet. Although the Chinese regard themselves as excellent traders (and indeed all over the world they are), trade and foreign direct investments are much more important in the Netherlands. Moreover, the Netherlands is mainly a service economy, while in China agriculture and industry are still dominant. Perhaps the most striking feature is that despite its large economy, China's income per capita (US $3000) is still sixteen times smaller than the Netherlands' (US $53 000). Although China has surpassed Japan as the world's second largest economy, it seems that it still has a long way to go

Table 6.1   Key statistics of China and the Netherlands (2008)

	China	Netherlands
Population (millions)	1325	16
Life expectancy at birth (years)	73	80
Mortality rate under 5 years of age (per 1000)	21	5
Internet users (per 100 people)	23	87
Improved sanitation facilities (% of urban population with access)	74	100
GDP (current US $, bn)	4327	871
GDP per capita, (in US $ at PPPs)	3267	52 963
Agriculture, value added (% of GDP)	11	2
Industry, value added (% of GDP)	49	25
Services, value added (% of GDP)	40	74
Average inflation (1990–2008, %)	7	2
Average real GDP growth (1990–2008, %)	10	3
Trade (US $, bn)	2553	1211
Trade as % of GDP	59	139
Net FDI inflow (current US $, bn)	148	−2
Net FDI inflow as % of GDP	3.4	−0.2

Source: World Development Indicators Database, OECD.

before reaching the development stage of the Netherlands or similar well-developed OECD countries.

6.4.2   Growth and Composition of Bilateral Trade

Notwithstanding the large differences and distance between China and the Netherlands, their bilateral trade has grown remarkably fast. Figure 6.3 shows the monthly import, export and total trade between China and the Netherlands between 1996 and 2010. The figure reveals that most of the trade growth between the Netherlands and China has been driven by imports from China. Figure 6.3 also shows that the trade growth really took off after 2001, the year in which China joined the World Trade Organization (WTO). Accession to organizations like the WTO has been shown to increase trade via direct effects such as tariff and quota reductions and indirect effects such as increased institutional quality, trust and the use of international standards. However, looking more closely at the trade-flow data suggests that there are two more important explanations for the prolific growth in China–Dutch trade. The first explanation is related to the function of distributor that the Netherlands plays between Asia and Europe, where, as mentioned before, re-exports and transit trade play an important role. A typical example of such re-export is computer hardware that is imported from

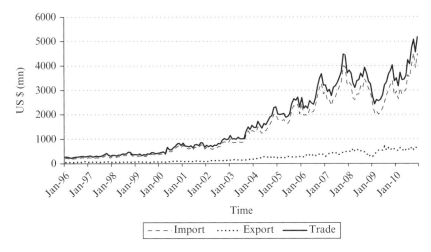

Time

| - - - Import   ······ Export   ——— Trade |

Source: CBS Statline.

Figure 6.3   Dutch trade with China

Asian countries, fitted with the proper (European) version of Windows, and exported throughout Europe.

The second explanation is related to outsourced offshoring to China. It seems that the Netherlands have outsourced production and assembly tasks to China. Trade statistics show that Dutch import of intermediate goods from China has risen more than 43 per cent per year between 1996 and 2006. But not only in absolute terms; the share of Chinese intermediate goods in Dutch import has also risen more than 30 per cent during the same period. Thus, China is becoming an increasingly important trade partner of the Netherlands in intermediate goods. This is a typical example of the Dutch skill in orchestrating production. It outsources the tasks with little or no comparative advantages and specializes in tasks where the labour force has specific skills.

A major reason in this section to take the China–Dutch trade as an illustration for the trade in tasks, and consequently for the role of transaction costs in a bilateral trade relationship, is that trade between these two countries has been growing even faster than China's trade growth with its main trading partners. Table 6.2 contains descriptive statistics and t-ratio tests on the difference between China's trade growth with its main partners and China's trade growth with the Netherlands. It shows that the Netherlands is one of China's main trading partners measured by trade value (data column 1), alongside economic giants such as the USA, Japan and India. Admittedly, trade between China's top 4 partners and the

Table 6.2   The relatively fast growth of China–Dutch trade

China's main trade partners	Total trade in 2010 (US $, bn)	Average trade growth (%)	Difference with the Netherlands (%-points)
Netherlands	48.75	19.29	–
World	2971.73	16.69	2.60** (1.18)
USA	385.44	15.76	3.53*** (1.19)
Japan	297.94	11.51	7.79*** (1.25)
Korea	207.24	16.80	2.49* (1.35)
Taiwan	145.34	14.68	4.61*** (1.43)
Australia	87.57	20.28	−0.99 (1.66)
Malaysia	74.22	21.66	−2.37 (1.49)
India	61.79	27.07	−7.78*** (1.45)
Singapore	57.05	14.73	4.56*** (1.38)
Thailand	52.96	20.29	−1.00 (1.31)
Indonesia	44.17	17.86	1.43 (1.88)
Philippines	27.76	21.66	−2.37 (1.59)

Notes: This table shows some descriptive statistics and t-ratio tests on the difference between China–Dutch monthly trade growth and China's trade growth with its main partners for the period Jan 1996–Dec 2010. Trade is defined as the sum of import and export values and computed from monthly logarithmic growth rates by comparing the same month in two successive years (to mitigate potential seasonal and month effects). The first column shows the total trade (in US $ bn) of China with its main trading partners in 2010. The second column shows the average of trade growth for the whole sample period (1996–2010). The final column shows the difference in growth rates between China's trade with its main partners and its trade with the Netherlands. We derive statistical inference by a simple t-test on these monthly differences. Standard errors are in parentheses and *, ** and *** represent significance at the 10%, 5% and 1% level respectively.

Source: Bloomberg.

Netherlands is considerably smaller. However, data columns 2 and 3 show that China–Dutch trade *growth* has in fact been significantly higher (on average) for the period 1996–2010 years than with these large trading partners. The largest difference is with Japan (8 percentage points) and Taiwan (5 percentage points). But also compared to the USA, China's number one trading partner, there is a substantial difference (4 percentage points). These differences are statistically significant for all top 4 trading partners.

Table 6.2 also shows that China–Dutch trade has been growing faster than China's overall trade with the world, a difference of almost 3 percentage points, significant at the 5 per cent level. The only country that has experienced significantly faster trade growth than China–Dutch trade is India–China trade. The difference is remarkable though (8 percentage points) and significant at the 1 per cent level. Trade with the Philippines, Thailand, Australia and Malaysia also grew faster than with the Netherlands, but the difference is insignificant at conventional levels. A reason for this can be that India, the Philippines, Thailand and Malaysia have export baskets that are very compatible with China's needs. India for example is naturally well-endowed with iron ore, which China needs for its production sector. In fact, in 2008, 52 per cent of Indian exports to China comprised iron ore. The Philippines and Thailand on the other hand are skilled in the production of several high-tech components, which China uses to assemble other high-tech goods. These patterns are, by the way, understandable from the Ricardian view of trade. The reason for the relatively high trade growth between China and Australia may be because China is a major merchandise export market for Australia.

However, for China–Dutch trade, Ricardian trade theory does not offer a satisfactory explanation. Table 6.3 shows the composition of China–Dutch trade according to the Standard International Trade Classification (SITC) in 1996 and 2010. The final 4 columns illustrate that the types of goods imported and exported to China are not as would be expected from the Ricardian perspective. From data columns 5 and 6, it appears that the bulk (62 per cent) of Dutch imports from China nowadays are goods classified as 'machinery and transport equipment' (MTE). A large part of these imported MTE goods are computers, telecommunication devices and components and parts of computers and office machinery.

Comparing data from 2010 to those of 1996 shows that the composition of imports of the Netherlands from China has become more high-tech in these 15 years. In 1996, MTE comprised only 27 per cent of imports from China, while 'miscellaneous manufactured articles' (MMA) such as footwear, clothes and handbags comprised the largest proportion of imports (39 per cent). A closer look at the data reveals that within the MTE category, computers and telecommunication devices have gained share at

Table 6.3 *Composition of China–Dutch trade*

Year	1996				2010 (Jan–Nov)			
SITC type	Import (US $, mn)	Import (%)	Export (US $, mn)	Export (%)	Import (US $, mn)	Import (%)	Export (US $, mn)	Export (%)
Food and live animals	116.0	4.7%	55.3	7.4%	537.7	1.4%	441.1	6.9%
Beverages and tobacco	4.5	0.2%	0.8	0.1%	18.8	0.1%	7.8	0.1%
Crude materials, inedible excl. fuels	200.5	8.0%	52.0	6.9%	619.3	1.7%	1438.1	22.4%
Mineral fuels, lubricants, related materials	23.0	0.9%	0.5	0.1%	61.5	0.2%	350.6	5.4%
Animal and vegetable oils, fats and waxes	1.6	0.1%	8.9	1.2%	7.9	0.0%	2.5	0.0%
Chemicals and related products	172.6	6.9%	211.9	28.3%	1180.0	3.2%	1369.1	21.3%
Manufactured goods classified by mat.	324.3	13.0%	56.0	7.5%	3059.0	8.2%	389.9	6.1%
Machinery and transport equipment	673.4	27.0%	345.7	46.1%	22930.9	61.7%	2165.5	33.7%
Miscellaneous manufactured articles	975.4	39.2%	18.5	2.5%	8727.2	23.5%	251.3	3.9%
Commodities not classified elsewhere	0.1	0.0%	0.2	0.0%	5.4	0.0%	17.2	0.3%
Total	2491.4	100.0%	749.9	100.0%	37147.8	100.0%	6433.2	100.0%

Note: This table shows the composition of trade between the Netherlands a-nd China in 1996 and 2010 (Jan–Nov) according to the Standard International Trade Classification (SITC).

Source: CBS Statline.

the cost of *inter alia* electrical machinery and apparatus. This is consistent with studies showing that China's export basket is becoming increasingly high-tech. This result is puzzling from a Ricardian perspective on trade since China is (given its natural resources) expected to have a comparative advantage in low-skilled labour-intensive products. On the other hand, the increased technology of China's export basket does not necessarily indicate technological advancement. There is much literature that China is adept in the assembly of high-tech goods with the use of production from other Asian countries, rather than in domestic production (for example, Gaulier et. al., 2007; Suyker and de Groot, 2006).

On the export side, Table 6.3 shows that goods exported to China are somewhat more in line with expectations based on traditional comparative advantages. The Netherlands mainly exports MTE, crude materials (CM), and chemical and related products (CRP) to China. Apart from the difference in composition, there is also a difference in size between exports and imports from and to China and the Netherlands. In 2010, Dutch exports to China were only around 15 per cent of total China–Dutch trade.

In summary, this overview of China–Dutch trade suggests that differences in comparative advantages based on natural factor endowments are an unsatisfactory explanation for the China–Dutch trade composition and evolution. China also seems to possess a comparative advantage in assembly, whereas the Netherlands exploits its traditional position as a trading nation and distributor to Europe, as outlined in Chapter 3.

6.4.3 Asset Specificity and China–Dutch Trade

The study by Den Butter and Hayat (2008) is linked to the perspective of transaction cost economics by following the network/search view of trade by Rauch (1999). This view provides an operational way to distinguish between goods that require relatively large relationship-specific investments and goods that do not. The argument is that an essential difference exists between homogeneous goods and differentiated goods. In this respect, Rauch distinguishes between three types of goods: goods that are traded on organized exchanges ('homogeneous goods'), goods that are not traded on organized exchanges but possess 'reference prices' ('reference priced goods') and all other goods ('differentiated goods').

As a rationale behind this distinction, Rauch proposes that the reason why some goods are traded on organized exchanges and some are not is that the latter cannot be distinguished from each other by observing their price alone. These goods are not homogeneous enough to be traded at an organized exchange. Their value has to be assessed on the basis of a number of characteristics across several dimensions.

Rauch gives two examples that support this view. Based on 'conventional wisdom', when comparing footwear (SITC classification 851) to lead (SITC 685), one would expect footwear to be traded on an organized exchange rather than lead because the market for lead (US $1.6 billion) is much smaller than the footwear market (US $27.3 billion). This is not the case, however. Footwear is not traded on an organized exchange, whereas lead is traded on the London Metal Exchange. Thus, there must be another reason why trade in lead is organized through an exchange whereas trade in footwear is not. The answer is that footwear is a typical example of a differentiated good: it can be subdivided into multiple categories across various dimensions (type, price, 'coolness', comfort, etc.). At the margins this subdivision may lead to a single supplier.

When considering the asset specificity of traded goods, Rauch makes the important observation that it is far more costly to match buyers and sellers in the market for footwear than for lead. There is much more information asymmetry between buyers and sellers of footwear than between buyers and sellers of lead, and this asymmetry cannot be overcome by the mere inception of an organized exchange on which the footwear can be listed as a homogeneous commodity, distinguishable only by price.

By contrast, there are also goods that are homogeneous, but are still not traded on an organized exchange (even though they might have large market sizes). According to Rauch, this is because these goods can only be compared to each other in terms of price through specialist information sources (for example, trade publications). Polymerization and copolymerization products (SITC 583) are examples of this type of goods. The market for these goods is larger than that of footwear (namely US $47.6 billion), but they are not traded on an organized exchange. This does not necessarily mean that polymerization and copolymerization products are differentiated goods. These goods have prices that are quoted weekly in the *Chemical Marketing Reporter*. Therefore, it seems likely that these products can be compared across geographical regions based on their quoted prices. However, it is also likely that getting this information is more costly and time-consuming than it is on an organized exchange.

Therefore, the main difference between goods traded on an organized exchange and goods that have reference prices is that the former have specialized traders that centralize price information (through the exchange), whereas the latter may not. This distinction is interesting for the empirical analysis of trade flows since it implies that the transaction costs associated with reference-priced goods are higher than those associated with homogeneous goods, but lower than those associated with differentiated goods. That is why Den Butter and Hayat explicitly make a distinction between these three types of goods in their empirical analysis of China–Dutch trade:

goods that are sold on an organized exchange, goods that are reference-priced and goods that are neither of these. In addition, it has been argued that trade in differentiated goods entails a lot more (relationship-specific) search costs than goods sold on an organized exchange. Trade in differentiated goods is thereby more prone to opportunistic behaviour.

Similarly Nunn (2007) argues that trade in differentiated products is more exposed to opportunistic behaviour than trade in homogeneous goods because less relationship-specific search costs have to be made to match buyers and sellers in the case of homogeneous goods. Furthermore, homogeneous goods have values that do not differ much within or outside a trade relationship because their market is thick (that is, it contains many buyers and sellers). In the case of differentiated goods, exposure to opportunistic behaviour is also increased because they are more prone to the verification problem. Their quality cannot be perfectly assessed by third parties because of their heterogeneity. This has an impeding effect on monitoring and enforcement. In addition, contracts for differentiated goods are more incomplete since more factors than price alone have to be considered. Overall, differentiated goods are more prone to the hold-up problem because of asset specificity and incomplete contracts and, thereby, transaction costs are higher for this type of goods.

6.4.4 Empirics for China–Dutch Trade

The overall conclusion of the empirical analysis of Den Butter and Hayat, using a gravity model for trade flows between China and the Netherlands, is that Dutch offshoring to China has significantly and positively affected trade growth between these two countries, namely through imports. Their estimation results suggest that Dutch firms have offshored in-house in the case of asset-specific goods and have offshored via the market in the case of homogeneous goods (that is, non-asset-specific goods). Dutch FDI to China seems to have a vertical rather than a horizontal character and thereby has been motivated mainly by production efficiency rather than market proximity. Tariffs seem to have been significant impediments to Dutch exports to China as well as to imports from China, although their contribution to the latter is modest. Moreover, the increased importance of Dutch re-exports has been found to have a significantly positive effect on the growth of Dutch imports from China but not for Dutch exports to China.

The effect of declining transportation costs seems to be statistically significant for reference-priced and homogeneous goods, but not for differentiated goods. Since transport costs have only declined 7 per cent in the reference period 1996–2006 of the study by Den Butter and Hayat, the overall economic effect, however, is negligible. Obviously, the most sizeable effects stem from Dutch and Chinese GDP growth. The elasticity between Dutch and Chinese GDP growth to import and export growth is close to unity, as gravity theory would suggest.

The analysis also shows that the choice of Dutch firms to move production to China by means of FDI or through outsourcing via the market is closely related to the character of the products. The asset specificity of the product largely determines how production in China has to be organized. It seems that when the asset specificity of the products is high, and thereby when there will be substantial coordination costs in the supply of goods though the market, the 'make or buy' decision will in general result in the 'make' decision of in-house production via FDI. This again highlights the importance of the asset specificity of producing goods or services in deciding how to move production abroad.

6.4.5   Conclusions for China–Dutch Trade

Outsourcing and offshoring as part of the worldwide process of globalization with trade in tasks have been major determinants of the strong China–Dutch trade growth. From this perspective, a major finding of the empirical investigation of the determinants of bilateral trade flows between China and the Netherlands is that Dutch offshoring to China has had a significant effect on China–Dutch trade growth. The effect of FDI on exports is also positive (although not significant), which indicates that FDI from the Netherlands to China has had a vertical rather than a horizontal character and is thereby mainly motivated by cost advantages rather than market proximity. Therefore, Dutch firms have moved parts of their production to China and have subsequently been importing intermediate inputs from China. The analysis suggests that Dutch offshoring to China has been mainly in-house rather than via the market. The decisions of Dutch firms to offshore to China in-house or via the market has been significantly influenced by the asset specificity (and thereby the transaction costs resulting from it) of the traded inputs. More specifically, the results show that FDI (representing in-house offshoring) has a positive and significant influence on the imports of differentiated goods, whereas outsourced offshoring has a positive and significant influence on the imports of reference-priced and homogeneous goods. The results indicate that differentiated goods are more sensitive to increases in Dutch re-export activities than are homogeneous and reference-priced goods. This reflects the fact that most re-exports of the Netherlands comprise differentiated goods. All of these empirical results from the gravity analysis seem to support the arguments of transaction management with respect to the types of transaction costs which are important determinants of bilateral trade flows.

The trade relationship between China and the Netherlands is one that takes place between two economically and politically dissimilar countries. This relationship is likely to have different dynamics from trade between countries that are similar in these dimensions. In addition, the comparative advantages of China and the Netherlands are different to the conventional advantages in, for example, high- or low-skilled labour-intensive goods. China, for example, is (next to low-skilled labour-intensive goods) skilful in assembly, whereas the Netherlands seems to be strong in reducing transaction costs through trade and orchestrating production. Nonetheless, the results strongly indicate that transaction costs matter (especially for trading nations). The knowledge of how transaction costs influence the working of the economy is, therefore, indispensable in understanding trade growth and the governance structures of multinational firms. That is how transaction management can contribute to value creation in a bilateral trade relationship such as that between China and the Netherlands.

6.4.6   Trade in Tasks in the BRIC Countries

Table 3.1 shows that China is not the only large economy which witnessed a fast economic development. This also holds true for two other BRIC countries, namely Brazil and India. Undeniably, this growth in the BRIC countries is because of increased outsourcing and trade in tasks. This trade in tasks is reflected in the trade in parts and components. By way of an illustration, consider the machine and transport industries, which cover 40 per cent of world trade in goods. In the period 2000–2006, trade in parts and components in these sectors increased by 129 per cent to US $1305 billion. This trade in parts and components grew considerably faster than the total trade in these sectors. A similar development can be seen with respect to total world trade in goods. The share of trade in parts and components in total world trade in goods increased from 8.9 per cent in 2000 to 10.9 per cent in 2006, an increase of 22.5 per cent.

Although trade in tasks is primarily located in industry, it is also becoming more important in services. This is partly because of the increasing demand for services in the form of transport and, in connection with the coordination function, in communication. However, it is a direct consequence of the fragmentation of production. Moreover, developments in ICT and in the software used, for example, in the automotive industry or in the design of aircraft make it feasible to conduct specific tasks with respect to technologically advanced production processes in a developing country such as India. According to data from the WTO, India and China have witnessed the strongest growth in exports of commercial services. Given these facts it is not surprising that nearly 60 per cent of trade in commercial services consists of trading in computer and communication services and in other business services.

The new role of the BRIC countries in the world economy and their strong output growth suggest that these countries are able to invest additional resources in education and R&D activities. In 2006, 882000 academic engineers graduated in these countries. This is 3.4 times the number of graduates in engineering in the United States, the United Kingdom and Germany combined. In a similar way, the R&D expenditures in the BRIC countries increased rapidly. The total expenditure is now equivalent to one-fifth of the R&D spending in OECD countries. Therefore, emerging economies are becoming more and more able to perform in world trade at technologically-advanced levels. The share of imports of high-technology products from non-OECD countries, which in 1990 consisted of about 13 per cent of the total imports of developed countries, had risen in 2004 to 22 per cent. The share of low-technology products fell from 41 per cent to 28 per cent.

6.5   LESSONS FOR TRANSACTION MANAGEMENT

Gravity equations are nowadays a widely-used empirical methodology to model the determinants of bilateral trade flows. The distance between the two respective trading countries is a major determinant of trade flows in these equations. Distance is not only measured as physical distance, representing transportation costs, but all kinds of other ways to describe 'distance' are included in the gravity equations and seem to contribute significantly to the explanation of trade flows. Whereas the physical distance, and hence the transportation costs, can be seen to represent the 'hard' transaction costs, the other indicators of distance in the equations stand for various types of 'soft' transaction costs, such as cultural distance, differences in legal institutions, informal trade barriers, etc.

These empirical studies of gravity equations provide proof of the growing importance of these 'soft' indicators of distance as determinants of trade. The size of the effects of changes in these 'soft' transaction costs on trade can be calculated by using the parameter estimates in the equations. In that sense they provide lessons for transaction management at the national level – but through it at the level of the industry and firms also – on what reductions of transaction costs will be most effective to foster trade. For example, the study by De Santis and Vicarelli (2007) using gravity equations shows that both the 'deeper' and the 'wider' strategies of trade integration have had a positive and significant effect on EU trade flows. The strategy of 'deepening' trade relates to the period from the late 1950s to the early 1990s, when trade integration was brought about through abolition of internal tariffs. Its result was the formation of the Single European Market. The aim of the strategy of 'widening' trade was to enhance trade between the EU and non-EU countries through preferential trade agreements (PTAs). Here, not only tariffs but also national and regional product standards, government procurement practices, rules of origin, etc., were looked at. The estimates of the gravity equations show that with respect to the 'deepening' strategy, countries belonging to the EU imported on average 125 per cent more amongst themselves than they did from outsiders. With respect to the 'widening' strategy it appears that EU PTA policies towards third countries enhanced trade by about 30 per cent.

The empirical studies discussed in the previous sections teach similar lessons for transaction management. The analyses of the influence of trust on trade show that, in line with the argumentation from new institutional economics, institutions which bring about trust, and which are trustworthy, have a positive effect on trade transactions. The gravity study on China–Dutch trade underlines the importance of transaction costs in the 'make or buy' decision in combination with the location decision. The extent of asset specificity appears to be a major determinant for these decisions.

6.5.1 Policy Implications

This knowledge from the gravity models is also useful for policies that aim to foster trade and, through trade, prosperity. Moving sections of actual production abroad, while keeping the coordination and trade function at home, can be a good productivity- and welfare-enhancing strategy for a transaction-oriented economy. The relative efficiency of such economies to reduce transaction costs – the core element of transaction management – is an important source of comparative advantage. Therefore, policy should stimulate investments in innovations that reduce these transaction costs. Part of these investments (for example, in knowledge and infrastructure) has the characteristics of a public good (since it is non-rival and non-excludable). Therefore, institutions that facilitate trade in a globalizing world should get special attention in government policy. These aspects are further elaborated in Chapter 9.

7.   Standards

This chapter explains how standards can contribute to reducing transaction costs. Standards come in many forms, and the ways they affect the working of the economy are also different. This chapter provides a characterization and classification of the various types of standards, and discusses in what way they contribute to value creation in transaction management. This discussion is illustrated by means of a number of practical examples.[1]

7.1   STANDARDIZATION AS AN IMPORTANT TOOL FOR TRANSACTION MANAGEMENT

In a globalizing world, with increased economic specialization and the fragmentation of production, coordination between different economic agents and countries with regard to international standards becomes ever more important. Standards are an effective means of reducing the transaction costs associated with trade. In that way they create value in trade transactions and contribute to international welfare. So far, this innovative role of standards in the reduction of transaction costs has remained somewhat undervalued in mainstream economic thinking. Yet it is a major tool in transaction management. This chapter discusses research into the successes and failures of the design of standards, and provides some guidelines on how to support the implementation of successful standards that create value and that, therefore, are profitable both for individual firms and for society as a whole. There are various types of standards, ranking from technical standards, rules and regulations, internal product and process standards of firms, external safety and quality standards, codes of conduct, accounting standards and standards for competencies. Some of these standards are just designed to make production more efficient, whereas others bring about network externalities – the standard creates more value when it is used by more people – and others are made to internalize external effects or prevent risks. A common element is that they reduce transaction costs both within a firm as well as among firms. Standards that reduce transaction costs within a firm will have a direct effect on the total costs of production, similar to technical innovations. When a standard reduces transaction costs among firms it becomes cheaper to trade. This induces more trade and allows more specialization of production so that comparative advantages can be exploited more. In most cases this is also associated with some form of (positive) externality.

The argumentation of this chapter shows how important it is to further increase knowledge about the successes and failures of the design of standards and to support the implementation of successful standards that are profitable both for individual firms and for society. Because modern ICT techniques are instrumental to such standardization in most cases, the knowledge of modern technology and a feel for the possibilities of using modern technologies for standardization is warranted. However, even more essential in setting standards is that all stakeholders, with often conflicting interests, come to an agreement about the one unique standard. This is much more a question of organizational and cultural knowledge than of technological knowledge. Moreover, setting standards may induce large sunk costs for those who contribute to the implementation of these standards. Therefore, there may be a free-rider problem, which gives standards the character of a public or a club good. For that reason it is essential to further study the design, development and implementation of standards, mainly by investigating case studies, to see how free-rider problems and lock-ins can be solved. A major development in this respect is the design of open standards and the economic explanation of the motivation of contributors to open software and open standards.

The container is an excellent example of what this chapter wants to illustrate, namely that standards, especially when they are used worldwide, can bring about a substantial reduction of transaction costs. In April 1956, a harbour crane in the American city of Newark loaded 58 containers into an old tanker. Five days later the tanker was unloaded in Houston where the containers were placed on 58 trucks to transport the containers to their final destinations. Since that moment, the container has conquered the world. Specialized ships can transport up to 13 000 containers at a time. This number is still rising. Cranes in specially-built container ports can move 30 to 40 containers per hour, and sometimes process 10 000 containers a day. One container ship can be unloaded and loaded again in 24 hours (see Levinson, 2006). Thanks to the standard sizes of containers, they will fit on all appropriate ships, vessels, trains and trucks at any location in the world. Considerably fewer people are now needed to organize transport from A to B. For instance, a truck driver used to have to wait for hours while his truck was loaded and unloaded. The container makes it possible just to connect and drive away with the trailer, which is adapted to the standards.

Figure 7.1   The container and other standards such as pallets, XBRL and bar codes: reduction of transaction costs by means of standardization

A container is nothing more than an empty box of steel or aluminium, with a wooden floor and a large door at one side, about seven feet wide and high, and slightly over 20 or 40 feet long – clearly no big technological breakthrough. Nevertheless, the container managed to enable an enormous productivity gain in trade and transport. It has resulted in a global revolution in the way goods are shipped and transported. Without the container, globalization on the scale we have seen during recent decades would have been unlikely. Therefore, the container can be regarded as an example of a major innovation, albeit not a high-tech one. The whole infrastructure for the transport of goods is nowadays adapted to containers (see Figure 7.1). The Chelsea Piers in New York, which were reserved for the traditional loading and unloading of freighters, have been transformed into an entertainment centre, as there was no longer enough traditional freight. Without the container, it would probably still have its old function. Similarly, in Rotterdam parts of the old harbour area have new functions nowadays: the 'Kop van Zuid' and the 'Loydskwartier' have become residential areas, and are no longer used for loading and unloading general cargo.

A second example of a standard in distribution, which has reduced transaction costs, is pallets. A standard prescribes how pallets should be made. They should have openings on all four sides, they must measure 120 cm by 100 cm and they should be able to carry at least 1000 kg of goods. This specification of the standardized characteristics of the pallet has the consequence that, ideally, transport can take place from the producer to the distributor and the retailer or end-user without having to repack the goods manually. In this way much time is saved in the supply chain and, therefore, the standardization of pallets contributes to lowering transaction costs. The flip-side of standardization in this case is that not every distributor can use its own warranted sizes, even though this would be more efficient for the individual distributor. It is likely that this disadvantage for firms to conform to the standard does not outweigh the benefits of using the standard, otherwise the firms would have opted to keep their own systems, which some firms do.

Because pallets do not need to be repacked, the use of standards reduces direct transport costs as part of transaction costs. An additional aspect of cost reduction in this case is that a single standard creates the possibility of leasing pallets instead of buying or making them. This general use of standardized pallets brings about economies of scale and network externalities. The logistics process as a whole becomes more efficient. The benefits are shared between producers, traders and retailers. In every part of the logistics chain, costs are reduced.

Another classic but more recent example of a successful standard is the GSM standard. This standard was developed in the 1980s by a group of telecom engineers and civil servants. Their task was to define the proper standards for one digital successor to a variety of analog standards for mobile telephony, to be adhered to by the European telecom industry at large. The use of chipcard technology allowed for the implementation of a sound business model for widespread international telephone traffic. The GSM standard has improved tremendously the ability for people 'to be in touch', thereby changing culture dramatically and globally. The GSM standard allowed for a much faster rate of development of the mobile phone industry in Europe than in the US, where no single standard was agreed upon until years later.

7.2   TYPES OF STANDARDS

Various types of standards can be distinguished. Figure 7.2 summarizes how these types of standards and their roles in the economy can be classified. The following definition roughly encapsulates these roles in the

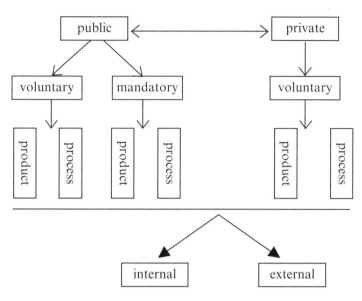

Figure 7.2   Classification of standards

economy: *a standard is the specification of the characteristics of goods and services that provides information on the quality of these goods and services and/or enhances their interoperability.* This section elaborates the classification of Figure 7.2 based on the characteristics of the various types of standards. This classification necessarily is somewhat fuzzy as the characteristics may differ in different circumstances, which makes a clear separation of roles impossible.

7.2.1   Classification of Standards: an Overview

The first distinction made in Figure 7.2 is between public and private standards. This classification refers to the way standards have been developed. Is the *market* (private sector) responsible for their development, or was it a *government* (public sector) initiative? The government has the ability to make the standards *mandatory* through the introduction of legislation. This is in contrast to *voluntary* standards.

The following distinction of Figure 7.2 is between standards that are related to products and those related to production processes. *Product standards* are requirements with respect to the characteristics of the product itself, whereas *process standards* are standards that prescribe how certain steps in the production process should take place. A problem is that often the question of whether a product meets a standard can only be answered by an inspection of the production process. This can be very costly or even impossible for products that are not produced domestically. The third categorization of Figure 7.2 is based on the difference between *internal and external* standards. Internal standards are subject to the control of firms that set them, whereas external standards are considered given for individual firms. Again, this distinction between internal and external standards is not clear-cut because standards may be developed as internal standards but may become external standards when they are adopted by consensus among firms. The remainder of this section provides a more detailed analysis of the classification in Figure 7.2.

7.2.2 Quality Standards and Product Differentiation

The extent of (product) differentiation is of importance for standards that prescribe the quality and specification of products and services. Economic theory distinguishes two main types of differentiation: vertical and horizontal differentiation. Vertical product differentiation has an ordinal character. To give an example: Rembrandt's 'The Syndics' controlled the quality of the 'laken' based on a list of characteristics, where a higher quality was assigned to products with superior characteristics. Horizontal product differentiation has no ordinal ordering and it is based solely on the individual tastes of consumers. Therefore, standards may influence the extent of product differentiation, where a more stringent standardization leads to reduced possibilities of product variation for the consumer.

A *private standard* is a standard that primarily focuses on the interests of the private stakeholders that develop the standard. These stakeholders will only take the interests of consumers into account to the extent that it benefits their own interests. Private standards can develop in different ways. For example, an individual firm may decide to share certain characteristics with other firms. The private standard can also originally be an internal standard (see later) that is subsequently adopted by other players in the market. An example is the barcode. Albert Heijn, the Dutch branch of the multinational grocery company Ahold, started to use the barcode within its own supermarkets and logistics, and forced all of its suppliers and business connections to make use of this standardized barcode system.

Alternatively a group of firms can decide to develop a standard together. Firms have often shared interests when they belong to the same industry and/or have the same suppliers and customers. When the standard can be used freely by third parties, it is called an 'open standard' (see Box 7.1). It is important to note that (contrary to popular belief) it is not the fact that the standard has no particular owner that makes it an open standard, but merely that it can be used freely. There may be confusion with 'open

BOX 7.1   XBRL AS AN EXAMPLE OF AN OPEN STANDARD

Standards may, through a reduction of transaction costs, contribute considerably to a growth in specialization and trade, and thereby to more economic welfare. This is especially true in the case of voluntary standards if these standards can be used by all players in the market at low costs, or even at no costs. Such a standard is characterized as 'open standard'. A recent example of a standard that has been developed as an open standard is the eXtensible Business Reporting Language (XBRL). XBRL is a standard that registers corporate records – for example, all kinds of book-keeping and financial data – in a unified manner, and which presents them to different stakeholders. XBRL is comparable with the example of the container. XBRL transports financial information in a standardized way just as the container transports goods. The standard enables different stakeholders to make compatible digital financial and non-financial data from their back office for external usage. External stakeholders can subsequently use the data in their own systems and extract information according to the specifications they need. It is like a computer language, where the syntax has been standardized, while at the same time providing every user with the possibility of providing their own interpretation of the semantics and using it in a way that suits their interests best (Dreyer and Willis, 2006). Tax statements are also made less complex, since collecting financial data has become more straightforward. This improves the effectiveness and efficiency of collecting data, increases access to the information and thereby results in a substantial reduction of costs for both the sender and the recipient of the information. There is no longer a need to make independent data collections for different usages. The receiver also knows for certain that the data has been calculated and reported using the appropriate definitions. The use of XBRL as a standard has been promoted by a consortium of both private actors and government agencies (with over 600 members in 2012). The actual implementation of the XBRL standard is primarily driven by regulators and governments. The XBRL implementation projects often differ in their approach and main objectives. Project goals vary from increase of financial market transparency, improvement of data quality and reduction of red tape. It makes XBRL a good example of a standard that originated in the market, while the government joined the initiative later on, and, in this case, even took the lead. Together these users of XBRL are a 'club' so that XBRL as a standard can also be considered a 'club good'. This path is often followed in the development of standards and it enables a good balance between private and public interests.

source', where the standard cannot only be used freely, but where it can also be changed to the desires of individual users. An open source standard is, because of this flexibility, less 'standard', which results in a better correspondence with the specific demands of users and allows for a larger product differentiation.

On other occasions – that is, when a standard is owned by a collective of private organizations – one can speak of a *club good* (see also Box 7.1). Here, the use of the standard is non-rival, but others (non-members) can be excluded from using the standard. In that case the standard does not have the full character of a collective good (which should be non-rival and non-excludable). A good example of such a club good is SWIFT. SWIFT is a collective of financial institutions that develops products for its members that deal with financial communication. To enable communication and interactions in a safe and trustful manner, SWIFT has developed several standards for such communication. Franchising is another interesting example of a standard as a club good. Through franchising, existing product formulas and networks can be used (which result, for example, in economies of scale in purchases, logistics and marketing), so that costs can be reduced. At the same time, consumers' information costs are substantially reduced: a hamburger at McDonald's in Moscow is the same as in Amsterdam, so the customer knows what he or she is agreeing to. This results in a competitive advantage and, therefore, makes it profitable for entrepreneurs to join such a formula. These are all examples of standards as club goods that can be made excludable. If this is not the case and the standard can be used freely by all users, payment for use of the standard should be made mandatory to exclude free-ridership with respect to the development and maintenance costs of the standard.

Other economic incentives and interests can also stimulate actors to develop a standard together. For example, consumer interest organizations can develop a standard to compare the quality of different kinds of products and services. Something similar holds for a trade union that tries to get good working conditions or safety standards introduced for its members. Many standards related to the ICT sector and the coordination between software and hardware have their roots in the private domain.

As *public standards* are standards imposed by government, they attempt to serve a public interest. Most public standards have a large and rather general scope. The design and implementation of these standards may become too complex to meet all the interests of the different stakeholders. This is even more difficult when some interests are opposing. Public standards, therefore, almost always require a political choice where the interests of different stakeholders are weighted against each other. Public standards are often a follow-up to earlier private standards, which have been adapted by the government to become public standards in order to bring them more in line with public interests. In this respect, the government may define the general conditions to which private standards have to comply. Public standards may also take private standards as models for defining specific characteristics.

7.2.3   Voluntary or Mandatory Standards

Public standards can be both voluntary and mandatory. A private standard is always a voluntary standard, unless the government has made that standard a public standard. Yet the threat of the government to make a standard mandatory can sometimes be a reason for private parties to introduce their own standards, which might be more in line with government demands while still serving their own interests better than in the case of a mandatory public standard. Examples are various codes of conduct – rules of appropriate behaviour for firms and their employees – that are the result of both ethical considerations and pressure from the government and other interest groups (for example, NGOs). For instance, Shell has introduced high ethical and ecological standards partially in reaction to pressure from governments, human rights organizations and environmental protest groups. Several types of self-regulation are based on similar 'voluntary' standards. The trigger mechanism behind these is that the costs of a reputation loss when the requirements of the standard have not been met can be very high.

7.2.4   Process and Product Standards

There are a number of rationales for process standards: (i) they may have a direct influence on product quality (for example, hygiene standards) or the quality of services (for example, ISO-9000 certification); (ii) they enhance production efficiency (for example, in the case of network externalities);

or (iii) they internalize external effects (as with environmental standards). Moreover, ethical considerations can play a role in the restrictions set by process standards, for example in the case of child labour.

Product standards specify the characteristics of the product. A technical specification enables different firms to make use of the same product as an input, because these firms can adapt their own production processes and products to the specifications of such standards. Because the container has standard sizes or, in this perspective its own technical specifications, it is possible for other firms to develop their applications on the technological specifications of the container. The example of the container shows how a technical specification can have a worldwide impact. This holds for all kinds of standards that prescribe universal sizes.

The automotive industry is an early example of the use of industry-wide technological specifications. These standards were needed because car producers had to rely on suppliers, a reliance that was relatively strong because of the complex nature of automobiles. An early example of a standard adopted by the automobile industry was the design of screws. These technological specifications made large-scale production possible so that economies of scale were exploited.

7.2.5 Internal and External Standards

Internal and external standards relate to different types of transaction costs (see Box 7.2). Internal standards are used to come to a better coordination and thereby lower transaction costs with respect to activities within the firm. External standards play a role in market transactions. These different roles of internal and external standards are linked to the way Coase (1937) describes the nature of the firm (see Chapter 4). According to the Coasean principle, a firm has its optimal size when marginal transaction costs, that are a result of (vertical) coordination via the hierarchy, are equal to marginal transaction costs that are a result of (horizontal) coordination via the market. Better internal standards enable a firm to become larger, whereas a relative improvement of external standards enhances the possibilities to make use of outsourcing, subcontracting or purchase through markets. This may reduce firm size.

7.2.6 Standards and Market Failure

A telephone would have no value for a consumer as a means of communication if he or she were the only user. The higher the market penetration of telephones, the higher is the value of the telephone for the consumers that are linked to a telephone network. This is the essence of *network*

BOX 7.2   MSD: AN EXAMPLE FOR THE PACKAGING OF DRUGS

The Dutch plant of the multinational pharmaceutical company Merck, Sharpe & Dohme (MSD) in the city of Haarlem provides an example of how internal and external standards can affect corporate management. MSD Netherlands delivers drugs from the mother company to customers and regions all over the world. The plant coordinates the logistics, packs the drugs and makes sure that all rules and legislative requirements have been met. Within MSD there used to exist an enormous diversity in packages. For example, different logos were used for the same product. A substantial part of this diversity was unnecessary. This unnecessary diversity can be considered an example of a suboptimal internal standard. Because the company is, to some extent, free to make decisions on the shape, size and design of the package, it can reduce transaction costs by setting unified standards for its packaging. In this way cost reductions were obtained through internal standardization and unification.

An external standard is ruled by mandatory requirements imposed by third parties. This can be the government (in this case with respect to the packaging of drugs), but it can also be a contract partner which has specifications that accord with the standard defined in the contract. Such external standards in packaging design play a major role in the case of MSD. MSD has to deal with many different prescriptions in various countries with respect to the packaging and distribution of drugs. These differences relate to texts and codified signs on the packaging, barcodes and medical descriptions and warnings on how to use the drugs. For example, it is prescribed that the medical descriptions are in the language(s) of the country where the drugs are used. Obviously, it would be beneficial to a multinational such as MSD that distributes its drugs all over the world if it could promote some harmonization of government legislation in this respect. Such harmonization could also be beneficial to public health when the harmonized standards would imply the use of best practices with respect to information on the drugs contained in the package.

Another example where external standards can reduce transaction costs would be a standardization of employee qualifications.

If diplomas in, for example, India, China and Eastern European nations provided the same reliable information on the different levels of skills of their incumbent workers, it would reduce transaction costs for firms that are outsourcing parts of their production processes to these countries and regions. However, in practice there is still a long way to go to arrive at some global standardization of qualification. Standardizing of diplomas among similarly developed countries already appears to be difficult due to differences in institutions and a high path-dependency of these institutions. An example is the requirements for Bar exams which even differ between the States in the US.

externalities. The value of the product is closely related to the size of the network. A standard can contribute to the development of a network that is large enough. Network externalities that arise when the size of the network grows are direct network externalities. Indirect network externalities arise when the number of complementary products available increases. An example of an indirect network externality is the combination of computers and software. As more software becomes available, the value of the computer to the user increases. This is best illustrated by the moment when the first operating system became available for the PC: it was especially after that time that the PC became a success. In the days that standardized operating systems were unavailable, only highly skilled professionals could use computers. Both internal and external network externalities are causes of market failure, which results in underinvestment in case there is no intervention from the government to repair the market failure. In the case of indirect network externalities, a standard can contribute to the reduction of market failure, because it makes different products compatible.

Apart from a coordination problem, two other forms of market failure can arise because of network externalities: *excess inertia* and *excess momentum*. Excess inertia occurs on the supply side of the market, when the introduction of new techniques is delayed. In such circumstances, firms are reluctant to bring their own technologies to market, since they take for granted that the technology of the market leader will be dominant and become standard. Excess momentum appears when buyers choose an inferior technique as standard. These two coordination problems are to be regarded as disadvantages of standardization. Another problem is that in the case of a private standard a monopoly position can be obtained. Here, Microsoft's monopoly on the market for operating systems is a well-known example. All software has to be compatible with the Windows operating system. Because Microsoft has refused to make the source code of its operating system public, it has been difficult for other producers to develop compatible software, and Microsoft has gradually monopolized the entire software market.

A further aspect in this context is incomplete information. High transaction costs bring about incomplete information when the transaction costs of acquiring the necessary information are higher than the (expected) gains in cost reduction, or profits, that the additional information yields. This argumentation shows that incomplete information does not exclude rational behaviour (see Section 4.2 on bounded rationality). Asymmetric information, which is a form of incomplete information, relates to a situation where the buyer cannot observe the quality or specific characteristics of products. In his famous article on signalling problems with asymmetric information, Akerlof (1970) gives the example of the secondhand car salesperson. The buyer does not know the quality of a car and, as a consequence, the bad cars (to use Akerlof's terms, the 'lemons') crowd the good cars ('peaches') out of the market. In this case, asymmetric information reduces the supply of good quality products.

Mandatory standards can result in the removal from the market of all products that do not comply with the minimum standard. This results (if the standard is set high enough) in the sufficient quality of supplied goods. Voluntary standards in combination with labelling can provide buyers with sufficient information on quality differences in a situation where both low and high quality products are supplied. Negative labels can be made mandatory by the government for producers of goods that do not comply with a standard. Positive labelling is used by firms to enable the consumer to distinguish (often more expensive) products that comply with high standards. Therefore, standards can reduce, or even take away, the problem of asymmetric information identified by Akerlof. By making information more symmetric and less incomplete, standards reduce the transaction costs because they enable more and better transactions. In this way, they provide a guarantee to the consumer that they can buy goods with confidence. It may also expand the market and potentially allow firms to economize on signalling expenditure, which is part of their transaction costs (Jones and Hudson, 1996).

From the perspective of information, economic analysis distinguishes three product types: (i) symmetric information products; (ii) experience products; and (iii) asymmetric information products. Symmetric products contain the information that is needed in advance in a way that is observable by the customer. In the case of experience products, the characteristics can be observed when using it. Asymmetric information products do not give the possibility of observing all relevant characteristics, not even after years of usage. Standards designed to solve the problem of incomplete information should focus on experience products and asymmetric information products. The above examples of labelling show that a standard enables the consumer to access information that he or she could not have obtained otherwise. Safety characteristics are an example of such information.

7.3 STANDARDS AS TRANSACTION COST-REDUCING DEVICES

As previously mentioned, standardization is a major tool of transaction management because standards may reduce transaction costs. This is because standardization decreases search and information costs, which are both part of transaction costs. When product specifications are standardized and known to trading partners, the bargaining process will cover only the price and conditions of delivery. When the product has not been standardized, bargaining will also be needed with respect to the specifications of the product. This leaves room for additional information costs, since the buyer does not avail themselves of all information needed. One example is the technical specifications of parts for the automotive industry referred to previously. After standards were introduced, it was no longer necessary to search for a supplier that could produce the parts that were needed in a specific situation. Search costs decreased and using external suppliers became more profitable. Apart from search costs, contracting costs were also reduced. Contracts between the producer and its suppliers no longer have to be specified extensively. Clearly this also reduces enforcement costs. In the early automotive industry, individual producers did not have much market power, so the benefits of standardization were entirely passed onto the consumer. Box 7.3 discusses two other practical examples.

The fact that standards reduce transaction costs has also been widely recognized in accounting theory. Watts and Zimmerman (1990) use the term 'contracting costs' for what this book calls transaction costs (in a broad sense). In their view, these contracting costs consist of direct transaction costs (for example, brokerage fees), agency costs (for example, monitoring costs, bonding costs and the residual loss from dysfunctional decisions), information costs, renegotiation costs and bankruptcy costs. According to Watts and Zimmerman, the existence of contracting costs is crucial to accounting choice, which makes accounting part

BOX 7.3   HOW STANDARDS CAN REDUCE TRANSACTION COSTS IN PRACTICE

In the case of XBRL many types of transaction costs are reduced. Administration becomes less complex with XBRL. Firms using the standard can also reduce costs since their internal control and reporting have become less complicated. Control by tax authorities will also be less time-consuming and thereby less costly. The translation of financial data from the back office system to a tax statement, warranted by the tax office, is no longer a complex process because it can be fully codified. For firms, it becomes much easier to serve different stakeholders with the information that they need, enabled by the right taxonomy and the simple push of a button. All sorts of reporting can take place more efficiently, in terms of both time and money. Additionally, daughter firms and branches can be managed more efficiently since it is no longer necessary to use complex internal reporting systems.

These cost reductions from the use of XBRL are in part a consequence of economies of scale and network externalities. For instance, it brings about considerable cost reductions for firms when external actors develop their own taxonomies that can be implemented in all systems of the firms where these external actors need information from. Reliability can also increase, since information has to be imported into the system only once. This development reduces accountancy costs. Management can also obtain more tailor-made strategic information, thereby improving the quality of the decision-making process. This results once again in a reduction of transaction costs, partially because the firm can make a better risk assessment.

At MSD, an internal standard has been developed to reduce packing costs, for example by using one package for a group of regions. Standardized packages can also improve the visibility of the firm and, through this marketing device, enhance reputation and reduce transaction costs. In other words, it reduces information costs. The firm will mainly benefit from the standardization by lower labour costs and more efficient inventory management. That is why the Dutch plant of MSD in Haarlem, in spite of relatively high local labour costs, has remained efficient in the worldwide distribution of drugs. To keep this position, R&D investments are needed to optimize standards that comply with the existing framework of legislation and regulation (which is demanding in this specific case of drug packaging). Because of this increased importance of R&D financing, a shift from variable costs towards sunk costs is taking place. Since MSD is critically assessing its own internal standards, it will also try to realize optimal external standards when interacting with governments. In the case of drugs packaging, it seemed that governments were open to discussion about the improvement and harmonization of standards. This is because for governments common arrangements in the form of standardized rules and regulations of what drug packaging should contain can also be efficient. This ensures that the registration of drugs in one country will be transmissible to other countries and that the rules and regulations are upgraded to best practices. Other producers can also benefit from these standardization efforts. This is why it is relevant to have externalities of these standardization processes internalized in club goods or through governments.

of the firm's efficient contracting technology. The standardization of accounting rules contributes to the reduction of these contracting costs both for the firm itself and at the macro level. There is a long history of the development of the International Financial Reporting Standards of the International Accounting Standards Board (IASB). Since 2005, its standards have held a dominant influence over the financial reporting of listed companies in the European Union, as well as in many other countries. Here, the question is whether these accounting standards should really be used worldwide or, for instance, also be applied to the US. There are obvious disadvantages in terms of transaction costs when there are two competing standards like in the US (the IASB rules versus the rules set by the Financial Accounting Standards Board (FASB), but Dye and Sunder (2001) also report a number of advantages deriving from the competition between standards. The arguments for competition are, among others, an increase in the likelihood that standards will be efficient and the better protection of standard-setters from the undue pressure of interest groups. Moreover, the choice between standards may provide the reporting firms with more flexibility with respect to their different clients. Such flexibility can be essential in the use of standards, as the example of XBRL shows. From this perspective, there is a fierce discussion over whether accounting standards should be rules-based or principles-based.

7.3.1   Standards and Trust

The previous chapter showed that trust is an important mechanism that enables the reduction of transaction costs, especially in the frequent cases of incomplete and/or asymmetric information. In such cases contracts can never be complete and trust will always play a role somewhere in the transaction process. Standards may very much contribute to such a formation of trust. The example of Rembrandt's 'The Syndics' shows that quality standards for 'laken' will only lead to lower transaction costs when all stakeholders trust the expertise and independence of the controlling authority. A painting by a well-known painter that shows distinguished gentlemen can help establish trust. This example illustrates the close relationship between standards and trust. The reputation and reliability of the quality labels have to be built up slowly, because the formation of a trustworthy reputation will need some time. The explanation of the standard and what it stands for to its users, as well as the adequate supervision and careful development of the reputation of trust and reliability, are needed to make the label a success. Here, a saying is that trust comes on foot, but leaves on horseback. There is an analogy with the fiduciary character of money. When everybody can be sure that his or her coins and notes are universally accepted as a means of payment, and when it is almost impossible to bring false money into circulation, money transactions can take place at low information costs. It is for that reason that central banks put great efforts in reducing opportunities to falsify money. Banknotes are printed on special paper and banks use high-tech printing techniques with hidden features and holograms to fight counterfeiting. The Dutch central bank has also used marketing campaigns to show the public how they can detect false banknotes, thereby making the job difficult for falsifiers. Similar methods are needed to make traders and consumers familiar with all kinds of (other) standards. Familiarity increases trust. In that way, brand names also play a role as standards, and can represent a high value for firms. For that reason, familiar and established brand names have been used to enhance trust in internet trade.

From that perspective, brand names can be valuable. This implies that calamities that reduce the trust and reputation that have been built up on brand names should be avoided as strongly as possible. Such a loss of trust and reputation may bring about huge costs, as is illustrated by the case of the Dutch 'Planta' margarine (which caused a skin disease with much itching) and the case of the French producer of mineral water Perrier. Another example is the case of Toyota, which in 2009 and 2010 had to recall a huge number of cars to repair defects. However, it seems that the company's openness about the seriousness of the problem ultimately restricted the harm to the reputation of the firm and brand.

7.4 INVESTING IN STANDARDIZATION

This section deals with incentives for the development of standards. Why standards are used and developed can be derived from the way they affect the economy. Even though standards are often developed in reaction to market incentives, as has been already argued above, market failures are present in other cases. This will result in too many or too few (or no) standards. Section 9.1 discusses more extensively how market failure can be an argument to legitimize government intervention.

7.4.1 Incentives to Standardize: Standardization and the Market

Standards play an important role in the ever-increasing fragmentation of production and the related process of globalization. Here, the chain of causality goes in two directions. On the one hand, the reduction of transaction costs through standardization creates possibilities for an increased division of labour and more specialization. On the other hand, more specialization and the reduction of other types of transaction costs that globalization brings about, for example through economies of scale and the better exploitation of comparative advantages in factor endowments, will enhance the need for worldwide standards. These cost reductions associated with the fragmentation of production (outsourcing) and standardization will usually not only benefit producers, but, by lowering product prices, will also eventually benefit consumers. How welfare gains of standardization are shared between producers and consumers depends largely on the extent to which producers are able to exclude others from using the standard. If, under the assumption of perfect competition, excluding competitors is impossible, every gain in productivity will eventually be passed on to consumers.

The presence of standards results in more competition, because the inter-compatibility of intermediate products and parts reduces switching costs (being part of total transaction costs). Joining such a standard reduces the dependence on specific suppliers (or on dominant customers). This increased competition will, generally and in the long run, benefit the consumer. However, if other producers cannot use the standard, the owner could acquire a monopoly position (see Box 7.4).

In some markets, network externalities (see the previous section) play an important role. Standards can be warranted in such markets, but there

BOX 7.4   STANDARDS AND THE CHIP MARKET

The chip market provides an interesting example of how standards affect profit-sharing between different players in markets. Intel plays an important role in setting standards in the chip market. These standards largely exclude other producers from using certain standards, especially since other producers (particularly AMD in the chip market, standing for Advanced Micro Devices) always have a technological lag relative to Intel, and can only start developing their own products after enough information about the newest generation of Intel chips has become available. In the market for other computer parts, there is much more competition. It is important for Intel that its chips have excellent compatibility with these parts, which means that Intel has to provide producers with information at an early stage of development, thereby enabling the newest generation of processors to be compatible with available motherboards. Other chip producers can, based on this information, only reconstruct what the design of the newest processor looks like (reverse engineering), whereas it is relatively easy for producers of motherboards to make a design that has good compatibility with the Intel processors. This enables Intel (which almost has a monopoly) to keep its profits high, while the producers of other parts (that are faced with almost perfect competition) have no, or compared with Intel, only very small profits.

are also pitfalls from the perspective of the functioning of these markets. For example, the GSM telephones in Europe – where only one standard was used – became an almost instant success, but never reached the same level of market penetration in the United States. This illustrates that under specific circumstances different producers have strong incentives to cooperate. At the same time, the case of the US makes it clear that this cooperation does not always take place. It can be that network externalities result in different players (both producers and consumers) waiting until the market has chosen a standard. Especially in the ICT sector, this inter-compatibility is of great importance. When a standard has reached a certain critical mass, it is highly likely to become (almost) *the* standard and will crowd out other possible standards.

An important incentive for firms to develop a standard can be the so-called *first-mover advantages*. The designer of the standard has a time advantage on its competitors when entering the market, which will usually give it the opportunity to maintain a large market share in the longer term. It also has a knowledge advantage. The presence of network externalities is usually amplified by the non-rival nature of standards. Every additional user increases the utility of all other users, but this does not come at the cost of all other users having to share the standard with the new users.

Economies of scale and network externalities make a preference for international standards over local standards plausible. Global standards provide the opportunity to realize even more economies of scale, now that there is not only the advantage of national compatibility but also that of international compatibility. This is becoming increasingly important in the globalizing world of today.

The possibility of obtaining the exclusive right to use a standard – by using patents and copyrights – is also an incentive to develop standards. When the standard is protected by copyrights or patents, it gives the owners the possibility to financially exploit their invention and to exercise market power. The possibility of excluding others from using the standard decreases the opportunities for free-riders. Especially in a situation of network externalities, the possibility of excluding others plays an important role. Here, producers and users have a strong economic incentive to use an identical standard, as soon as it has become the dominant standard in the market. Therefore, the monetary value of this standard will be very large for its owner. This is the problem of the 'winner takes all' approach.

When free-rider behaviour becomes possible, and first-mover advantages become smaller, producers will take a more passive approach in the development and implementation of a new standard. In that case, it pays to wait until another producer has introduced a standard, and then adopt that standard. The producer that developed the standard will bear all the development costs, whereas the benefits of the standard are the same for all players on the market. This will result in a clear competitive disadvantage for the innovating firm. In situations like this, it can take a considerable amount of time before a standard is introduced into the market.

Section 7.2.6 discussed how so-called asymmetric information products have characteristics that cannot even be observed after the products have been used. Large players in a market (with well-known brands) can communicate these characteristics by building a good reputation. Yet, small players often lack this possibility. In such a situation the producers of products with a relatively high quality have a strong incentive to join a quality standard. Whether it pays to introduce a new standard depends on the extent to which existing standards are present and on the costs that are needed to introduce such a new standard (for example, marketing costs to familiarize the public with the standard). It is striking that in most industries there is only one quality standard. Producers that meet the minimum requirements of this standard would often also meet the requirements of a higher quality standard. There are several reasons why in such cases it is not profitable for these producers to come up with their own standards. First, the costs of the new standard would have to be shared between a smaller number of firms. Second, the consumer can only respond to a limited amount of information, which means that every additional standard necessitates even larger marketing costs and will also increase the information costs for the consumer.

These arguments illustrate again that the possibility of excluding others from using a standard plays an essential role. A quality standard makes little sense when products of inferior quality cannot be excluded from making use of the standard (for instance, when producers pretend that they comply with the quality standard in their marketing campaigns).

7.4.2 How are Standards Set?

Sometimes, an existing technology somewhat fortuitously becomes a standard. In cases like this, the standard has an ad hoc character. The standard is just there, without the pretence or plan to make it a standard. Standards that are developed as club goods may rather soon become profitable, since the costs can be shared while the club can still exercise some market power. In many other cases, however, a lot of coordination is needed to come up with a standard. This is especially true for public standards, since in such cases it is less likely that the benefits of developing the standard are large enough for only one or a few producers to develop and implement it. Yet, from the perspective of social welfare, the development of such public standards could be warranted if the welfare gains of all stakeholders exceeded the costs of the development of the standard. In such a case there is a role for government to play.

This role for governments is also evident in the attempts to come to unified standards in the EU (see the next section). Here, the use of one EU-wide standard instead of different national standards can reduce transaction costs and bring about more network externalities. By contrast, welfare losses may occur when national preferences with respect to standards are different or when an EU standard is not able to encompass these differences. This can, for instance, be the case when there are higher minimum quality requirements in richer member states than there are in poorer member states. European benchmarking with respect to best practices would in that case be unwarranted. Therefore, setting EU standards requires good negotiations between EU member states and much flexibility in the design. In this respect, Casella's (2001) argument is noteworthy.

Using a formal model from game theory, she argues that it may be beneficial for international trade if worldwide standards are developed as club goods by an international coalition of firms instead of being the result of negotiations between governments.

Standardization agencies, such as the German DIN or CELENEC in Europe, constitute another important institutional arrangement through which standards can be developed. In the Netherlands the Electronic Commerce Platform *Nederland* plays such a role with regard to ICT. A large number of standards, with a more or less official characteristic, have been developed in this way. The development of standards by standardization agencies often takes place via a trajectory of consultation and discussion with different stakeholders because consensus formation and creating support for the use of the standard is essential. To get patents and copyrights recognized as a standard, standardizing organizations usually demand that they can be used at no cost or at relatively low costs. This is relevant in case these standards were originally excludable as a private good or club good. In the case of complete exclusion, there will be potential users that do not use the standard (for example, when the price set by the owner is too high or access to the standard has been denied to them completely) while the marginal revenues of using the standard would still be larger for them than the marginal costs. This is inefficient from a welfare point of view. When the designer of the standard has the possibility of asking a certain price from users of the standard (to stimulate the development of new standards), a trade-off occurs.

A choice has to be made between the efficient usage of existing standards on the one hand, and speeding up the development of new and improved standards on the other hand. Sometimes, when the owner can exclude others from using the standard, it can turn into a 'winner takes all' situation. The previously mentioned dominant positions of Microsoft and Intel in the computer world are good examples of that. By contrast, standardizing agencies have an incentive to produce as many standards as possible, which could result in over-standardization.

Farell (1996) models the process of political negotiation that takes place when standardizing organizations adopt a new standard. He considers a situation where several producers want to have a high quality standard implemented. When these stakeholders have large vested interests, it can be very profitable for them to get their own standard adopted, even if there is a better standard available (note that the concept of competitive advantages does not take into account efficiency gains that are equal for all firms). The willingness to wait plays an important role here. Since a high degree of consensus is needed to implement the standard, a stakeholder that can wait for a long time (gaining a strong bargaining position in the meantime) has a strong incentive not to agree with a proposed standard that is of high quality but very different from its own standard. This stakeholder hopes that the fast implementation of a standard will be of such importance for the other stakeholders that they will eventually agree to an inferior standard. An interesting conclusion by Farell is, however, that the player with the best standard will usually have the largest preparedness to wait. Therefore, he argues that the negotiation process is mainly a process of screening, where the different stakeholders rank each other's preparedness to wait. This eventually results in an *ex ante* standard of high quality, but can be very time-consuming.

ICT improvements have somewhat increased the speed at which new standards are adopted by standardizing agencies, but they have had almost no effect on the screening process where the players explore each other's preparedness to wait. The time that is needed to get a new standard implemented was, in the mid 2000s, still over three years. This was an improvement compared with the situation ten years earlier, when, according to the annual report of 1995, more than five years were needed. Yet the process remains very slow. Especially when existing interests are large (usually when there are multiple stakeholders with large market shares), it can be efficient to increase the speed of the process, even if this comes at the cost of the adoption of a suboptimal standard (Farell, 1996).

When setting a standard, the interests of the end users (often consumers) usually receive less attention than those of the producers. The interests of individual producers are often very large so that even for one producer it can be profitable to contribute actively to the development of a standard. Additionally, the number of producers is often somewhat limited, which makes it easy to introduce a standard in a coordinated action. The users of the standard are often a large mass where the individual interests related to the standard are small. However, when their number is sufficiently large (as is mostly the case), their combined interest can easily be larger than that of the producers.

7.4.3   The Welfare Economics of Standards

By reducing transaction costs, standards generally have a positive effect on the economy and enhance social welfare. This is especially true when standards are voluntary and can be used (almost) freely by all market players. An example is the open source standards that are often developed by the users themselves (a well-known example is the operating system Linux). An intriguing question from the economic perspective is about the incentives for the contributors of these freely-available open sources. These open source standards seem to give much opportunity for free-riders, while there are no direct revenues for the contributors to the standard. However, it seems that informal hierarchies between the contributors build up, where only a limited number of key programmers have the power to decide which additions are included in the system. Joining such a group of experts may increase the prospects of finding a (well-) paid job related to the open source development. Apart from that, intrinsic motivation often plays an important role for these contributors.

Standards may also have a negative effect on the economy and be welfare-diminishing. This is especially the case when they are used worldwide and there is a large existing infrastructure with high sunk costs. In such cases, the existing standard can make further innovation almost impossible because of the high transition costs (that are also part of transaction costs) of switching to a new and better standard. A well-known example is the QWERTY keyboard, introduced in the late nineteenth century to prevent typing machines from jamming. In this era of computers, it would be possible to switch to a keyboard design that maximizes typing speed. However, the costs of such a change are very high, since everyone would have to learn typing all over again.

Large network externalities can be a major cause of these *lock-in* effects. Here, the costs of being the first one to switch to a new standard that is not compatible with the old one can be extremely high. This will block innovation until the revenues of the new standard have become very high. This difficulty in switching to a new technology because of high sunk investments and switching costs (transaction costs) is called the bandwagon effect. A good example is fuel engines. The whole infrastructure, with roads, the automotive industry and gas stations makes it almost impossible to abandon this standard in favour of another. The economics of these kinds of technological transitions have been extensively studied, especially with respect to new standards and technologies that are more efficient in energy use and thereby enhance environmental quality (see for example Den Butter and Hofkes, 2006). By contrast, Liebowitz and Margolis (1990, 1994, 1996) argue that the danger of lock-ins due to the network externalities of standards has been exaggerated in some cases.

There is a clear relationship between standards and innovations: several studies have found a positive relationship. A study of the DIN (2000) of the effects of standards on the German economy concludes that the impact of standards on the growth of the economy exceeds that of other types of innovation. However, standards can also be harmful to innovation so that the relationship becomes negative. Standardization can, for example, decrease the speed at which other major innovations are developed. Innovations requiring a standard that is not (yet) used worldwide with sufficient network externalities will be costly to develop because the revenues from the innovations will be low, at least in the short run. In addition, the 'winner takes all' effect tends to increase the risks for innovators. The chance that in the end the technology of another developer becomes the standard is large in such cases. If so, there will be no revenues at all but only the sunk development costs. Because a higher rate of return is demanded from investment opportunities with the same expected return but a higher risk, this risk premium implies a lower net present value of investments in new technologies. External effects, however, may result in additional revenues for the owner of the standard. This might also result in higher revenues from products that are compatible with the standard. On the one hand, Blind (2004) reports that, according to some studies, industries with a high R&D intensity are characterized by a relatively low number of existing standards. Therefore, it seems that causality exists in two directions here: innovating industries do not standardize as much as other industries, and strongly standardized industries innovate less. Other studies find, however, that there is not necessarily a causal relationship between standardization and R&D expenditure (Blind, 2004).

The increased risks when the innovations are dependent on standards seem to be an important reason for firms to join collective standardization projects. In this way, the risks of R&D projects can be substantially reduced (DIN, 2000). Additionally, empirical evidence shows that forces other than standards are of far more importance as barriers for innovation (DIN, 2000). Moreover, as soon as innovations have become implemented as standards, these new technologies find their way into the production process and to the end users at a much higher speed than when standards play no role in the innovations. This may (more than) compensate for the risk premium and, consequently, decrease investment in innovations. In particular, standardizing agencies play an important role in this respect. When new technologies are well specified in a standard, and available to all stakeholders at no or low costs, the diffusion of the new technology will accelerate. Overall standardization seems to reduce investment in new technologies, but at the same time bring about a better usage and broader application of the new technologies. Since this last effect seems of far more importance than the first, the relationship with innovation seems (strongly) positive from that perspective.

7.5   STANDARDIZATION IN THE EUROPEAN UNION

The extent to which standardization reduces transaction costs depends on the level at which the standards are used. National standards have less impact than standards that are used all over the world, such as in the example of containers. This implies that at the European level it is preferable to set uniform standards for the European Union, provided that no differences in preferences between member states stand in the way, for example because of differences over quality. Yet, in the case of uniform standards in the EU, the benefits of such standards should outweigh their costs. For such standards to be effective, new institutions at the EU have to be set up. Such institutions can also contribute to the reduction of transaction costs, under some circumstances, but can be the source of ambiguities, due to problems of governance of standards. The euro provides a striking illustration of these ambiguities.

The following proposal for the design of a standard at the EU level provides an example from the financial world where up till now, because of regulatory differences between European member states, a lock-in with respect to standardization exists. In this case, standardization at the EU level can bring about significant cost savings. It seems that here the benefits will outweigh the costs of institutionalizing at the EU level.

7.5.1   Examples of European Standards: EU Standards for Financial Transactions in Capital Markets[2]

Financial transactions in capital markets are an area where the EU currently lags behind the US with respect to transaction costs and where the development of EU standards is urgently needed. According to data from the BIS, in 2005 financial transactions in worldwide capital markets amounted to about US $1400 trillion. However, the direct costs of handling these financial transactions between EU member states are two to six times as high as in the US. The European Commission aims at a future reduction in the cost of these transactions to a level similar to that in the US (The Giovanni Group, 2001). However, the trading of financial assets involves transaction costs that go far beyond direct and easily quantifiable trading costs. For example, the London Stock Exchange (2002) calculates that the formation of a European clearing and settlement platform can incur a saving in direct transaction costs of €1.6 billion per year. Moreover, the potential cost savings on indirect costs vary from €5 billion to €40 billion per year. The successful completion of a transaction largely depends on the quality of the transaction and the speed of communication. The opportunity cost of failed and missed transactions can be reduced by improving direct handling procedures and by standardizing communication. The size of these opportunity costs is, based on data from the Harvard Research Group (2003), estimated to be US $7 billion per year, which is the value of missed transactions. If the settlement of the entire asset trade can be speeded up by two days, a (rough) estimate of the savings amounts to US $2.7 billion per year. However, besides institutional reforms, there is an obvious need for a better standardization of the handling of financial asset transactions at EU level. Here, because of differences in the types and sizes of the various stock exchange markets between the EU and US, a mere copy of the American means of regulation at the EU level seems unwarranted. Therefore, the EU should develop its own standard to reduce transaction costs based on product harmonization.

The major differences between the US and EU asset trade are that the US asset trade is more specialized in specific financial products and derivatives and has – as evidenced by BIS statistics – large trade turnovers. This specialization (in niche markets) increases the asset specificity of the trade. This large asset specificity requires specialist knowledge of how to trade these financial product and derivatives. This increases, in principle, the transaction costs. However, it also offers opportunities for professionals to create value in the transactions and to exploit economies of scale in trading large volumes. That in turn may reduce transaction costs. In the EU there is also a kind of asset specificity in the financial assets trade but it has a different character in the US. These contrasting characteristics are mainly national differences in property rights and regulations that lead to product differentiation. This again increases the transaction costs in the EU.

Given these characteristics of the financial assets in the EU, there are two ways an EU standard can be set up. One possibility is the creation of a standard where legal and fiscal product harmonization is imposed by the EU. This means, in the terminology of Section 7.2, an external standard. To this end, the EU can use a 'best practice' from the market or set a number of conditions to which the various types of financial products have to comply. The latter implies a flexible standard. The advantage of such a flexible standard is that it favours market dynamics and innovative strength. However, the infrastructural complexity is only partially reduced, so the infrastructure is capital-intensive with substantial transaction costs. This increases the coordination problems with respect to the design and implementation of one standard. The alternative of a more stringent standard under 'best practice' brings about fewer coordination problems with respect to the design of an EU standard, so transaction costs are lower from that perspective. The main problem here, however, is the rigidity of the standard. Such a fixed standard may suffocate innovation and thereby the ability to reduce transaction costs through specialization and complementarity.

Both standards have their specific advantages. The flexible standard is dynamic and innovative but a 'best practice' standard is easier and cheaper to realize. A good escape from this dilemma seems to be to adopt and implement two standards. In that way, the EU can benefit by introducing a 'best practice' standard to be adopted for the majority of financial asset transactions. This can be done, for example, for the extensive traditional stock exchange trade in bonds and shares. By contrast, gains in reducing transaction costs can be achieved using a flexible standard that formulates guidelines for trading conditions with respect to the more specialized financial products with less voluminous turnovers on EU financial markets. This flexible standard is fitted for the types of financial assets that are complementary to the 'best practice' standard assets, such as options, swaps and other derivates complementary to bonds and shares. Therefore, the best way to reduce transaction costs in the EU seems to be to use two standards or a shared dual standard. The EU can learn from the US about how to deal with large trade volumes (the 'best practice' standard) and specialist products (the flexible standard). The task for the EU, therefore, is to legally define and formalize which types of assets should be subjected to the 'best practice' standard and for which types of financial products flexible conditions of regulation should be allowed. Then, the implementation of these standards to further infrastructural standardization can be left to market stakeholders. Financial market participants have in the past been able to develop appropriate standards (for example, SWIFT) and can come to collective decisions about these matters. Here, the EU will only have a coordinating role.

Such infrastructural standardization (or harmonization) of financial asset trade in the EU reduces information costs and negotiation costs because search and matching become simplified. Yet a harmonization at EU level implies that cultural differences should be overcome. This process will be time-consuming rather than costly. These harmonization costs can be regarded as soft transaction costs. The benefits of a harmonized trading system, however, are (a reduction of) hard transaction costs and will take effect immediately. With a low-cost EU-wide financial trading system, using a comprehensive standard, the EU can play an important role in the global financial capital markets and can compete with the US in this respect.

7.5.2 Regulation and Standards in the EU[3]

Public standards are often set up as part of regulatory measures which aim at internalizing externalities. In such cases, the welfare benefits of regulation should outweigh the implementation costs of regulation (see Section 10.1). However, the growth of regulatory standards has contributed to the growth of the administrative burden, and this has led to growing concern

Table 7.1   Administrative costs by member states as a share of GDP

Austria	4.6%	Netherlands	3.7%
Belgium and Luxembourg	2.8%	Poland	5.0%
Czech Republic	3.3%	Portugal	4.6%
Denmark	1.9%	RE*	6.8%
Finland	1.5%	Slovakia	4.6%
France	3.7%	Slovenia	4.1%
Germany	1.9%	Spain	4.6%
Hungary	2.4%	Sweden	1.5%
Ireland	2.4%	UK	1.5%
Italy	4.6%	EU25	3.5%

Note: *RE combines the Baltic member states, Malta and Cyprus.

Source: COM689 (2006); based on Kox (2005).

Table 7.2   The distribution of administrative costs in Denmark and the Netherlands

Share of administrative costs by origin of legislation	Denmark	Netherlands
Originates directly in international law	28%	43%
International origin but implemented nationally	15%	13%
National origin	57%	44%

Source: COM689 (2006); based on Danish and Dutch baseline measurements.

in the EU as well as in some individual countries. The EU has estimated administrative costs by member states (Table 7.1), and has calculated that a reduction in the administrative burden by 25 per cent would eventually lead to an increase in EU GDP of 1.6 per cent.

The source of the administrative burden arises from four different levels: (i) international; (ii) EU; (iii) national; and (iv) sub-national. The split shown in Table 7.2 suggests that the most important source of burden comes from national governments, although this may change as the EU expands its regulatory activities. Specifying where the burden originates can be difficult. Often a measure originates at, say, EU level but is implemented at national and then sub-national level. Often the original impetus also comes from an international standards agency such as the ISO. At each stage of the chain, there is the potential to add to the original obligation, a process termed 'gold plating'. International law always needs 'transposition'. This is also the case for EU directives, but not for EU regulations, which are directly applicable.

The EU's role is twofold: controlling its own administrative burden and persuading all member states to follow. There is enthusiasm among some member states to do this – the Netherlands, Denmark, the Czech Republic and the UK are well down this path. However, other states seem less enthusiastic and without EU pressure would probably only make limited progress. Apart from the four countries listed above, Austria, Belgium and Germany have substantial plans in place and Poland plans in several areas. However, France, Ireland, Italy, Finland and Latvia have relatively few plans. As such, the EU Commission has set a target for the whole of the EU to reduce administrative costs by 25 per cent. In addition, it is envisaged that targets will also be set in specific policy areas where both the administrative burden is particularly heavy and there is the potential for significant cuts. The EU believes these figures are reasonable and cites results from the four states that have carried out baseline measurements that there is a potential for reductions of this size by focusing on costs originating at both the EU and the national level.

7.6   CONCLUSIONS

This chapter provides a transaction-cost perspective on the economics of standardization. By providing a number of examples, it describes the mechanisms by which standards have an impact on the economy. It discusses how standards are an important means to reduce transaction costs. They may reduce uncertainties, risks and other information problems, they may exploit economies of scale and network externalities and they may enhance the coordination of production processes. Thanks to standards, more transactions can take place, which is beneficial to social welfare.

There is a large diversity of standards, ranging from standards used within a certain firm to those used at a global level. This has resulted in fundamental changes in transaction and trade technologies and infrastructure. The container is a good example of the latter. It is sometimes difficult to draw a line between what can be called a standard, legislation, institutionalization or technology. One could even say that a common language or a common value system within a society can be considered a standard. At the least, similar processes that reduce transaction costs play a role here. For example, empirical evidence shows that countries with similar legislations have relatively large bilateral trade flows (see Chapter 6). From that perspective, the International Bureau for Fiscal Documentation attempts to harmonize the tax legislation of different countries throughout the world. The empirical research of Islam and Reshef (2006) shows that good and reliable institutions are even more important for international trade than the harmonization of these institutions. Therefore, standards should also play an important role in controlling the quality and reliability of institutions.

There is a definition problem with respect to what can be called a standard and what an innovation. Many of the examples in this book show that standards can often be considered innovations themselves – again the container is an obvious example. However, it is often less technological sophistication – it is a mistake to focus innovation policy exclusively on 'high-tech' – and more organizational efforts that are particularly needed to get a new technological standard implemented and accepted by different stakeholders. The relationship between innovations and standards is yet another dimension. On the one hand, the existence of a standard can result in a large number of other additional innovations within the system of the standard, where these innovations derive their values from the standard. On the other hand, because of high sunk costs, a standard can result in a lock-in situation, where innovations that do not comply with the dominant standard no longer take place. This problem of the lock-in, and that of the high transition costs of escaping from it, also occurs when a much better alternative for the old standard becomes available that would improve social welfare in the long-term. In that sense standards can also harm welfare.

In the EU many of the standards and regulations have grown in recent years because of: (i) technical change; (ii) rising standards; (iii) changes in the state of the world; and (iv) globalization. Technical change means that products can now be produced that were not previously possible, but the health and safety of products such as mobile phones and GM foods need to be regulated. Rising standards mean that we have legislation that we did not have previously simply because we now expect more from products and production processes. Changes in the state of the world can be political, such as the growth of the EU; or non-political, such as climate change and the appearance of new diseases. Globalization is relevant because increasingly we are buying products produced in diverse parts of the world, just as many products in any one country will have a more widespread market than previously and these need to be regulated. All of these reasons help explain the growth of standards, legislation and regulatory activity. In this sense, it is almost inevitable that the business burden has been increasing over time. However, not all the trends are negative. The development of the computer and the internet will have substantially reduced the compliance costs of, for example, collecting VAT for the government. The growth of the EU and international standards will have reduced considerably the administrative costs to firms trading internationally. Nonetheless, it is probably true that the pressures on the administrative burden will tend to be upwards in the coming years. This means that if it is a target of government policy to stabilize or even reduce that burden, then finding more efficient ways of doing things, rather than doing fewer things, is probably essential.

Nowadays, it should be recognized that standards increasingly come from the EU rather than from national governments and that increasingly they have as their bases an international standard. Many such standards are 'voluntary' and thereby are left out of all the calculations of administrative burdens. Examples are the ISO-9000 and the 14 000 series of standards relating to product quality and environmental management. Yet, for many firms these are essential badges to be obtained, demanded by some large multinationals and even governments. They too are a cost on business. By contrast, many standards, particularly but not just interface standards, impose a relatively small burden on business but offer substantial benefits that also reduce the cost of business.

This chapter only provides a qualitative review of the way standards reduce transaction costs and of the consequent welfare gains. The quantification of these welfare gains and of the costs of the introduction and implementation of standards has barely taken place. This is a promising field for further research.

NOTES

1. Based on Den Butter et al. (2007).
2. Based on Den Butter and Corveleijn (2007).
3. Based on Den Butter et al. (2009).

8.   Innovation through transaction management

This chapter discusses the importance of innovations that reduce transaction costs. These trade innovations, or transaction innovations, include a large knowledge component. Because these innovations can bring about positive externalities, the government should pay attention to them. Finally, this chapter discusses the complementary relationship between transaction management and Lean management, the latter being an amply applied business management method of organizational innovations that bring about cost reduction.

8.1   PRODUCT AND TRADE INNOVATIONS

The examples on standardization in the previous chapter show that innovation and knowledge creation play an important role in a transaction economy. However, innovation and knowledge creation are commonly associated with technological innovation. From that viewpoint, the goal is to increase productivity by making better products and by using better production processes. Investment in R&D is supposed to be an engine for such innovations and knowledge creation. The proposition here is that R&D-driven technological progress leads to an increase in productivity within the links of the production chain (Figure 5.1).

Chapter 5 assesses how, from the perspective of the fragmentation of production, two sources of comparative advantage can be distinguished. Process and product innovations within the various parts of the production chain result in lower production costs. This increase in productivity within that part of the production chain can bring about a comparative advantage for production. By contrast, innovations that reduce the transaction costs of linking the various parts of the production chain create value and increase productivity in the orchestrating function. This provides a comparative advantage in the coordination and organization of production.

An important empirical question is whether the productivity increases in industry can be attributed to product innovations (within the parts of the chain) or transaction innovations, as they are labelled by Jacobs and Waalkens (2001), which relate to connecting the parts of the chain. Den Butter et al. (2008) call these latter innovations *trade innovations* and show in an empirical study based on rough indicators at the macro level that the contribution of trade innovations to productivity increases in the Netherlands is at least as large as the contribution of investments in R&D to productivity increases. Productivity is in this study measured as total factor productivity. This large contribution of trade innovations is confirmed in a study by Den Butter and Pattipeilohy (2007), where in a production function the contribution of offshoring to productivity growth is estimated. The estimation shows that when adding R&D as a control variable, it yields hardly any additional explanation for productivity growth.

8.1.1 Further Research is Needed to Assess the Influence of Trade Innovations

These empirical analyses provide only a first attempt to separate the influence of product and trade innovations on productivity. It leaves much scope for future research. First, the proxy used to measure transaction costs measures the effect of lowering transaction costs and not the expenditures on innovations lowering these costs. Here, an adequate data set with longitudinal data at the plant level is warranted. Sets with micro data at the firm or even plant level have now become available for various countries. The empirical analyses using these data sets have already enhanced our knowledge on the relationship between innovation in the organization of production and productivity (see for example Federico, 2010, and the papers and discussions of a conference on 'Productivity and Internationalization: a Micro-data Approach' in The Hague in September 2010). However, a strict separation between R&D and trade innovations will be difficult to make because R&D data also partially measure innovations lowering transaction costs. It may be useful to make a further breakdown into various types of investments that enhance the division of labour and productivity. Spillovers between these different types of knowledge investments will complicate the analysis but can also indicate the need of government intervention in the case of externalities.

Second, the existence of reverse causality between productivity and trade innovations can influence the results. This reverse causality, or more precisely the proposition that the causality runs from productivity to trade, is a much-discussed issue in the literature. It is in fact part of a more general discussion on the determinants of the 'make or buy' decision, where transaction costs and R&D spillovers play an important role. From a transaction cost perspective there is reason to assume that causality (also) runs from innovative skills to reduce transaction costs to productivity.

Third, the empirical analyses discussed here only consider the impact of R&D and trade innovations in the Netherlands, and only for a historical reference period. A further research question is whether major differences exist between the impact of R&D and trade innovations on (total factor) productivity among countries. A preliminary analysis has indeed revealed such differences for a number of OECD countries. A first conclusion, therefore, is that a 'one size fits all' approach to focus solely on R&D expenditures for enhancing growth and the competitive position might not be justified for all OECD countries. However, such a conclusion warrants a more sophisticated empirical analysis. It would be interesting to have such analysis focused upon the structural differences of countries that can be regarded as production-based economies, with possibly high levels of technological R&D, and transaction economies that are more (but not solely) oriented towards trade and services in the transaction sector.

Another question for further research regards the impact of these trade innovations on employment at home and abroad. Up till now, the focus has been on employment changes and labour market dynamics because of an international rearrangement of jobs in the production sector, including the 'production' of services. Little attention has been paid to the transition of workers from the production to the transaction sectors or to the world-wide division of labour in this respect. Future research may deal with these problems and provide further empirical evidence on the contribution of trade innovations to productivity growth.

In addition to innovations that facilitate commercial transactions *between* firms, these issues also relate to the organizational innovations that reduce transaction costs *within* firms. Especially in the case of large international enterprises, it is difficult to distinguish between these different types of transaction innovations. Nevertheless, it clearly shows that better transaction management enhances productivity and that this can be regarded as a kind of innovation. A similar observation holds for social innovation as described by Volberda et al. (2007).

As yet, data on investments in R&D mainly include expenditure on technological research that leads to an increase in productivity within parts of the production chain. In its traditional form, innovation policy focuses primarily on the promotion of such research and on internalizing the positive external effects of such technological knowledge. The consequence is that the investments in knowledge capital that enhances productivity in the orchestration function and the external effects of spillovers of that type of knowledge remain largely out of sight of innovation policy.

8.1.2 The Role of Innovation in the Traditional Theory of Economic Growth

An important reason for this focus of productivity analysis on product and process innovation lies in the traditional theory of economic growth. This theory considers production as the outcome of a production process with capital and labour (and sometimes energy) as inputs. The more effective utilization of these production factors enhances productivity. Therefore, by using the same amount of capital and labour, better and/ or more products can be made. This is technological progress. In early growth theory, these technological innovations came to us, in the words of Joan Robinson, as *'manna from heaven given to us by God and the engineers'*, so that technological progress was considered exogenous. However, modern growth theory emphasizes the fact that technological progress is created endogenously. Investments in R&D are seen as the driving force. Therefore, it is obvious to link investments in R&D with innovation: the guiding principle is that innovations that lead to better products and production processes are the consequence of investment in R&D. The result is that the industry can supply products at better value for money, and that productivity increases. This has a positive impact on the competitiveness, economic growth and thereby on the welfare of a country. Chapter 4 previously mentioned that in this version of growth theory the organization of production is not yet endogenized.

A key observation in the literature is that many investments in R&D bring about spillover effects. The knowledge obtained through learning and through investments in new technologies leads to an increase in human capital, so that labour is used more efficiently as a production factor. This leads to an increase in labour productivity. These knowledge spillovers yield positive externalities, which should be internalized by the government through providing additional incentives for such knowledge investments. By contrast, knowledge investment may also involve negative externalities, for example when old technologies are replaced quickly by new technologies when the development costs of these old technologies have not yet been recovered. Yet the positive externalities are usually considered to dominate the negative ones, so that the internalization of these externalities forms a viable argument for the government's technology policy and for its focus on innovation and investment in R&D. This argument is central to current thinking about the knowledge economy. As mentioned, modern ideas in innovation policy in the context of growth theory mainly relate to technological innovation through R&D. In her review article, Sena (2004) shows that, besides these spillovers that enhance productivity, various forms of cooperation in R&D and the extent to which the intellectual property rights resulting from investment in R&D can be protected nowadays constitute major topics of economic research in this field.

It is also noteworthy that the recent theories of international trade that focus on the fragmentation of production mainly explain differences in productivity (and in the heterogeneity of productivity) within parts of the production chain (see Helpman, 2006). Although the costs of trading ('trade costs') play a role in these models, it is remarkable that, apart from the focus on incomplete contracts, the possibility of heterogeneity of productivity and productivity differences in the orchestration function – namely, one firm being better able to organize production and manage transaction costs than the other – is not explicitly addressed. However, recent literature shows that a significant empirical link exists among trade, productivity and economic growth. For instance, the empirical study of Noguer and Siscart (2005) uses a detailed data analysis to show that, in addition to other determinants, trade has a direct positive influence on income. Herrendorf and Teixeira (2005) find a negative effect of international trade barriers on productivity. From the study of Dollar and Kraay (2003) it seems that in the long run the volume of trade in a country combined with good institutions proves to be an important determinant of economic growth. In the short run it is primarily the volume of trade itself that determines the growth rate.

8.2 TRANSACTION MANAGEMENT IS A KEY FACTOR OF THE KNOWLEDGE ECONOMY

Innovations such as standards that reduce transaction costs require a good combination of technical, social and cultural knowledge (see Box 8.1). As such, there is no reason for policy and for strategic decision-makers in the business sector to make – as is sometimes suggested – a choice for the future of a country between a 'knowledge economy' and a 'transaction economy' or 'trading nation'. These two aspects of economic development are purely complementary and cannot be separated. Therefore, it is untrue that the only knowledge a trading nation needs is to know where goods, services and parts and components can be purchased at the lowest prices, and where products and services can be sold at the highest prices. Technological knowledge and science are essential for a transaction economy to function properly. Many new technologies can indeed be purchased and the development of open source standards takes place on a global scale. However, it is of utmost importance to really understand the new possibilities and to know how to assess the benefits, as well as to

BOX 8.1   THE RELATIONSHIP BETWEEN
          INNOVATION AND TRANSACTION
          MANAGEMENT

In the traditional economic view of innovation, which focuses on production and technological progress in production, innovation is particularly associated with technological innovation, resulting from investment in R&D. From this perspective, economic policy analysis emphasizes the need for a sufficiently high level of R&D for a country to be competitive in the global technology race. From this viewpoint, underinvestment in R&D will cause a loss of competitive position and lead to relegation from the premier league of advanced economies. Hence, the so-called Lisbon Agenda of the European Union, which in 2000 aimed at making the EU the most competitive and knowledge-intensive economic bloc in the world, sees the level of investment in R&D as an important indicator. A level of 3 per cent of GDP was taken as the standard for reaching the objective.

However, this book advocates a more balanced description of innovation. In a broad sense, innovation can be characterized by the 3 Cs: creativity, coordination and communication. The emphasis on technological innovation, which relates closely to fundamental knowledge on science and technology, focuses on *creativity.* This may also include practical ingenuity that yields useful inventions. Yet such creativity, inventiveness and even serendipity have to be organized and facilitated. This brings *coordination,* and thereby good transaction management, into play. In this context the skill of connecting people and thoughts can be regarded as an important prerequisite for innovation. In fact, it is very much related to the formation of networks. It is by fostering dialogue, preferably between different disciplines and skills, and by making unusual combinations, that fine ideas to create new products, or to reduce transaction costs, originate. Finally, innovation does not automatically lead to higher productivity and a competitive advantage. Knowledge about new technologies and the applications of ideas should also be communicated. A core competency of a transaction economy and trading nation is to be knowledgeable about how to collect information on what, where and from whom to buy, on what new applications there will be, and on what the world needs. Therefore, good *communication* is essential for making profitable transactions, which would otherwise not have taken place.

be aware of the risks associated with new technological developments. Therefore, a transaction economy should not only be able to understand how valuable new knowledge can be for trade, but should also actively contribute to the development of new knowledge and technology.

The real scientific geniuses who conduct basic research moving the frontiers of knowledge forward should be nurtured. Because these scientific geniuses are homogeneously distributed across the world, it is expected that countries such as China and India, with an increased access to education, will deliver many of these brilliant researchers in the future. For that reason, to be able to collect the fruits of the new technological developments, it is recommended to set up a good scouting system for high potential among young researchers and where possible to let researchers in the home countries benefit from the creativity of foreign researchers early in their careers. This also means that researchers in the home countries should not just be focused on their own research, but that the focus should be directed to organizing creativity and serendipity. These qualities are highly valuable in a combined knowledge and transaction economy. Therefore, the education system should support not only theoretically interested scientists and technologists, but especially scientists and technologists who are keen on practical applications and who know how good ideas can be born and exploited.

In this context, the knowledge of mathematics is often regarded as scientific knowledge. This is not justified in the sense that nowadays disciplines other than the traditional scientific disciplines also require an extensive knowledge of relevant mathematics. This holds true for economics, psychology, some areas of law and sociology and even for linguistics and history ('cliometrics'). This kind of science-oriented knowledge ('beta-knowledge'), which is much broader than the technical knowledge of engineers and which can be labelled '*beta-plus*', is necessary in an economy where orchestration is becoming increasingly important. In such an economy there should be a good climate for attracting foreign firms and knowledge workers. From that perspective there is a need in transaction economies to promote investment in academic knowledge that is directed to answering the research questions of the business sector.

The transition from a production-oriented to an orchestration-oriented economy also has important implications for the required knowledge and skills of the workforce. Jobs that relate to direct production will disappear. Instead, new jobs will be created with an emphasis on orchestration and the implementation of knowledge. This simultaneous job destruction and job creation where the economy adjusts to changing circumstances is, incidentally, a well-known phenomenon. For instance, data on labour market dynamics in the Netherlands suggest (depending on the proper definition of a job: see Bruil et al., 2010) that in this country each year around 500000 old jobs disappear and that, depending on the stance of the business cycle, around 500000 new permanent jobs are created. Here, it must be noted that the change in the nature of jobs is only partly because of the relocation of activities abroad. Outsourcing, and the related destruction and creation of jobs, takes place more frequently in domestic production. Section 5.4 shows that the construction industry, which can be regarded as almost a prototype of the manufacturing industry, is a good example. As mentioned, the construction industry can achieve significant productivity gains by saving on transaction costs associated with the coordination problems related to subcontracting. The transition from a production-oriented economy to an orchestration- and globally-oriented economy also implies that workers in the home country will have to deal much more with foreign colleagues. This requires not only additional cultural and communicative knowledge, but also a change in the mindset of many workers, which should change from a local to a global orientation (see Box 8.2).

8.3 THE RELATIONSHIP BETWEEN LEAN MANAGEMENT AND TRANSACTION MANAGEMENT[1]

As already indicated in the introductory chapter, this book deliberately promotes the skill of managing transaction costs as *not* simply another 'management method'. As Chapter 4 reports, its theoretical basis can be found in transaction cost economics, with three Nobel Prize winners (Coase, North and Williamson) as intellectual fathers. It combines elements of modern growth theory, the theory of the firm, international economics, new institutional economics and industrial organization. Yet one claim of transaction management is that it can contribute to making profitable strategic decisions for individual firms. Therefore, it seems reasonable to compare the methodology of transaction management with more targeted methods from the management literature that purport to reduce costs in production processes. From that perspective, this section discusses similarities and complementarities between transaction management and a well-established practical management method, namely Lean management. A major reason for this comparison with Lean management is that during a presentation of transaction management, management consultants asked about differences and similarities with Lean.

Lean management directly aims at improving production processes and

BOX 8.2   GLOBAL JOBS

'Working together' has been the motto of the Balkenende cabinet in the Netherlands. In a modern society where horizontal working relationships prevail, 'working together' means that we really have to do the job together. It is only possible to do so when we truly enjoy working together in good agreement and harmony. To understand each other and to distribute tasks between each other as much as possible according to our wishes and abilities is what makes working together really enjoyable and profitable. 'Cooperate and do not obstruct' is the adage. Nothing is worse for work and the economy than when colleagues strive to be allotted with only the most rewarding tasks, and give each other poor information or simply hate each other. This makes the intrinsic motivation to do the job properly disappear, and urges management to come up with more and more rules, regulations and complicated job descriptions. In that case costly extrinsic motivation crowds out intrinsic motivation.

The microeconomic perspective is that we should derive utility beyond sheer payment in money from the job. This can be called the 'satisfaction argument' of employment. When work is challenging and an individual can fulfil his or her personal interests and capabilities, but also when work provides the opportunity to meet and work with interesting colleagues, one will be willing to work harder and longer than when it involves routine and boredom. In these times of ageing, which requires high participation from the working age population, this is also good for society as a whole. Satisfaction at work will be enhanced when there is more flexibility over the time and place of work, and when the job enables participation in private networks where one's reputation of professionalism can be developed and honoured. Modern ways of employment are also characterized by working based on contracts in different settings rather than the traditional permanent job for life with the same employer. Moreover, in the future the working career will be longer and longer, with a postponement of the pension as long as one wants or is able. Then, it is essential that the working career itself becomes less stressful with less strain during the 'rush hour of life'.

The focus on trade in tasks and the international division of labour which globalization brings about require excellent communication skills and a good talent to cooperate. Global outsourcing also implies that it is essential that the ability to cooperate and understand each other now includes understanding other cultures and customs as well. Trading nations traditionally have such abilities and these must be properly nurtured. Working together will much more than before become 'working globally together'. These skills will gain importance and, whereas technical knowledge and expertise remain indispensable, the jobs of the future will increasingly be jobs in the organization of global production. Our colleagues will no longer mainly live in the next village or suburb, but will also live in Bangalore, Shanghai, Moscow and São Paulo. When we keep a close eye on these trends, it is true that direct manufacturing jobs at home will be destroyed and disappear, but plenty of other jobs, with a global character, will be created instead.

Moreover, because of the ageing population, numerous new domestic jobs will be created in medical and social care for the elderly, and more broadly to satisfy the needs of the old age pensioners who will be relatively wealthy. One can think of specialized travel agents, education and organizing cultural events and financial services for the elderly. One could even speak of an 'ageing-related industry'. It is obvious that this 'industry' requires good networking skills as well, and, therefore, will profit from good transaction management.

at value creation by cost reduction. The focus is on production within a firm, or otherwise on the total value chain of a specific product. In addition, transaction management may provide a more general strategic view in which a balancing of costs in the short and long term plays a central role. It is in principle focused on the external organization of firms and production processes. Moreover, transaction management is also applicable in the public sphere of social organization.

The suggestion may be that because Lean management is directed at cost reductions in production, the application of Lean management will bring about product and process innovations; whereas transaction management, which is directed at cost reduction in coordination and organising exchange, will bring about trade innovations and institutional innovations. However, the following assessment of Lean in relation to transaction management shows that such strict separation between the two types of innovations is not justified in this case.

8.3.1   Lean Management

The 'Lean management' philosophy originated at Toyota in the automotive industry but is now also used in many other industries. Lean management is very much customer-oriented. It helps to optimize the entire production chain, where as many as possible components of the chain, and transitions in the chain, which do not directly contribute value to the customer, are removed. Moreover, production processes that are designed according to the principle of Lean management provide the possibility of taking the wishes of customers into account, without parting from the principle that products should be based on combining a limited number of standardized parts.

Lean is a label for a philosophy also known as the Toyota Production System (TPS). In the 1980s, it was discovered that Toyota scored significantly better on a number of aspects of efficient production than the Western automobile industry did. For example: there was less effort required to design, manufacture and sell its products; there were fewer accidents; fewer investments were needed to achieve a certain production capacity; there were fewer faulty products produced; the required stocks were lower; and the cycles of 'concept-to-launch', 'order-to-delivery' and 'problem-to repair' were shorter.

Lean is often linked to the smart organization of production, and thus focuses on the entire value chain. From this perspective, it is a philosophy that concentrates on providing added value for customers by eliminating all forms of waste. The category 'muda' is for most people the most recognizable form of waste. Muda includes waste resulting from:

- Transportation;
- Waiting;
- Overproduction;
- Defects;
- Realocation;
- Stocks; and
- Additional.

Yet, mura (unevenness) and muri (overburden) can also be considered important sources of waste. Mura comprises all efforts, such as quality control, that arise because the quality of a product is not predictable. Muri involves the utilization of human effort and machines above or below their capacities.

Various management tools are useful when a firm decides to embrace the Lean philosophy. Important in this respect are 'value stream mapping' and 'Kaizen'. Value stream mapping is used to analyse a process to detect forms of waste. This relates not only to the flow of goods, but also to the stream of information. Kaizen means continuous, gradual improvement, which is a typical Oriental approach to changing an organization. In this respect Kaizen, and in a more general sense, Lean management are also concerned with aspects of human resource management (HRM). The name Lean management does not come from Toyota itself. The term 'Lean' was first used by Krafcik (1988), and it should be noted that the idea of Lean manufacturing actually goes back to the introduction of mass production lines of cars by Henry Ford. Ford foresaw the importance of not wasting materials during production and of organizing production efficiently by assembling standard components. The difference between the static conceptions of Ford and the more modern way of organizing production according to the principles of Lean is that nowadays production takes place in a much more dynamic environment where rapid responses to changes in customer preferences and the flexibility of the production process are essential.

8.3.2 Lean and Six Sigma

Lean management includes different perspectives on the organization of production. One example is the integration of Lean with Six Sigma. Six Sigma was developed by Motorola and has since been applied by many US companies including General Electric and Allied Signal. The concept of Six Sigma is that in assembling products from many different parts, the quality of the product depends on the probability that one of those parts does not function properly. In cases of defects in the weakest links in production, the tolerance for error margins of those components must be much smaller than the usual twice the standard deviation (2σ). When the tolerance is reduced to six times the standard deviation (6σ) and thereby higher quality standards are required for the components in the production than are often supplied by others, the costs of failure due to product failure will become considerably less. In that sense, Six Sigma complements Lean management because it strives to reduce the costs of failure as far as possible.

8.3.3 Combining Lean and Transaction Management

Likewise a combination of the principles of Lean management and transaction management seems conceivable. The greatest similarity between Lean management and transaction management is that both methods focus on controlling costs. However, whereas transaction management makes a distinction between direct production costs and additional trans-action costs, Lean management focuses on avoiding unnecessary costs in total production. In this sense, Lean management is complementary to transaction management because, unlike transaction management, it focuses on total production costs, including direct production costs. It implies that Lean management also pays attention to transaction costs, albeit without explicitly naming them and without explicitly distinguishing them from direct production costs.

The above description of Lean management in relation to transaction management gives a first impression of the similarities and differences. Lean management specifically aims at avoiding unnecessary costs in the production process. Transaction management considers the organization of production, but it has a much broader perspective and also focuses on what value can be created through transactions. Although many experts in Lean management and many examples of case studies in Lean manage-ment are available, there are fewer for transaction management. In this respect Lean management can be regarded as an established method to reduce costs, whereas transaction management is yet to prove useful.

Chapter 4 explains that the specificity of the production process or service is an important concept in the theory of transaction costs. This asset specificity refers to the degree to which the transaction costs incurred in the first transaction do not have to be re-incurred in subsequent trans-actions. This applies to the exchange of goods or services that have spe-cific characteristics. For example, in the case of outsourcing tasks, when these specifications have been established and approved in a first round, less detailed supervision for the next round is needed so that transaction costs are now lower. This can be seen as a process of learning. However, the more goods or services are tailored to the individual needs of the buyer, the higher asset specificity is. Thus, asset specificity also determines the extent to which trading partners are bound to lasting relationships (Williamson, 1985). If there is no asset specificity, there is free entry to markets for such goods or services, and traders will not be interested in investing in mutual relationships. The degree of asset specificity is a major determinant of transaction costs and, consequently, how transaction man-agement can create value.

In addition, there is a relationship between asset specificity and stand-ardization (see Chapter 7). Uniform standards ensure that suppliers and customers become less dependent on each other and thus, from that per-spective, reduce transaction costs. By contrast, the requirements in the case of the supply of parts, components or tasks can be specific to a par-ticular situation so that standards are developed for that situation only. This makes the mutual investment costs, which the supplier and customer have to make in their relationship, bigger. In this respect, asset specificity also plays a prominent role in the strategic alliances of a firm with its suppliers, as discussed earlier in the IHC case. Choi and Krause (2006) define the *supply base* as the portion of a supply network that is actively managed by the buying company and show that the complexity of the supply base is key in the external organization of the firm. Reduction of supply base complexity, for instance by standardization, may reduce transaction costs. On the other hand, too much reduction of complexity may affect the competitive position of the firm, as asset specificity can be associated with innovative product development.

Case studies of Lean management from the literature show that that asset specificity – although not in this exact wording – plays an important role in this methodology. Bruce et al. (2004) describe the strategies of four firms from the textile and clothing industry. These firms operate at sub-markets that differ in the ways in which the needs of customers are to be met. In general, the market for clothing is characterized by short product cycles and a changeability of the client, where impulse-buying behaviour and a quick response to the latest fashion trends are major features. This implies that the clothing industry must be able to respond quickly in their production lines to rapid developments. Moreover, these production lines may entail many links in a fragmented production chain. The required response time for each producer depends on the specific market characteristics. A firm that serves traditional clients is able to outsource parts of the production process to low-wage countries. The additional time and effort associated with this outsourcing is compensated by the gain from lower manufacturing costs. In addition, contacts with suppliers in the home country are kept up for the development of new clothing and fashion to comply with the more sensitive parts of demand. For another firm, however, the gains from lower production costs by outsourcing to low-wage countries do not compensate for the loss of response time to new developments in fashion. This firm focuses on the upper segment of the home market where tastes change quickly. Finally, there is a firm that is particularly keen on maintaining contacts with reliable suppliers, so that communication and coordination when adjusting the requirements involve fewer costs. From the perspective of Lean management, this case study shows the necessity of balancing costs between the cost savings of applying the Lean philosophy and the value of being flexible to respond to the changing needs of customers.

An addition that the perspective of transaction management can make to this case is that the balance between self-producing and domestic or foreign outsourcing depends on the asset specificity of the product. There is a trade-off between different types of transaction costs where the costs of coordination, the costs of lowering the lead time and the costs of building up an efficient trust relationship are to be balanced with each other.

Gabriel (1997) shows how the Lean philosophy has proven useful in project management. He describes two major building projects in the public domain in the United Kingdom: the construction of a new wing at the National Gallery and the new Glyndebourne Opera House. Both projects are organized in such a way that the communication lines are as short as possible. Project managers were employed by the clients, but each operated the projects as independently as possible. In addition, the project teams consisted of representatives of all the contractors and subcontractors who were responsible for their parts of the projects. The project teams looked after the necessary budgets and deadlines. This method of organization made sure that no unnecessary loss through miscommunication and misunderstandings occurred. This example of Lean project management is consistent with transaction management's finding that insight into the interests of various stakeholders and organizing discourse between the many interested parties may lead to a compromise, which can save on transaction costs. It is what Chapter 10 refers to as the 'polder model'.

However, the principles of Lean management are also criticized in the literature. Cox and Chicksand (2005) indicate how in the process of food and meat production, and in the links of this production chain with retailers, the application of Lean management can be problematic. For individual firms, Lean management principles may be profitable, but for the production chain as a whole there are disadvantages. The reason is that in the production chain the customers, which in this case are the retailers, obtain too much power. This makes the suppliers too dependent so that they are no longer able to organize their productions in an optimal way. Lean management seems not to take these costs of uneven power positions into account. Cox and Chicksand illustrate this phenomenon by the supply of fresh and frozen meat in the United Kingdom. In fact, the question here is about the distribution of added value in the production chain. Transaction management can in such cases exploit modern theories about the organization of production and trade (Antràs and Rossi-Hansberg, 2009). From a societal perspective it is important that all parts of the production chain are linked in an optimal way at the lowest possible costs in the long run, and that the aim to reduce the outsourcing costs of production in the short run, through negotiating sharp contracts with suppliers, does not bring about high transaction costs in the long run because the suppliers are no longer able to comply with the contracts. This means that the orchestrator in the production chain, for example in the way IHC fulfils this role in the dredging industry (see Section 5.3), should ensure that the distribution of the profits from value creation in the chain takes place in an appropriate manner. To give incentives to suppliers to provide innovative solutions during the full extent of the trade relationship, it is necessary that the proceeds from these successful solutions also accrue to those suppliers. This is the long-term perspective that the orchestrator should always respect and for which transaction management provides the arguments.

One of the most underrated aspects of Lean management is that much time is required for cultural changes to be fully effected. In fact, this is a major issue of the Lean philosophy. Cultural changes are an important prerequisite to adjusting the organization of production within a firm in order to adapt to changing circumstances. This is what 'Kaizen' empha-sizes in the Lean approach. It is obvious that the way these gradual changes in the business organization are realized, or rather provoked, depends on the cultural background of employees in the firm. In an Eastern-oriented business, a successful strategy might be different compared with where Western mentality and standards apply. In transaction management, the costs incurred by the transition from one organization of production to another are part of the overall transaction costs. These costs may relate to the cost of the transition to a different standard as discussed in the previ-ous chapter. However, bridging cultural differences is also a concern for transaction management. In this sense, transaction management comple-ments the concept of Kaizen and the resulting implications for HRM. In this respect Beauvallet and Houy (2010) argue in their survey on Lean HRM that the Toyota model may not have universal relevance and that the Scandinavian and German production models may act as counterex-amples. The upshot is that firms must organize themselves in accordance with the economic and social context in which they evolve and, hence, define their own 'productive model'. This is also true for the transition to a new way of organising production. Of course, the cultural component in the transition costs is difficult to quantify and such a transition requires responsible management.

Another aspect of Lean HRM, which can lead to a reduction of trans-action costs, is concerned with the relationship between operators and managers in the production process. Managers should inspire operators not to be content with performing their production tasks as they are, but to be eager to submit proposals to improve the process. This is especially true if problems arise in the production line. Operators should look for the reasons for faults. It is related to the Lean strategy of Right First Time (RFT). RFT is defined as the willingness by a firm to deal with faults immediately when they arise and, hence, control its processes perfectly. It implies that the incentives for the operators should be to detect faults and inefficiencies, and not to hide them or cover them up, or let openness on faults and inefficiencies lead to loss of face. Obviously for management to get these incentives right will strongly depend on the cultural background of the personnel.

The discussion in Section 5.3 of the specific relationship IHC can establish with respect to both procurement from suppliers and to customer demand, provides an excellent example of how insights from Lean management can be complementary to those of transaction management. That is because Lean management is also concerned with cases where benefits from outside the organization are to be collected. In such instances, a firm will enter into strategic alliances with a limited number of suppliers and customers (Piercy and Rich, 2009). Then, these suppliers and customers must be involved in the Lean philosophy of the organization. Dyer et al. (2001) studied the success factors for an effective strategic alliance. The main conclusion is that someone just below the top of an organization should be appointed to deal with such strategic alliances and be a partner in all strategic discussions of the firm. A target for strategic alliances within the Lean philosophy (Dyer et al., 2001; Piercy and Rich, 2009) is to reduce transaction costs for both suppliers and customers. Obviously, this literature on strategic alliances implicitly makes a connection between Lean management and transaction management (see also Dyer, 1997). Additionally, Dyer and Nobeoka (2000) show that Toyota itself as the birthplace of Lean management was able to save on costs by knowing how the network of suppliers should be organized in order to enhance the efficiency of production. Oxley (1997, 1999) discusses these strategic alliances from the perspective of transaction cost economics. Her main concern is about the technology leakages, the so-called 'appropriability hazards' and about their implications for governance between members of the strategic alliance. It seems that the most important factors contributing to appropriability hazards in inter-firm alliances are related to transaction characteristics: the type and scope of the transaction explain a large fraction of the variation in the alliance form. In accordance with the logic of transaction cost theory, more 'hierarchical' alliances are chosen for transactions and cooperation where these hazards are more severe. This is, for instance, the case when allying with firms from countries where intellectual property protection is weak.

Quite another example where Lean management can be complementary to transaction management concerns the case where decisions to outsource work and jobs abroad may imply the dismissal of employees in the establishment at home. It can lead to social unrest, which in turn entails many transaction costs. In this respect Lean management is concerned with the interaction between HRM and other bundles of Lean manufacturing practices, such as just-in-time management (JIT), total quality management (TQM) and total preventive maintenance (TPM) (see Shah and Ward, 2003). HRM should anticipate and avoid as much as possible the costs that social unrest due to sourcing decisions brings about. That is particularly important because of the spillovers that such unrest will have to the other bundles of Lean manufacturing practices, so that it becomes more difficult to control costs with respect to these practices as well.

8.3.4   Conclusion

Lean management is a well-established method for organizing the production process. It is particularly suited to the establishment of production processes in what transaction cost economics considers products or services with high 'asset specificity'. This illustrates how Lean management and transaction management are related to each other. In both cases there is a strong focus on cost reduction within the production chain. Yet the difference here is that Lean management focuses on all costs in the production process, whereas transaction management focuses specifically on the transaction costs that the organization of production brings about. Both approaches have different backgrounds. Transaction management does not label itself as a management technique, but rather as a way of thinking that provides a practical application of recent developments in trade theory, and in the theories of new institutional economics and industrial organization. Lean management stems directly from the practice of the organization and is an elaboration of how Toyota successfully organizes its supply chain and production processes.

Nevertheless both methods have a lot to offer one another as complementary approaches. They partly even overlap, though a different mindset and contrasting terminology are used. However, there are also significant differences in the way both methods balance costs, for instance between one-off and recurrent costs, between costs in the short run and long run and between costs associated with risks and expenses to avoid risks. Moreover, transaction management makes an important distinction between vertical costs (through the hierarchy within the firm) and horizontal costs (through the market). This distinction is particularly relevant for the 'make or buy' and location decisions for outsourcing. Lean management places great emphasis on avoiding unnecessary costs and on the extent to which costs are needed to generate value for the customer. Especially because of these differences, both methods can complement one another. Admittedly, Lean management has already earned its spurs, whereas transaction management has yet to be proven profitable in such business-case applications.

The human aspect forms another important issue on which the two methods complement each other. One of the elements that Lean considers 'wasteful' is the overloading of staff: it is called 'muri'. In transaction management, the human factor plays an implicit role in soft transaction costs. For example, in procurement various dimensions of sustainability play important roles in strategic decision-making within the firm (see Section 4.6). Soft transaction costs also include the costs of unhappy staff. Lean makes this aspect more explicit by referring to the costs of such frustration in cases where transactions are poorly organized. This may apply to both government and industry. Another overlap relates to the seven types of waste Lean distinguishes, namely transportation, waiting, overproduction, defects, relocation, stocks and additional processing. These concepts, which in Lean are strongly associated with the production process, can also be applied on a more abstract level to transactions. This can provide a helpful tool for the relevant categorization of transactions and thereby a distinction between various types of transaction costs.

Both Lean and transaction management try to avoid unnecessary costs ('waste'), but whereas Lean is focused in particular on costs within an organization, transaction management seeks to organize the whole production chain at the lowest costs. Looking beyond the walls of the firm, as transaction management does, may even reduce costs within the walls of the firm. The fact that a transaction is executed in a certain way may create waste in the organization, such as an unnecessary stock. Now all effort can be made to minimize the inventory within the firm, but it seems better to coordinate the transaction with the customer or supplier. Here, the risk of Lean is to be 'penny-wise, pound-foolish': when the organization is made 'Lean', circumstances may change so that waste is created again. This can happen in times of crisis, allowing organizations to fall back into old habits. From that perspective, transaction management states that all partners in the supply chain should discuss the optimization of the transaction together. When such an orchestration of the supply chain is performed within an organization, the introduction of Lean in that organization is bound to be easier. The people doing the work know best what is possible and what is not. They are also the best to know the implications of changes to their work.

All in all it seems that Lean is an effective and well-proven method to eliminate all forms of waste within the firm or production chain, whereas transaction management focuses on the links between organization of production within the firm and the outside options in a globalizing world. It implies that there are, as indicated above, differences in the strategic horizon of the two methods: the major concern for Lean is the internal organization of the firm whereas transaction management mainly considers the external repercussions of decisions about how to produce. In that sense, Lean and transaction management complement each other very well. As yet, there are no cases available where both methods are applied in combination. Therefore, in order to obtain a better understanding of how combining both methods can be exploited in the best possible way, it is essential to avail ourselves of such practical cases. Hopefully that practical experience can now be gained as quickly as possible. It may add to the knowledge on how transaction innovations can enhance productivity.

NOTE

1. Based on Boons and Den Butter (2011).

9. Government intervention and transaction management

This chapter shows, from a normative economic perspective, how the government can contribute, by linking trade and innovation policy, to reducing transaction costs and thereby achieving welfare gains. The main argument is that a major reason for government intervention is to repair market failures. Therefore, government trade and innovation policy should concentrate on knowledge spillovers in transaction management that bring about positive externalities. An example of the provision of public goods in this respect is national branding. Here, government should ensure that no damage is done to the reputation of trustworthy trading partners. By way of an example, the possible role of the government in SCM is considered. The chapter also pays ample attention to the question of whether trade and innovation policy should be targeted to specific industrial sectors. This links to the discussion of how to conduct industrial policy without invoking international retaliation.

9.1 ARGUMENTS FOR GOVERNMENT INTERVENTION

This section discusses what the modern textbooks on 'public sector economics' generally consider the arguments for government intervention. It should be clearly stated that this perception of what the government should and should not do stems from the welfare theory of economics, and that the tasks of government that other disciplines may consider relevant are ignored here. Moreover, this economic theory of the public sector has a strong normative character: it is the idea that government aims to maximize societal welfare that *prescribes* how it has to operate. Hence from this perspective the role of government is formulated in terms of what the government *should* do. This contrasts with the approach of public choice theory and of behavioural economics, which explain why the government has responded to policy problems as it has, and why politicians and civil servants act as they do.

Under this normative approach there seems to be no role for government in a theoretically ideal world of perfectly-functioning markets and of perfect information. When all scarce resources are distributed in a fair manner, the invisible hand sees to it that through the price mechanism in the market economy a socially-optimal situation is reached automatically (see Box 2.1). Therefore, when seeking arguments of government intervention that are justified from an economic point of view, one must always ask why the market does not fulfil its task properly. In other words it is necessary to answer the question why and in what way government intervention would bring about higher social welfare than when the supply of goods and services had been left entirely to the market. Government policy requires a thorough argumentation in this respect. The argument in this case is over the reason why the visible hand of government intervention and the budget mechanism is to be preferred to the invisible hand of the market. In that respect, the way government intervention should be shaped aligns with the prescriptions from new institutional economics.

Economic theory provides several arguments for why the market mechanism is not (fully) working and why, consequently, government intervention can take place. The emphasis here is on 'can' take place, because it is not necessarily always true that the government 'should' act when markets are not fully functioning. Sometimes government intervention may bring about sizeable efficiency losses, high transaction costs or a poor assessment of social preferences. This may be so costly that the welfare gain due to intervention in the market is smaller than the welfare loss that government intervention brings about. In such a case of major *government failure,* no government intervention is better than a government intervention that aims at making the markets function better.

9.1.1 Redistribution

The first valid argument for government intervention is the *redistribution argument.* In this case, the functioning of the market yields a distribution of social welfare that can be improved by redistribution by the government, for example through progressive income taxes and providing social security. There is a need for such redistribution in the case of a 'too' uneven distribution between rich and poor (or between the old and the young), which does not sufficiently take into account the social preferences with respect to questions of equity and solidarity. It should be stressed that the political scene determines these views on social welfare, and thereby the warranted extent of redistribution, rather than economists. The task of economists is to design the redistribution scheme with a minimum loss of efficiency, given the political preferences for equity ('second best' solution).

9.1.2   Public Goods

A second argument for government intervention is the *provision of public goods.* These are goods and services not provided by the market because they are non-rival and non-excludable. Chapter 7 on standards has already provided some examples. Other well-known examples include defence, the legal infrastructure and various forms of physical infrastructure such as seawalls and polder dykes. When these public goods and services are supplied by the private sector, there is the problem of 'free-ridership' as mentioned in discussing the provision of standards. Economic actors tend to wait to provide such goods and services until others do so, and then take a free ride. If everyone waits for others to take the initiative – the famous *prisoner's dilemma* shows that this non-cooperative behaviour is rational in the sense that it is the Nash equilibrium solution in a one-shot game – there will be no provision of public goods and services. Thus, the government must solve this dilemma. However, the discussion on which goods and services the government should provide is not solely an economic one: political preferences also play a role, especially in the case of so-called *semi public goods.* This is linked to the discussion on the *core competence* of the government in safeguarding the public interest.

9.1.3   Repair of Market Failure

A third argument for government intervention, which is highly relevant from the perspective of innovation, is *market failure.* This concerns the occurrence of *external effects,* such as the network externalities mentioned in Chapter 7. Furthermore, a situation of information asymmetry, increasing returns to scale or monopoly may cause market failure. Externalities can be positive or negative. A positive externality occurs when actions by private agents provide benefits to other agents, whereas these private agents do not receive compensation for those benefits. Therefore, the results of those actions may, in a way, gain the character of a public good, although they may also be made excludable, which reduces the social benefit. Government intervention to correct these market failures can take the form of additional funding (subsidies) or tax relief. In the case of negative externalities, the activities of private agents damage other agents, whereas this damage is not taken into account when the agents decide on their activities. Safety standards and regulatory taxes play a role to internalize such externalities.

9.1.4 Make the Market Work

The situation of a market that does not function well provides a final argument for government intervention. It can, incidentally, also be regarded as a type of market failure. In this case, the government should not seek to become a (structural) substitute for the role of the market, but must allow the market to function in a better way. This is a policy of promoting or restoring *the functioning of the market mechanism.* This type of policy is usually concerned with the prevention of cartels and monopolies and is closely related to *competition policy.*

9.2   GOVERNMENT AND INNOVATION POLICY

How can these various arguments for government intervention be translated into an innovation policy that seeks to fully exploit the strengths and opportunities of a transaction economy in this era of globalization and the fragmentation of production? All the preceding arguments may be relevant to government intervention in the case of the transition of the country from a production-oriented economy to an orchestration-oriented economy. The *redistribution argument* will only play a minor role in this case, but it still cannot entirely be ignored. As a matter of fact, the transition from production to orchestration will bring about value creation in transactions and in the organization of production. The question then is how the distribution of productivity gains associated with that value creation will take place, and whether the government wants to interfere with such an allocation because of political preferences. This may relate both to the distribution of earnings between producers and consumers, and to the distribution of value creation between the home country and abroad. From a (narrow) national interest, the question is how the welfare gains from the innovations reducing the transaction costs – which are additions to the consumer and producer surplus – can be retained in the home country. This distribution problem that the transition to orchestration brings about should be of more concern to governmental policy. From that perspective, Visser (2005) studied the impact of FDI on economic development and advocates against slowing down outgoing FDI because it acts as a form of protection. A liberal policy with respect to outgoing FDI yields most welfare benefits. The (political) problem is that the benefits of FDI are not directly observable and have positive effects especially in the long run, whereas the disadvantages (for example, destruction of production jobs) show up in the short run, and are directly visible. This also applies more broadly to aspects of globalization and the fragmentation of production.

The second argument for government intervention, the *provision of public goods*, has a more direct link with the subject of this book. Two aspects can be distinguished here. In the first place, for a country that is moving more and more towards the orchestration function, the extent to which it is trusted is becoming increasingly important (see Chapter 6). This implies that 'branding' the country becomes important. When foreign trading partners and clients are aware of the good qualities of the traders and firms in the country, it reduces transaction costs and promotes good relations, which are needed in the orchestration function. The flip-side of building up this trust and a good reputation as a trading partner is that there is a major risk factor related to the bad behaviour ('scandals') of individual firms. Here, the government can play an active role to try, through adequate branding, to build up a good reputation for reliability (as a form of social capital) and avoid through regulation and supervision any damage to that reputation from unwarranted actions by individual firms. This would destroy the social capital of the good reputation. The second form of the provision of public goods that is relevant from the perspective of the transition to a transaction economy concerns education. The transition to more orchestration will, as previously noted, imply that production workers with particular skills in the home production of goods and services will have to extend these skills with the complementary competencies necessary to minimize transaction costs when tasks are outsourced to others. The organization of teaching these skills is in principle a public task, but such teaching can also be organized by associations founded for that purpose by specific branches in the industry and service sectors.

The most prominent role for government policy in a transaction economy relates to the repair of *market failure*. The main argument for government intervention here is that knowledge investments generally bring about positive externalities. Therefore, individual firms tend to underinvest in such innovations from the perspective of social welfare because they cannot exclusively reap the fruits of those investments. As mentioned before, in the case of the transition of a production-oriented economy to an orchestration-oriented economy, the (measured) investments in R&D are not the only things that matter. There is a much wider range of knowledge investments that reduce transaction costs. Partitioning knowledge through patents and other forms of protecting intellectual property rights is one option, but often that is not optimal from a societal perspective because it blocks the profitable use of that knowledge by others.

9.2.1 Arguments for Innovation Policy

Innovation policy should, therefore, see to it that these external effects are exploited, by facilitating and promoting cooperation in research and the transfer of knowledge with respect to these trade transactions. This may include a targeted subsidy (see Section 9.5). In that case, it should be clear that such a subsidy supports investments with positive externalities. It cannot be, as is often still the case in actual industrial policy, that these subsidy schemes involve a lot of administrative arrangements that, in particular, enhance government employment. It is important that the benefits of the schemes are weighed against the costs. These costs are much larger than the actual amount of money of the subsidy itself. Indeed, the arrangements are associated with various types of transaction costs for applicants and grant-providers. The firm may have made the investment even if no subsidy were available. This is the *deadweight loss* that plays a role in the granting of subsidies. It means that in the case of funding knowledge investments for innovation, it has to be made very clear, both by the firm or interest group of a cluster of firms requesting the grant, and by the government, how the subsidy is bound to internalize the positive externalities and how these externalities are to be exploited. In other words, the transaction costs that the application and granting of subsidies for innovation entail, should, in addition to the amount of the subsidy, be lower than the social benefits of internalizing the positive externalities.

That is why innovation policy finds its legitimacy largely in the repair of market failures and in preventing underinvestment in innovative knowledge. Because of the limited scope of measured R&D and growth theory, which is oriented to production rather than to the organization of production, industrial policy and innovation policy almost exclusively focus on product and process innovation. This relates to productivity gains through the innovation achieved within the parts of the production chain as depicted in part A of Figure 5.1. This kind of innovation fits the traditional image of the own-production-oriented manufacturing industry. However, in an industrial organization where orchestration plays a major role, innovations in transaction management will be most productive. Again, these innovations bring about knowledge spillovers that give rise to positive externalities, although much research is still to be performed to find out the best ways to exploit these spillovers. For example, internalizing positive externalities from knowledge spillovers on how to organize production can also be performed by establishing government institutions which facilitate these knowledge spillovers. Another way is to change rules with respect to regulating spillovers. An important issue in this respect, which requires more research, is the trade-off between the positive welfare effects of cooperation because of knowledge spillovers versus the negative welfare effects because of collusion between cooperating firms. Here innovation policy is in conflict with competition policy.

9.2.2   Transaction Innovation by the Church

In history it has often been the church that acted as a replacement for the state in providing social care. The example in Box 9.1 illustrates that the church has, in the Middle Ages, also been instrumental in facilitating coordination in production. Through church bells it acted as a promoter of innovations enhancing the productivity of the population by reducing the transaction costs of villagers and farmers in coordinating their activities.

9.3   FACILITATING THE ORCHESTRATING FUNCTION

The previous argumentation indicates that part of the innovation policy of the government relates to facilitating the transition from a production-oriented economy to an orchestration-oriented economy. Therefore, internalizing the positive externalities of knowledge investments in the transition process is a target for government policy. Here, not only is the (measured) investment in R&D to be considered, but also a much wider range of knowledge investments that reduce transaction costs.

From that perspective, it is relevant to look at literature on the relationship between innovation and the orchestration function resulting from the fragmentation of production. It seems that being exposed to foreign competition is essential for firms to converge on the most efficient means of production (technology efficiency frontier). This is partly because of knowledge spillovers induced by international competition (see for example Peter et al., 2004). Another interesting development in this respect is that firms are increasingly outsourcing innovation to international networks – a form of open innovation (Naghavi and Ottaviano, 2006). For example, Procter & Gamble wanted to outsource in 2010 half of the development of ideas for new products to such networks, as compared to 2006 when that was the case for only 20 per cent.

The government can promote the transition to the role as orchestrators of incumbent firms by focusing the policy on this type of knowledge transfer. Prusak and Weiss (2007) discuss the opportunities for firms to

---

**BOX 9.1   TRANSACTION MANAGEMENT IN THE
MIDDLE AGES**

St-Gengoux-le-National is a picturesque medieval French town,
nestled among the vineyards of southern Burgundy (Figure 9.12).
As in all old medieval towns, the church tower dominates the
view. The church bells are heard for miles around. Every quarter
of an hour a bell rings, namely once at quarter past the hour,
twice on every half hour, three times a quarter before the hour
and four times when a new hour begins. Then, the number of
strokes of a different bell in the tower indicates the new hour. That
is how villagers and farmers were to know the time. In France, it is
usual that the bell indicating the new hour rings twice: if you forget
to listen the first time, or if you are confused about the number of
strokes, you get a second chance.

In the Middle Ages, the ringing of church bells was regarded
as an important form of transaction management. Landes (1998,
p. 67) explains how the ringing of church bells brought order and
regularity, so that people could coordinate without interference
from or directives by others. Remember that in those days people
did not have watches. Farmers could determine how much
time they had spent working on a piece of land. Appointments
between villagers and/or farmers, which were settled for a specific hour, were facilitated by the time indicated by the church
bell. Therefore, the church bells contributed to the reduction of
transaction costs and brought about an increase in productivity.

Remarkably, as the picture shows, in St-Gengoux-le-National
two church towers stand side by side, and are connected by a
wooden bridge. The deeper significance of this form of transaction management is, however, unknown to the author of this book.

---

reduce the transaction costs of the accumulation of knowledge within the
organization. These are the costs for finding, linking and using expertise.
Proximity of knowledge centres and building trust between the knowledge
workers are instrumental in reducing these kinds of transaction costs. It is
obvious that the government should contribute to affect such knowledge
transfers so that the externalities are internalized. In a way, this is what the
recent industrial policy in the Netherlands tried to achieve when identifying the key economic sectors to pursue a policy of 'backing winners' (see
Section 9.5). By organizing a beauty contest, knowledge workers from the

Figure 9.1   St-Gengoux-le-National

same sector were urged to cooperate, whereas before that they were operating independently of each other.

Given this aim of innovation policy to repair market failures in these
types of knowledge investments and knowledge spillovers, it is necessary to know how knowledge investments that reduce transaction costs
bring about social benefits. This may include the fact that the knowledge
required for making profitable trade transactions – part of the 'real'
entrepreneurial spirit – often has a more specific nature than innovative
knowledge that enhances productivity within the parts of the production
chain. This applies in particular to the knowledge and skills when dealing
with incomplete contracts in transactions. The idea is that a commercial
relationship can never fully be settled in a legal contract (or that a full contract bears transaction costs that are too high). Therefore, in the end, trade
contracts are always *incomplete*. Section 4.2 discussed how the incompleteness of contracts constitutes a focal point in the theory of new institutional
economics. This incompleteness implies that legal disputes in the case of
non-compliance with the contract are difficult and costly to settle. The
more the trade relationship has a specific character ('asset specificity'), the
greater is the open nature of the trade contracts for trade (Nunn, 2007).

Countries and firms, depending on their cultural and legal backgrounds,
may have different approaches to deal with such incomplete contracts.
Thus, the way a country or firm negotiates and operates in such a situation

may give a competitive advantage (or disadvantage). The assumption is that trading nations have comparative advances in dealing with such incomplete contracts and relational exchanges. This implies that the knowledge of how these skills for orchestration and good entrepreneurship in trade can be protected from use by free-riders, but can be exploited for societal benefits, differs from how innovation policy directed at product and process innovations deals with such knowledge transfers. This marks the challenge for the way trade policy should be combined with innovation policy. Besides an active and even proactive direct government involvement in such knowledge transfers, it is also a major task for the government to provide a good institutional and physical infrastructure for trade transactions and knowledge transfers in that field.

Moreover, a focus of government policy on the transition to the orchestrating function is also relevant in the view of the problem of ageing, which many OECD countries are facing. This is especially true in countries where a substantial pension capital has been built up to enable pension payments in the years to come, when the baby boom generation finally retires. The risk is that the country becomes a nation of rentiers where the proceeds from the pension capital come from abroad, but where the country loses its competitiveness. This should be avoided (see Box 9.2).

9.4   GOVERNMENT POLICY AND SUPPLY CHAIN MANAGEMENT

Section 2.3 discussed the role of supply chain management (SCM) in relation to transaction management in the globalizing world with the increased fragmentation of production and specialization. The question now is which of the arguments for government intervention are relevant for SCM policy. It is likely that the redistribution argument in this respect plays a minor role. The only reason to consider this argument here lies in the question of whether the income from government intervention, such as contributing to international standards, could be retained for the home country, or how the costs of setting such standards can be shared in a 'honest' or 'fair' way between the various countries.

The main arguments for government intervention with respect to SCM are the provision of public goods and the repair of market failures by internalizing external effects. As shown in Chapter 7, standardization plays an important role in this respect. The extent to which standards have the character of a public good is essential for the way standards affect the working of the economy through SCM. A standard is often created and then generally accepted and implemented by the efforts of a

BOX 9.2   OUTSOURCING AND ORCHESTRATION AS RELIEF FOR THE AGEING POPULATION

An important policy issue in many OECD countries is the ageing and dejuvenation of the population. This leads to a growing number of retirees and fewer workers in the future. Although this demographic development has already been foreseen for several decades, the urgency of the problem has only been fully recognized in the policy debate relatively recently. All kinds of policy measures to enhance the participation rate in the employment of the baby boomers generation – the elderly aged between 55 and 65 years – are taken. The problems are becoming very severe in some Eastern and Southern European countries and markedly in Japan where, due to serious dejuvenation, fertility rates are far below 2.1, which is necessary for a constant population size.

Many of these OECD countries have accumulated a lot of savings for retirement. But there should also be enough labour as a production factor to complement and use the pension capital to be productive. Without labour the rate of return to the capital will be zero. The growing participation rates of the baby boomers generation, which is a result of incentives offered in recent policy measures to remain employed, will provide some relief in the next few years to come. A major issue here is to delay the retirement age, which is also needed because the life expectancy of the retired is increasing. As things stand, the relative number of pensioners as compared to the working population will increase dramatically. This leaves us with three options.

The first option is to allow more immigrants to work in the country. Of course, it is useful to have skilled immigrants and the country must be generous to them and not make their stays difficult by strict rules and regulations (which bring about large transaction costs). Quantitatively, however, it is a drop in the ocean.

The second option is to place our fate in the hands of those who seek the best possible investments for our pension capital. This means that capital will be invested in those countries where the highest returns can be expected. This will mainly be countries where the age structure of the population is a mirror-image of that in Western countries, namely that they contain many young people who can work and relatively few elderly people. These are mainly countries in South and East Asia (China excepted!) and Latin America. But should we rely on this, invest all of our money in these countries and wait and see? This seems risky, especially since pension funds have not been lucky in their capital investments in recent times. Moreover, it will give a country the character of a nation of rentiers, where the part of the population that is still employed earns its money primarily for the care of older people who, in this way, spend their pension incomes.

Therefore, a third option is best. This scenario implies that optimal use is made of foreign workforces and skills by outsourcing those parts of the production chain where outsourcing is profitable. Good transaction management may reduce the transaction costs of outsourcing so that it becomes more profitable. In fact, this third option scenario can be regarded as an alternative to the first option of enhancing the domestic workforce by immigration in the sense that the additional foreign workforce does not migrate but stays in its country of origin. The organization of the production remains in the hands of domestic entrepreneurs. The difference compared with the first option is that production is now organized globally instead of locally. This third scenario makes the orchestrating function and the skills to orchestrate more important. These skills have always been valuable in transaction economies. Think, for instance, of the activities of the multinational firms in terms of worldwide purchasing, production and sales. Think of the important roles of countries such as the Netherlands, Belgium and Switzerland in the financial world, although that position is at risk in the aftermath of the credit crisis. Yet, many small and medium-sized firms are also providing services that are important for the orchestration and the management of transactions. Therefore, the best remedy for the ageing population is to fully exploit and develop the necessary knowledge for the orchestration and organization of production on a global scale.

dominant player or a club in the private sector. To avoid free-ridership and recover the investment and implementation costs of the standard, non-contributing parties should be excluded from using the standard. However, in the case of network externalities exclusion from a standard is socially undesirable.

In international standardization, free-ridership can also be a menace.

This risk from free-ridership occurs when there is a failure to share fairly the costs of standardization that benefits all parties. These are the problems that the EU is facing in its efforts for uniform standardization. If no proper arrangements are made on a multilateral basis, this problem can easily arise: no country has an incentive to contribute to the development and implementation of the standards. A country that does not contribute will ultimately gain almost the same rewards as the countries that do. When most other countries decide not to contribute, it will often still be the best for a country not to contribute either, because otherwise the country has to bear a very large proportion of the costs. This leads to the prisoner's dilemma, where eventually everyone is collectively worse off than if there were cooperation. Such a (dangerous) development is currently also evident in the case of road taxation of foreign cars in the EU. Here, governments have the ability to impose taxes on citizens of other countries. For example, if every country in Europe taxes cars upon entrance to the country in a separate and uncoordinated way, it leads to the somewhat medieval situation where car-drivers are forced to pay at each border for entrance into the country. This is in conflict with the idea of the free movement of persons. Moreover, as the tax rates and the way the tax is levied (tax base) would be different for all countries, it would imply higher transaction costs and make Europe collectively worse off. This example stresses the importance of cooperation in the development of uniform standards and agreements about sharing costs. In fact, the provision of a coordinated Europe-wide infrastructure can be regarded as the provision of a public good. In that case, differences in use of the infrastructure in the various European countries – some countries need more infrastructure for international transport than others – can be dealt with through a differentiated system of cost-sharing. Then there should also be a uniform system regarding whether the costs are financed through targeted or general taxes, in order to provide a level playing field for pan-European transport.

The argument of making the market work is important in this context of SCM, in the sense that the joint development of technologies and standards that reduce transaction costs may result in collaboration and knowledge transfers among firms. If competition policy is so stringent that such cooperation is frustrated, then these cost advantages are lost. By contrast, through this cooperation, cartels that fix a common price that distorts competition should not be prevented. This could be harmful to social welfare when the losses from the cartel formation exceed the gains from cooperation in setting common standards. Likewise, it can be harmful to social welfare when such cooperation leads to the exclusion of other firms if it is suboptimal from the perspective of exploiting network externalities.

In that case, the government can increase social welfare by contributing to the formation of a sufficiently large 'club' of stakeholders and even by making membership of the club compulsory.

The arguments above show that there are several ways the government can be involved in the provision of an infrastructure that contributes to the reduction of transaction costs in SCM. Such reductions can be obtained:

1. By supporting the initiatives of firms to form a club for the development of standards and other types of infrastructure that bring about network externalities;
2. By promoting that a privately developed standard will have full implementation;
3. Through a (monetary) contribution to the development of a standard and of other forms of infrastructure;
4. By taking the initiative for development and avoiding a situation of free-ridership; or
5. By providing a niche for, and protection of, new technologies and standards so that a potential lock-in of an existing dominant technology or standard can be broken.

These recommendations imply for SCM that government interventions and provisions should not be narrowly focused on logistics and transport only, but that these facilities should be beneficial to the entire supply chain. It is important that the impacts of soft transaction costs are recognized. Obviously ICT can be helpful to establish such fully-fledged facilities. However, not all knowledge that leads to a reduction of transaction costs can be codified and thereby standards may not always be useful. The management of the supply chain partly depends on tacit knowledge – that is, knowledge that is not explicit, but stored in the minds of people. This means that standards and procedural rules should be flexible enough to exploit this tacit knowledge. In this sense it is also preferable to make use of open standards and open forms of innovation for a further reduction of transaction costs in the production chain.

Road transport provides an example of the linkage between externalities and the public good character of knowledge. GPS-based navigation systems are increasingly used for routing in road transport (see also Box 9.3). It is likely that, with the introduction of forms of road pricing, these navigation systems will also be able to take the user costs of roads and the duration of the journey into account when determining which route to choose. In that case, knowledge of the choice of transport routes and the timing of the trip is not only important for the individual road-users but

BOX 9.3   STANDARDS FOR SUPPLY CHAIN
           MANAGEMENT

In the field of SCM (see Section 2.3), standards can be helpful to make processes more efficient. An example of a standard in this field is the GS1 Data Alignment Service, operated by the GS1 standard organization. This system allows, via a central database, the exchange of databases with information on merchandise goods between suppliers and retailers. It is important that the information includes the whole hierarchy of the merchandise goods – not` only the data on the consumer units, but also on the packaging and pallets. Such standards make the introduction of just-in-time principles easier and cheaper. A major reason is that such standards bring about lower soft transaction costs. If such a standard is introduced and used in a way that enables a certain critical mass to be reached, new users are keen to join. The technical specifications are available at virtually no cost, and there is no need for a long process of negotiations with a group of firms to come to a common standard. Such standards have already been developed in specific sectors of supply management. It is noticeable that these sectors are often dominated by a few large players. These large players, such as car manufacturers, can 'impose' such a standard on their suppliers. This is because, for such a player with a large amount of market power, finding a new supplier is typically much less costly than it is for the supplier to find a new customer. This does not imply that the introduction of such standards in markets with no major players exploiting their coordinating role is less profitable. Government intervention, preferably delegated to a standards organization, may be desirable in such cases.

   Another example of a standard that in the future may play a role in SCM is RFID (Radio Frequency Identification, a possible successor to the barcode). By processing a tag the size of a rice grain, goods or pieces of cargo can easily be identified by electronic systems, and thereby linked to information stored in databases. This allows a better monitoring of goods flows and makes the automated handling of goods easier. Through these RFID tags, the property of goods can also be better secured and it can be exactly tracked where and when the goods were produced and what route they subsequently followed.

also for fellow road-users. This gives the choice for the routing and timing of an individual road-user the character of a public good. Therefore, it would be a public task (or the task for a club of road-users) to centrally collect the data on the chosen routes and to provide feedback to the individual road-users. In that case the choice of the routes and travel times can be made dependent on the choices just made by others. In this way, the optimal utilization of the capacity of the road network can be made, given the preferences for the payment and travel time of individual road-users. Of course, for the implementation of such an information and communication infrastructure it is essential that all information is obtained and processed according to the same standard. Ultimately this could become a global standard for integrated road pricing and routing systems. Moreover, it is even conceivable that such an integrated system be linked to a central information system for public transport, so that an optimal route as a combination of private transport and public transport can be calculated in real time.

Overall, it seems that standardization and the modern use of ICT may lead to a substantial reduction of transaction costs in SCM. However, coordinating the various parts of the production chain will always involve transaction costs. Discretionary decisions cannot be avoided in the management of the supply chain. Certainly this is true with respect to the written and unwritten rules of government in relation to the business sector. These costs of the implementation of government regulation in G2B relationships are the subject of the next chapter.

9.5   GOVERNMENT POLICY AND STANDARDIZATION

Whereas the previous section focused on government intervention with respect to supply chain management, with an important role for standardization, this section discusses more generally how government can contribute to more efficient management of transaction costs by promoting standardization.

9.5.1   Failure of the Private Sector to Standardize

There are many reasons why private standards sometimes fail to be developed, or why multiple standards sometimes emerge simultaneously, whereas from the perspective of social welfare it is generally desirable that only one standard is created. If some large parties decide to develop their own standards, it will create uncertainty among users and the benefits typical of a standard cannot be exploited. If there are many small parties, they might be unable to organize and make a standard by themselves. In both cases, public authorities should organize consultation and facilitate coordination, preferably through a standardization organization. Their role includes bringing parties together and formalizing and distributing the exact definition of the standard.

This may even play a role with Radio Frequency Identification (RFID) (see Box 9.3). Government may set a standard defining how RFID tags should function, and may establish an infrastructure where member organizations can retrieve information with respect to specific RFID tags. Government can simultaneously monitor the privacy of citizens by not allowing all users to retrieve all available information. For example, when all bicycles have a RFID tag, the manufacturer and the distributor can easily read the address of the retailer where each bike has to be delivered. Then, the retailer immediately knows which customer has ordered each bike and what the price is. Other services may use the same tag. For example, customs can easily verify that the item is a bike that belongs to a delivery for the local market and is not a bunch of weapons intended for export to a country with a dictatorial regime. Such RFID tags can also simplify the work of tax authorities. At a later stage, after the bike has been sold to its owner, the police can use a scanning device to easily find out whether the bike has been stolen or not. Moreover, this reading of information from RFID tags can be organized in such a way that the police (after compliance with privacy regulations) can see whose bike was stolen, but an unauthorized person with a scanning device cannot find out the address of a cyclist passing by. In this way, information flows can be processed much more efficiently than before, and the transaction costs of both government and the participating firms can be further reduced without sacrificing the privacy of citizens.

In a more general sense, the argumentation above also shows that government regulation is needed for the use of these standards by private parties. These new standardized technologies can easily be misused by profit-seeking firms and bring about negative externalities. The previous argumentation (and that in Chapter 7) shows that leaving the development of standards entirely to the market may sometimes result in solutions that are suboptimal from the perspective of social welfare. Here, market failure is an argument for government intervention. The following subsections contain a more extensive review of the various aspects of market failure and the role that government can play. First, aspects of asymmetric information and network externalities as sources of market failure are discussed. Section 9.5.3 considers the role of government in making the use of standards excludable by protecting intellectual property rights.

9.5.2 Asymmetric Information

In some cases, asymmetric information, where the producer usually has better access to information than its customers do, can result in inefficiencies. This is a clear case of market failure, since the assumption of full information is no longer met. When asymmetric information results in the inability of customers to include some relevant aspects of the product in their buying decision, it is possible that only products that score low on these aspects are offered in the market, since they cost less. This is undesirable and, albeit under certain conditions, could be legitimate grounds for government intervention.

The government can take several measures to repair these market failures. One possibility is to force the producers to label their products. Another possibility is a complete ban on products that do not comply with a certain minimum level of quality. The latter is often inefficient, since there may also be demand for lower quality products. For instance, some customers might not derive any utility from the fact that a good has been produced in an ecologically responsible manner.

Apart from internalizing negative externalities, it is especially by reducing information problems that the government can benefit society through the introduction of a quality label that informs the user on several relevant aspects. Such a multidimensional quality label facilitates the supply of products with various quality levels. This system aims at promoting product differentiation, which enhances consumer welfare. Although such a standard no longer implies a unified set of minimum requirements that all products should comply with, it can still be regarded as a standard. Joining this type of standard can be voluntary or mandatory. It is likely that producers that have a low score on certain dimensions will not voluntarily join the standard in the hope that customers will expect an average quality of the product in the absence of information. This can be undesirable. Therefore, the EU energy label, for example, is mandatory and must be used by all producers.

Definitions with a subjective character pose another type of asymmetric information problem. For example, the definition of chocolate has been specified in a standard that prescribes, among other things, a minimum percentage of cacao. Producers are not allowed to label products that do not comply with the standard definition of chocolate as 'chocolate'. Such (mandatory) standards are desirable from a social welfare point of view, since they reduce the opportunities to misuse asymmetric information. In this way, they reduce the chances of miscommunication and, consequently, the information costs for consumers. However, it is important that such standards are closely related to popular definitions of the products that are covered by them. In other words, it is important that what is defined as 'chocolate' in the minimum standard is in line with what is generally considered chocolate.

9.5.3   Exclusivity and the Protection of Intellectual Property Rights

When third parties cannot be excluded from using a new (improved) standard, it will less often become profitable to invest in the development of such a standard. By contrast, a standard protected by copyrights or patents provides the owners with the possibility to exercise market power. This raises the price of using the innovative standards and, consequently, yields an incentive to increase the supply of innovative standards, while their usage will at the same time decrease. There is a clear trade-off in this situation. Farell (1995) shows that in the presence of network externalities a less-than-full protection is justified from the perspective of social welfare. Two types of inefficiencies accumulate here: (i) the individual does not use the standard while his or her gain in utility is higher than the marginal costs; and (ii) the decrease in the utility of the other users caused by the non-participation of this additional user. Empirical evidence shows that the presence of patents is an important motivation to standardize (Blind, 2004). In this respect, Matutes and Regibeau (1996) argue that private standards can be used by incumbents to prevent the entry of other firms into the market. When an incumbent already uses a network for its standard, a new entrant using another standard will not be able to compete with the incumbent. To tackle this problem, international standardization might be used as a means to level the playing field in order to create a free and competitive market. However, such a harmonization of international standards may be hindered by the fact that the level of the standard depends on the income level of the country. Therefore (demanding) standards set by developed countries may be harmful to developing countries in that the latter are unable to meet them (Hudson and Jones, 2003). In this respect Casella (2001) notes that national differences in standards and regulations are often used by governments to protect local industries now that formal trade barriers, such as import duties, have been reduced through WTO agreements. Therefore, in a sense this protectionist use of standards can be regarded as creating soft transaction costs that aim to prevent transactions.

When several producers engage in the development of a new standard at the same time, as was the case with the development of the DVD player and the VCR, all producers will ultimately have to switch to the technology that succeeds at reaching a critical mass of users first. A similar selection of a standard occurred in 2008 when Blu-ray became the leading standard over HD-DVD. In such situations, the contributions of individual producers do not really play a part in the development of the standard as it is but rather in developing it a little bit faster or better than the others develop. Here, the first producer who gets his or her finding patented is rewarded with all the revenues. The presence of strong network externalities even makes it possible that a standard chosen somewhat arbitrarily (for example, it is not outstanding with respect to quality compared with the other technologies that competed to become the standard) becomes protected by copyrights or patents anyway. Therefore, most standardizing agencies require that the standard that is adopted is available free or at a reasonable price.

Legislation by competition authorities, which prevents cartel formation, may exclude inventions that have become a standard because of the protection by property rights. This can happen in cases where this protection results in decreased market competition. Measures that have been taken against Microsoft are a well-known example. At first sight, it seems somewhat unfair, because it implies that findings that are 'somewhat' useful are protected, whereas a finding that becomes 'very' useful at a certain point in time loses this protection. However, it is plausible that making such exceptions benefits social welfare. Moreover, since the large profitability of these findings stems mainly from the fact that they have become a standard, and not so much because of the exceptional quality of the innovation itself, it can be regarded as unjust that the owner of the standard obtains a monopoly. Blind (2004) points out that a lot of useful standards started as patented technologies – something that is clearly positive – while these same patents can (especially when the standard has become a success) substantially reduce technological progress afterwards since others are not allowed to develop it further and since the diffusion of the standard is limited. In that case 'standing on shoulders', which is a major source of technological progress, is no longer possible.

Apart from the arguments above with respect to the externalities of standardization, governments can also standardize their own services. A special case relates to services provided to multinational enterprises. These enterprises often have to take into account all sorts of differences in rules and legislations that exist between different countries. This can bring about high transaction costs for them. In particular, small countries with legislation that differs substantially from that of other nations will make themselves less interesting for multinationals. For small open economies it is, therefore, important to take this aspect of international compatibility into account when redesigning the legal system. Harmonization and less complexity can enhance the ability of a nation to attract foreign investment. To keep such a country attractive as a trade nation it is important to be one of the first in designing and adopting new international standards, especially with respect to government services. An example is harmonization and reducing transaction costs with respect to customs regulations, where many changes have already been made through the World Customs Organization (WCO) (see also Chapter 10 on Authorized Economic Operators (AEOs)). In general, international arbitrage with respect to trade disputes may reduce transaction costs. It has been shown that in international negotiations on standards, a dispute settlement procedure may enhance the welfare effects of standardization by reducing information asymmetry during negotiations.

Finally, ineffective governance with respect to standardization can result in a strengthening of the negative lock-in effects discussed in Chapter 7. When the government strongly supports a certain standard, and when it can be changed only through lengthy procedures, the introduction of a new and better standard will be much more difficult. This is once again a plea for a well-designed standardization policy that is preferably organized through standardizing agencies. These agencies can devote special attention to policies that attempt to reduce lock-in effects by promoting and supporting the introduction and development of new and better standards. The government can subsequently play a helpful role as an early adopter.

9.5.4 Conclusions

The extent to which the standard has the character of a public good seems essential for the way standards affect the economy. Often a technology or specification becomes a standard after a dominant market player in the private sector makes efforts to get it accepted within the market. To guard against free-riders and earn back the investment and implementation costs of the standard, it should be made possible to exclude others from using the standard. However, the exclusion of others becomes undesirable from the perspective of social welfare when the use of a standard brings about network externalities. In cases of market failure, incentives to invest in the development of standards can be too low. In such cases, government intervention is needed. A similar argument holds for government support to escape from lock-in effects and to come to the faster implementation of newer and better standards. It is difficult, however, to organize this government intervention in an effective and efficient way.

Standards and associated regulatory activities represent a business cost, but it is not a cost without benefits for either society or firms. Standards that ensure product quality, particularly when related to safety, provide a clear benefit to consumers. However, they also benefit the firm in several ways. First, they provide a guarantee to the consumer that they can buy goods with confidence, which will economize on individual search costs, possibly expand the market and potentially allow firms to economize on signalling expenditure (Jones and Hudson, 1996). This is of particular importance for firms trading over borders, especially within Europe. Second, firms also benefit from such guarantees. In agriculture, for example, standards can reduce the spread of infectious diseases among livestock. Other standards and regulatory activity ensure the health and safety of the workforce. This is also an advantage to society and to good employers, who do not have to unfairly compete against firms with less rigorous standards. In addition, it has been argued that by establishing guidelines of good practice, firms can benefit directly, for example by reducing waste that is 'non-profitable output'. Third, there are environmental standards that again deliver clear benefits to society.

Of course, administrative costs which relate to the costs of complying with such regulations have to be taken into account. Moreover, there is the negative effect of standards, mentioned in Chapter 7, that they can cause lock-ins and be too rigid to allow diversity. For instance, in the case of standards in agriculture, there is the ecological argument (from scientists, not from political ecology) that standardization also reduces biological diversity, thus exposing the world to major diseases and their rapid dissemination.

9.6   THE PROS AND CONS OF A TARGETED INNOVATION AND TRADE POLICY[1]

9.6.1   Transaction Management is a Key Competence in Innovation Policy

Economists are sceptical about an innovation (or industrial) policy of 'picking winners' or 'backing winners', or even 'backing challengers'. This kind of targeted innovation policy has been criticized via the argument that backing or picking winners may lead to the protection of existing structures, institutions and interests. It excludes innovative outsiders that do not yet have the strength and size to qualify as winners. Moreover, it is unclear why winners need government support anyhow. A related reason for this scepticism is that it is questionable that the government has more knowledge than entrepreneurs about which parts of the business sector have a good chance of becoming global players. After all, these entrepreneurs can make a lot of money by making the correct strategic decisions.

Another aspect, as the previous argumentation shows, is that innovative transaction management does not focus on specific industries or knowledge disciplines. Transaction management, if properly applied, is valuable to all sectors that are able to grasp the benefits of globalization. In this context, it is noteworthy that the Dutch government identified the creative industry as a key 'sector' for targeted support. The labelling 'creative industry' is undoubtedly inspired by Richard Florida's (2002) description of the 'creative class'. This relates to all kinds of creative minds who operate in networks in a highly developed knowledge economy. The creative industry is not a 'normal' sector, as defined in the NA. On the contrary, members of the creative industry exploit their knowledge and creativity in every area of an innovation-oriented economy. Think of the many text writers, web designers and marketing experts active in industry. In general, many knowledge workers, such as doctors, lawyers, financial advisors and scientists, are regarded as belonging to the creative class. In the United States this is approximately 30 per cent of the workforce. This finding also provides a perspective on how a transaction economy can improve competitiveness through innovation, namely by identifying and promoting the development of key competences that will be required in future for the transaction function. To be good at transaction management is, in a general sense, such a key competence.

Given this scepticism, the following discusses the options for a targeted industrial and innovation policy from the perspective of a strategic game among firms or sectors. Here, the welfare effects of such a targeted policy may stem from cost reduction and industry-wide profit creation. Government support may take various forms and the usual debate around the benefits and the scepticisms of industrial/public/trade policies all matter one way or another. For a small, open economy most government intervention, especially when it relates to innovation policy, will naturally take the feature of international trade policy. Although the conventional wisdom of laisser-faire is valid in an idealized world of perfect competition, it has been identified that a strategic incentive to intervene with international trade under imperfectly competitive market structures may exist (for example, Brander and Spencer, 1983, 1985). Such a shift in the theoretical stance was made from the recognition of the interactive feature among firms and governments, which contrasts with the conventional economic reasoning based on the terms-of-trade advantage. The arguments received criticisms as well, which were mainly clustered upon the 'beggar-thy-neighbour' feature and the possibility of a mutually destructive trade war. A unilaterally optimal policy may in this argumentation lead to the distortion of international competition and retaliating responses may follow, in which case the policy has a negative instead of the warranted positive effect on national welfare.

9.6.2   The Scope for a Non-uniform Innovation Policy

Although conventional discussions have occurred around the structure of uniform policy, Jo (2010) shows that a non-uniform policy may further strengthen strategic trade intervention incentives: aggregate profits in the whole industry can be newly created without affecting the other trading partners and, therefore, without the usual retaliatory concern. This feature is particularly strengthened when public policy aims to encourage R&D activities by firms. Domestic firms can be unequally treated to create an asymmetric structure of the firms' effective marginal costs. The restructured cost conditions among the firms then set a new game rule for the firms to rationalize their output decisions, which may serve to save overall production costs in the market for the benefit of the policy-imposing country's profit improvement. This profit creation can be sustained even for a technology without economies of scale. This contrasts with the conventional profit-creating argument in the literature, which is valid only when economies of scale prevail in the production technology. In addition, since this new profit-creation aspect of strategic R&D subsidy remains valid without affecting the other trade-involved countries, it is robust to the usual trade-war concern.

The main question with the finding of Jo (2010) that a targeted innovation policy may, under the conditions mentioned above, be preferable to a non-targeted policy, however, is about the practical implementation. The theoretical model has three relevant parameters, namely the initial marginal costs of an 'investment in R&D' that brings about a 'unit' of innovation (c); the extent an innovation subsidy contributes to reduce such costs for other firms (α) (the spillover effect); and the extent to which the innovation subsidy reduces these investment costs for the firm itself (β):

$$k = c - \alpha \, (S - s) - \beta s \qquad (9.1)$$

Here, k is the after-subsidy marginal cost of a firm with s the amount of subsidy to that firm and $S = ns$ is the total R&D expenditure by the government, where n is the number of firms that receive a subsidy. When c, α and β are equal for each firm or sector, or when the government is unable to discriminate between firms or sectors with respect to these parameters, the policy of picking winners according to this analysis boils down to throwing a dice. Obviously such a policy is not feasible in practice. First, it will be legally unviable to select the recipients of subsidies by a purely random selection mechanism. In reality, however, the parameters c, α and β will indeed differ among firms and sectors. In that case, it seems reasonable to select those firms or sectors that have the lowest value of c and the highest values of α and β so that subsidizing these firms or sectors is most efficient. Then, the next questions are: how does the government assess differences in c, α and β in selecting winners to be backed; and how do firms or sectors react when the government is uncertain about the true values of these parameters?

In these cases, the government may find out by utilizing the existing data to derive detailed intuitions about these parameters before and after R&D subsidies were imposed. To sustain welfare improvement, it is now important to design and operate the mechanism through which the preferential selection of firms can be made in an efficient way. A well-designed mechanism may bring about an additional benefit to the economy by inducing firms to take extra efforts to improve their pre-policy efficiency to be eligible for the subsidy rewards. By contrast, the risk of rent-seeking behaviour is present when the government's discriminatory policy is designed based on the observed performances of the firms. Therefore, the successful implementation of the policy has to be one through which all the agents get to internalize the costs and benefits within their own behavioural incentive systems. Below, such issues related to the informational details and behavioural incentives of the firms are addressed. Transaction cost issues arising from opportunistic behaviour are also discussed.

9.6.3   Incomplete Information

One of the major scepticisms regarding interventionism is that it presumes that policy-makers have good information on industry details such as cost, demand, the mode of competition, and so on. The policy authority, however, is only informed to a limited degree. The first natural observation is that firms could behave opportunistically to influence their entitlements to policy benefits. Overinvestment can be a consequence. In such a situation of asymmetric and incomplete information, a government may invent a policy menu combining a reward and a penalty through which firms are motivated to reveal their true types. This is so that the government can reflect on the actions taken by the firms to come up with the appropriate form of discriminatory policy (a separating equilibrium in the terminology of game theory). In that the uniform policy would be the alternative if the screening effort fails and the ex ante private information were not revealed (pooling equilibrium), well-designed mechanisms would be inevitable for the successful realization of the best welfare outcome. On the contrary, a separating equilibrium is not always a better option than a pooling equilibrium because of the transaction costs that may arise from the former. In this regard, a policy-maker should pay extra attention to the details of the incomplete information when designing an innovation policy.

9.6.4 An Additional Benefit of Inducing Efficiency-improving Efforts

When an innovation policy is to be imposed in a discriminatory way based on the pre-policy efficiency level of firms, firms would take it as an incentive scheme and would try to enhance their productivities even before the subsidy is assigned to them. A virtuous cycle of high productivity–high subsidy–high productivity will further separate good firms from bad firms, and the preferential subsidy mechanism can set a binding platform for this self-selecting process. This additional efficiency-gaining effect is distinguished from the usual screening mechanism, which is often useful under an asymmetric information situation. The latter solely aims to separate good firms from bad firms, whereas the proposed R&D policy implementation mechanism would drive even the less efficient firms to improve their efforts rather than to lag further behind. Thus, not only the separating equilibrium but also the pooling equilibrium may bring a welfare gain from the national perspective. To compensate those firms who improved in efficiency yet ended up receiving lower subsidies because of their lower-than-average productivity improvements, the government may introduce an additional subsidy if available.

9.6.5 Concern Of Rent-seeking Behaviour and Other Transaction Costs

When selecting the right firms is the central focus of the mechanism, firms' efforts to receive a high subsidy may lead them to adhere to the selection mechanism only. This rent-seeking behaviour may prevail before the actual subsidy assignment. The rent-seeking incentive typically leads to the prisoners' dilemma in which all firms tend to behave only to be picked for a higher subsidy but with no practical contribution towards meaningful efficiency improvements yielding a socially undesirable outcome. This phenomenon can clearly be captured by designing a game in which the order of movements between the firms and government is reversed. If the government assigns subsidies *after* firms take an action to signal their types in terms of their productivities, all firms would have an incentive to overinvest for a lower cost to be eligible for a more beneficial subsidy. This subsidy assignment mechanism can help mitigate such an incentive if it contains a self-adjusting system, in which those who received a higher subsidy (yet did not show a meaningful performance in productivity gain ex post) are further penalized later through a lower subsidy.

The plausibility of an effective incentive mechanism for genuine cost-reducing efforts prior to the subsidy assignment can be seen through the framework of the repeated games in game theory. Firms would select to play opportunistically when the game is played only once or just a few finite times. However, when the firms are conscious of the thorough monitoring mechanism in which the policy authority regularly updates the details, they will necessarily weigh the potential gains and losses from such opportunistic behaviour. In this regard, a deliberately designed follow-up program of industrial policy is needed to manipulate subsidy recipients to aim for a socially desirable outcome. The productivity-gaining efforts by a firm to be eligible for a higher subsidy could be exercised through a visible investment in new technology or penetrating into a new market to realize a higher scale economy. Alternatively, firms might seek an efficiency gain through non-tangible resources. Operational, technical and managerial resources might not have been optimally exercised and the R&D policy mechanism would induce firms to reach their optimal utilization for all possible business areas. These all contribute towards reducing transaction costs, which need to be counted as a positive feature of the mechanism. Transaction costs can be saved on the policy authority side as well throughout the whole procedure of sorting out the recipients – assigning subsidies – and monitoring the outcome for the next rounds of subsidy imposition.

9.6.6   R&D Joint Venture versus Adversarial Approach

As another meaningful insight, the relative sizes of α and β in Eq. 9.1 can shed light on the debate about which policy between an R&D joint venture – that is, cooperation between the firms – and adversarial approach is to be adopted. One concern about the adversarial approach is that it provides a firm with an incentive to overinvest or underinvest. The former matters if the spillover effect is negligible and thereby a firm has an incentive to more-than-optimally invest to give itself a strategic advantage against its rivals in subsequent product market competition. The latter becomes real if the spillover effect is substantial but is not fully internalized in the private decision process. As such, encouraging an R&D joint venture could be an alternative option. Given the double-edged potential sub-optimality of an outcome when an adversarial approach is adopted, a rule-of-thumb criterion can be suggested on the matter: when the spill-over effects (α) dominate the own cost-reducing effect (β), a R&D joint venture is better encouraged through which the cost-reducing effect of the R&D policy will be maximized even though the aggregate profit creation may not be obtainable. Otherwise an adversarial policy through an asymmetric treatment of individual firms should be given priority. It is noteworthy that the Dutch government, in its beauty contest to select the key innovative sectors in the Netherlands, very much favoured those sectors where firms seemed able to present themselves jointly in the beauty contest. The implicit insight behind this design of the contest may be the desire to enhance future spillover effects in addition to finding out which sectors already contained joint R&D ventures.

9.6.7 Corrective Objective versus Strategic Objective

While the main part of the analysis in this section focuses on the strategic objective of an industrial policy, a policy authority may also have a distortion corrective objective in mind. In particular, in connection with R&D activities by the private firms that are to be influenced by an R&D policy, the possible sub-optimality of the private firm-level investment as discussed previously might induce a government to try to catch both rabbits. Therefore, it has to be understood that the optimal form of the industrial policy – subsidy or tax – depends on which incentive outweighs the other. From a corrective policy perspective, a tax would have to be imposed if the spillover effect of an R&D subsidy caused overinvestment in a firm; and a subsidy would be optimal if underinvestment were caused. Yet the optimal form of policy from a strategic perspective depends on other factors such as consumer demand and the completion mode among the firms. If both motives reinforce each other, it is not a concern. However, if the two motives are counteractive, the relative importance of the two objectives has to be weighed up before a preferential redesign of the policy is introduced.

9.6.8 A Political Economic Concern: Redistribution Scheme

From the usual perspective of positive economics, when the winners' gains are larger than the losers' losses, an appropriate domestic redistribution scheme is necessary to ensure that all participants gain. However, in light of the specific purpose of innovation policy, one may even leave the outcome as it is. In that way, it can be used as an incentive scheme for the firms to improve their technology and cost conditions to further guarantee a higher subsidy. In a good scenario, the incentive scheme will lead all firms in the industry to higher efficiency in absolute terms. The subsidy redesign then relies on the relative measure of efficiency gains to reward only those with high efficiency improvements while those firms with a below-average efficiency gain will be penalized and receive a lower subsidy. The government may take another stance by rewarding all those with an efficiency gain, yet in a discriminatory way. The firms' efforts will be praised, although unevenly. Of course, such a non-uniform policy of 'backing strong winners' and 'backing ordinary winners' requires an additional fund. The opportunity costs of the public fund will become an issue again, and the government will have to weigh all the related costs and benefits. The costs side would involve both the visible costs and the invisible transaction costs, whereas the benefits should entail the screening effects in this asymmetric information environment to effectively distinguish the low-cost firms from the high-cost firms as well as the usual cost-saving encouraging benefits.

9.6.9   Conclusion

This section discusses policy options for industrial and innovation policy using a new feature in strategic trade policy. The starting point is the theoretical case where, under an international oligopolistic market, a non-uniform innovation policy through R&D subsidies is superior to a uniform policy in its national welfare-enhancing effect. This theoretical argument provides a benchmark in the debate on whether a targeted innovation policy is warranted when the government 'picks' winners.

Whereas the benchmark model relates to a fantasy world with identical firms, this section considers the more realistic cases of ex ante asymmetric costs where the cost-saving effect on the firms or sectors of R&D subsides will instead be differentiated. This implies that the government will have to exploit a priori information on the differences in cost reduction that the R&D subsidy might bring about. This is especially true for the size of the spillover effects that are positive externalities and may lead to underinvestment in R&D unless it is internalized within the system or through an industrial policy. The problem is that the government has incomplete information on the true initial efficiency levels of the firms and on the extent of the cost reduction that the innovation policy will accomplish. Firms may behave strategically to impress the government, which could even lead to overinvestment and rent seeking. Therefore, the government must design a carefully deliberated strategy for innovation policy and show consistency in its implementation. It is warranted that the policymaker can sort out the informational asymmetry to clearly configure the right form of the optimal policy. Furthermore, it may bring about the additional benefit of inducing extra efforts on the firms' sides.

From this perspective, the analysis discusses the various strategic issues for a targeted innovation policy. Informational configuration about the current efficiency conditions of market participants has to be preceded and the potential efficiency gains through the policy have to be estimated, while potential opportunistic behaviour by the firms should be discouraged. A carefully-designed mechanism to provide firms with the right incentives and to monitor their post-policy behaviour should be combined as well. In addition, the 'challengers' should not be completely isolated from the whole picture and the strategic details of the policy should entail backing the right winners – both existing and potential.

This analysis does not rule out the possibility that the ex ante optimal form of the policy may be indeterminate or that the informational complexity may lead to a substantial transaction cost loss, so that eventually it has negative welfare implications. The above discussion of these policy options only has a qualitative character and it is based on modern theory of strategic firm behaviour. A fully-fledged analysis would need to formally treat the specific strategies. Then, a quantification of the net welfare effects that the optimal design of the policy strategies can bring about could be made. These net welfare effects may turn out to be positive, but could also very well be negative. In other words, in spite of the fantasy model, which provides an argument for backing winners, in practice the cons of such a policy may outweigh the pros. Moreover, a major argument of this book is that it is not so much investments in R&D that may foster productivity and enhance welfare, but more investments in trade innovations through transaction management. Picking winners by selecting strong economic sectors or firms is less relevant from that perspective than 'picking key competencies' that foster trade innovations and bring about positive externalities through knowledge spillovers on the international organization of production.

NOTE

1.   Based on Den Butter and Jo (2009).

10. Transaction management and the implementation of government policy

This chapter argues that the government should also utilize transaction management to reduce the implementation costs of laws and regulations. This relates to transaction management in the relationship between the government and business sector (G2B relationship), which can be seen as a principal/agent relationship. In accordance with the Dutch polder model of compromising on policy issues, it is good to consult with all stakeholders to obtain support for the law and regulations. This reduces implementation costs because this public support enhances the intrinsic motivation to comply with the rules. By way of an example, the prospects for a more customer-oriented and trust-based handling of customs formalities (that is, the Authorized Economic Operator (AEO) certification) are reviewed. Here, the emphasis is on trust and reputation effects in the cooperation between customs and the participating firms.

10.1 TRANSACTION MANAGEMENT IN A PRINCIPAL/AGENT RELATIONSHIP

The previous chapter discussed the relationship between government intervention and transaction management from the perspective of government's role in enhancing social welfare. Arguments from the theory of public sector economics indicate in what way government should interfere, for instance, in relationships between businesses (B2B relationships) in the case of externalities. However, the implementation of government regulation to internalize such externalities, as well as regulation with respect to tax collection or the provision of public goods, will bring about costs both for the government itself and for the private sector. The implementation costs of government regulation can be regarded as transaction costs of a sort (as was also discussed in Section 9.6 with respect to various strategies in innovation policy). These costs arise because, under government regulation, citizens and businesses should provide the government with

---

BOX 10.1   THE PRINCIPAL/AGENT RELATIONSHIP

The principal/agent relationship (or 'agency relation') describes the vertical (hierarchical) cooperation between a commissioner or client (the principal) and a supplier or subcontractor (the agent). This relationship is characterized by information asymmetry: the agent has more information about how the 'contract' can be fulfilled than the principal. An example is a travelling salesperson who is better informed of the wishes and whims of the customers in his or her area than the boss and principal who is head of the sales department.

The problem in the principal/agent relationship is how the contractor as agent can be bound through an implicit or explicit contract ('a performance contract'), so that he or she acts in accordance with the aims and wishes of the principal. In practice, there are many kinds of principal/agent relationships. It is not just about a salesman and his or her boss, but the relationship between a government and its citizens can also be seen as a principal/agent relationship where citizens have more knowledge about their individual circumstances than the government, though they must comply with the laws and regulations of the government. Another example is the relationship between the shareholders (as principals) and the management of firms (as agents).

---

information and certain services to show that they comply with the regulation. The government incurs costs because it has to collect, control and monitor this information and these services. Think, for example, of regulation through legislation to comply with environmental policy. In economic terms the implementation of such a regulatory policy implies a principal/agent (agency) relationship between the government (as principal) and the citizens and businesses (as agents) (see Box 10.1).

It is because of information asymmetry, where firms have more information about the additional costs of complying with government regulation than the government itself, that the regulatory relationship between the government and the business sector can be seen as a principal/agent relationship. In doing so, the concept of the transaction (or implementation) costs of government regulation is equivalent to the vertical transaction costs within the hierarchy of the firm considered by Coase (1937).

The principal/agent relationship distinguishes three types of costs that are all part of the total transaction costs of regulation:

1. *Monitoring costs* of the government: costs of the preparation of regulation and monitoring compliance;
2. *Bonding costs* of citizens and businesses: costs of the preparation and application of permits or subsidies, payment of (regulatory) levies, and the delivering of products and/or services in accordance with legal obligations and prescriptions; and
3. *Residual loss* because of the incomplete fulfilment of the wishes of the principal by the agent.

The first type, monitoring costs, are the costs for the government itself. Parts of these are administration or enforcement costs, but additional costs also come with the design of regulatory measures. Therefore, implementation or enforcement costs for the government are generally considerably higher than the amounts that appear in the budget (payment of subsidies, receipts of levies). The additional costs include the salaries of civil servants engaged in policy preparation, the implementation of regulatory measures and other monitoring activities. Monitoring costs also relate to subsidies that are not granted and allowances for tax exemptions. Whereas the costs that appear explicitly in the budget can be seen as hard transaction costs, the other costs can be seen as soft. Hard transaction costs are relatively easy to quantify and calculate, but soft transaction costs are not. They may, however, also appear in the budget, albeit implicitly.

The second type of costs are the bonding costs for businesses. Here, all compliance costs incurred because of government regulation should be taken into account. They are the direct financial costs such as levies, but also capital investments and all other remaining costs incurred when meeting the obligations of laws and legislation. These compliance costs also include the costs of informing the government (sheer bonding costs). Calculating total compliance costs can, however, be rather complicated. For instance, when firms meet the requirements of environmental legislation or safety regulations, they have to make all kinds of investments in the production processes and management procedures of the firm. These costs can only be partly counted as the transaction costs of government policy because some would be made in any case from the commercial perspective of the firm. Therefore, there is a need to separate these kinds of compliance costs into external compliance costs, which are added to the transaction costs, and internal compliance costs, which are not transaction costs originating from government regulation. Of course, such a split between external and internal compliance costs has, to some extent, an arbitrary character and requires good insight into the management of the firm. Here, an analogy exists with the sources of standards that firms are willing or supposed to comply with. From that perspective, Chapter 7 made a distinction between internal and external standards.

There is some practical experience about how to calculate these various types of compliance costs for specific cases (Nijsen, 2008; UK Government, 2008). The size of these compliance costs from existing government regulation can be calculated by using the Standard Cost Model (Nijsen, 2008, 2012). This is an activity-based accounting model that aggregates the costs for businesses with respect to all the direct costs of complying with legal information obligations. The focus of the Standard Cost Model is on providing indicators of the administrative burden of government regulation at the macro level (costs for all laws) and at the micro level (costs for one law), which is a useful device for policy discussions on the size of that burden (macro level) and on reduction policies (micro level). However, the costs of businesses involved in providing the required information to facilitate monitoring by the government are just part of the total business costs of government regulation. To comply with *substantive* and *financial obligations* by businesses or civilians in a direct way, for example to take care of safe labour circumstances, minimize CO_2 pollution according to the legal standards or pay the due income tax, further costs have to be made. These costs relate to the direct achievement of the public goals themselves. The aggregation of these costs over all relevant information obligations, financial obligations and substantive obligations yields an estimate of the total direct compliance costs of government regulation for the regulated part of the business sector, the so-called norm addressees. Besides the direct compliance costs of the regulated businesses or norm addressees, there are also secondary or indirect compliance effects for the economy as a whole. To obtain a full picture of all relevant implementation costs, both to the business sector and to the government, the Standard Cost Model should be extended to include these costs (see Nijsen, 2012).

The third type of costs, the societal costs of the residual loss, are much more difficult to assess. These arise because the reaction of the agents to government regulation will never be in complete agreement with the objectives of government. The difference is the residual loss. Principal/ agent contracts should be designed in such a way that the total agency costs (monitoring costs, bonding costs and residual loss) are minimized. This implies that agency contracts should not focus on reducing only one particular type of costs, but there should be a good balance between all three types.

This discussion shows that the principal/agent relationship provides an adequate framework for the categorization of the transaction costs of government regulation. The total transaction costs of government regulation consist of the netted sum of the three components. The expression 'netted sum' indicates that, for example, subsidies granted by the government to private agents are counted as costs of the government, but as benefits (or cost reductions) for the private agents. In that case the 'netted sum' is zero. In the above discussion, which considers principal/agent costs as transaction costs, the concept of the transaction costs of government regulation is equivalent to the vertical transaction costs within the hierarchy of the firm considered by Coase (1937). Moreover, these implementation costs as the netted sum of the three components from the principal/agent theory provide a quantification of the 'gross' transaction costs of regulation. In fact, the aim of regulation is to enhance welfare, often by internalizing externalities (Chapter 9). For regulation to be effective, the benefits of regulation, in terms of welfare gains, should be higher than the implementation costs. Otherwise government failure is higher than market failure and society is better off without regulation.

Williamson (1996) extensively discusses the differences and similarities between the principal/agent (or agency) theory and transaction cost economics. Both perspectives deviate from the traditional neoclassical assumption of frictionless transactions. However, in Williamson's wording, transaction cost economics regards the firm as a governance structure whereas agency theory considers it a nexus of contracts. Although both theories are concerned with incomplete contracts and the resulting hazards of opportunism, agency theory examines contract predominantly ex ante from an incentive alignment point of view, while transaction cost economics is more concerned with crafting ex post governance structures within which the integrity of the contract is decided. Whereas agency theory is little concerned with dispute resolution, which is, according to Williamson, a characteristic of all ex ante approaches to contract, dispute avoidance and the machinery for processing disputes are central to transaction cost economics. Assessing the comparative efficacy of alternative governance structures for harmonizing ex post contractual relations is the distinctive focus and contribution of transaction cost economics. In spite of these differences between transaction cost economics and the principal/agent theory asserted by Williamson, his 'objective view' is that these two perspectives are mainly complementary. Therefore, this chapter draws on this aspect of complementarity by using the concepts of the principal/agent theory for categorizing the different types of transaction costs in G2B relationships, whereas the arguments for governance in the institutional set-up of AEO certification of Section 10.3 are based on the theory of transaction cost economics. Yet when using the distinction made in agency theory between monitoring costs, bonding costs and residual loss for categorizing all transaction costs associated with implementation of government regulation in G2B relationships, both ex ante and ex post cost arguments are looked at (see also Section 4.3).

10.1.1   Taxonomy of Transaction Costs of Government Regulation

Table 10.1 lists the various types of transaction costs of government regulation that can be distinguished from the perspective of the three cost categories of the principal/agent framework in the various stages of the design and execution of the regulation.

Theoretical aspects and the measurement of the transaction costs of environmental regulation have already been extensively investigated by McCann and Easter (2000) and McCann et al. (2005). Although these authors do not explicitly consider the transaction costs of government regulation from the principal/agent perspective, their typology of transaction costs with public policies follows a similar line to that shown in Table 10.1. McCann and Easter distinguish the following types of transaction costs: (i) research and information; (ii) enactment or litigation; (iii) design and implementation; (iv) support and administration; (v) contracting; (vi) monitoring/detection; and (vii) prosecution/enforcement. Moreover, these authors emphasize the chronology of when transaction costs occur and when they should be measured. Some costs are made early in the period of regulation, some costs are recurrent during the whole period of regulation and some costs appear at a later stage of implementation (for example, monitoring and enforcement). Finally, McCann and Easter also make a distinction between the ex post measurement of transaction costs of government regulation and the ex ante evaluation of the costs of regulatory measures. The latter type of measurement can also be useful for the design of new measures of regulation or for making existing regulation more cost efficient. This is the focus of the following subsections.

10.1.2   Cost–benefit Analysis of Government Regulation

The previous argumentation of the transaction costs of government regulation take existing regulations as given. This allows focusing on the costs of regulation, which is in line with political pressure (and pressure from the business sector) to reduce the administrative burden of government regulation. However, as argued before, government regulation aims at enhancing social welfare so that the benefits of regulation should exceed the costs. This is the case, for instance, with environmental regulation, or regulation with respect to safety measures. The benefits of such regulations are not always directly visible and often relate to long-term

Table 10.1 *Criteria for the types of hard (in italics) and soft transaction costs of government regulation*

Policy cycle	**Principal: Government**: monitoring costs/ enforcing costs	**Agent: Businesses**: bonding costs/compliance costs	**Society**: residual losses	**Secondary macro economic effects**
Agenda setting	salaries of civil servants engaged in agenda setting	salaries of employees and consultants involved in lobbying		
Goal setting	salaries of civil servants engaged in goal setting	salaries of employees and consultants involved in lobbying	misalignment costs in goal (target) setting: goals set by the government do not completely reflect the optimal goals from the perspective of societal welfare	
Designing policy measures	salaries of civil servants engaged in designing policy measures	salaries of employees and consultants involved in discussions on the design of the regulatory measures		
Decision-making	salaries of civil servants engaged in decision-making	salaries of employees and consultants involved in decisions on how to cope with the regulation (for example, avoiding the regulation: avoidance costs)		

Implementation	• *payments of subsidies minus receipts of levies* • salaries of civil servants for monitoring, control and enforcement	• *direct financial compliance costs (payments of levies minus receipts of subsidies)* • substantive compliance costs (capital investments, etc.) minus business-as-usual costs • informational compliance costs: incl. salaries of employees involved in reporting and networking	• costs because of inadequate reactions of agents to government regulation (goals are not met when businesses comply with regulations) • competition • economic growth • employment
Evaluation	salaries of civil servants engaged in evaluation	salaries of employees and consultants involved in elaborating new strategies to cope with the regulation	Societal costs because of social discontent with the outcomes of regulation

benefits for society, whereas the direct costs are more tangible and are borne by specific stakeholders, the norm addressees or, more specifically, the regulated businesses. The obligation to comply with environmental standards, for example, does not seem to bring benefits for businesses, but these standards are set by the government to internalize or prevent negative external effects, which would otherwise be harmful to society and in an indirect way also for the business sector. Even the benefits of pure financial regulations are not always directly visible or easy to measure. An example is the obligation for firms to publish an annual report. What are the benefits? In this case, such reports reduce the transaction costs for those who want to obtain information on the financial positions and strategic behaviour of the firms, for instance when they are involved in business transactions with these firms or want to buy shares. Then, it is useful that the financial reporting is conducted according to some international standard, which makes the interpretation of the financial position more transparent. However, these benefits for society are difficult if not impossible to quantify.

Good government institutions for the design and implementation of regulation can be helpful to reduce the implementation costs for all parties concerned. This requires a combination of well-designed standards that fully exploit the modern possibilities of ICT (for example, a standardized and uniform application form for licensing, which can be downloaded and submitted online), and the institutionalization of consultations between all relevant stakeholders. This consultation and seeking to come to an agreement (or 'participation' – see the following section on 'matching zones') is essential for making the stakeholders understand government regulation. It breeds an understanding and acceptance of policies, and thereby increases the intrinsic motivation of citizens and businesses to comply and act accordingly. Such organized, or even institutionalized, consultation and participation will lead to much lower transaction costs than when the regulation has to be enforced and can only be implemented through extrinsic motivation. Reducing administrative burden is part of the policy-oriented effort of the government to reduce transaction costs. In this case, it is also better for the government when citizens and businesses meet their reporting obligations through intrinsic motivation.

The various transaction costs that the implementation of government regulation brings about are partly unavoidable. However, given the policy goals, it is important to keep these costs as low as possible. This implies that government intervention should be designed in such a way that, in accordance with the arguments of the previous chapter, social welfare is maximized. Therefore, it is essential to consider all costs of government regulation from the perspective of welfare analysis. This is particularly relevant when the argument for government intervention is the repair of market failure. As discussed in the previous chapter, a major reason for government regulation in this respect is to internalize external effects. This government intervention has both direct and indirect effects. The indirect effects relate to the transmission of the regulatory measures to other markets: at the macro level these are, for instance, the effects on economic growth and employment.

In the case of government regulation that aims to repair market failure by the internalization of externalities, a distinction should be made between positive and negative externalities. Laws and regulations that aim to internalize positive external effects purport to facilitate economic activity where the revenues are not fully collected by those who do business. Internalization usually takes place by means of grants and subsidies, or through a reduction in the payment of taxes. A negative externality occurs when the economic activity of one actor poses a welfare loss for others. Such an externality can be internalized through a (regulatory) fee and/or all sorts of rules and regulations. Here, the implementation costs for the businesses relate to compliance with laws and regulations. In this case, one can think of various types of legislation and procedures, for example regulatory taxes in environmental policy, but also the obligation to comply with conditions set in permits in connection with spatial planning and zoning. The costs of providing information and administrative charges are part of these implementation costs.

Determining the size of the transaction costs of government regulation, both for the government itself and for citizens and businesses, is in principle a part of the measurement of the net welfare effects of the (proposed) laws and regulations. The quantification of such welfare effects is usually based on a societal cost–benefit analysis (see Box 10.2). In such an analysis, only direct welfare costs (and benefits) for the various stakeholders are typically quantified, whereas a number of indirect costs and benefits are only listed as a pro memori (pm) post. Such a pm post can also indicate that the respective costs or benefits are difficult to assess.

It should be noted, however, that these costs and benefits, included as pm posts, can be substantial and, moreover, may differ considerably when analysing alternative policy options (or, in this specific case, alternative regulatory measures). Likewise, these costs may, in a proper design of government regulation that aims at internalizing externalities, be much lower than in the case of the existing law and/or regulation, which serves as a null alternative in the cost–benefit analysis. Hence, a better understanding of these different forms of transaction costs is essential for a proper consideration of alternatives in a societal cost–benefit analysis.

BOX 10.2   COST–BENEFIT ANALYSIS

Cost–benefit analysis (CBA) is a proven tool in making strategic decisions. For decisions at a firm level, CBA lists the costs and benefits of various options and selects the option where the benefits minus the costs yields the highest gain. CBA is also applied in public decision-making. In that case, it is based on welfare theory, and the balance between the social costs and benefits is calculated. The outcome of such a social CBA will differ from the outcome of a CBA at a firm level in the sense that the former takes into account the external effects and the costs and benefits for various stakeholders, or the provision of a public good, whereas the latter ignores these welfare aspects.

The principle of CBA is very simple. To come to a decision about a project, all costs and benefits of this project are calculated and added together. When the expected benefits outweigh the costs, it is desirable to implement the project. In practice, however, it seldom or never happens that the outcome of the CBA can be summarized in a single number as the result of the confrontation of benefits and costs. This is especially true for (large) infrastructure projects, such as the building of a new railroad, extension of harbour facilities or the development of a new business quarter, where decisions are usually only partly based on CBAs. A first complication in the calculation is how to define the project and its alternatives and to see what the reference situation is for the calculation of costs and benefits, the so-called null alternative.

Take, for example, the CBA conducted to find out the best way to expand the configuration of runways at Schiphol Airport. Here, the configuration of the five runways including the new 'polder' runway was taken as the null alternative. This alternative describes the constraints that the airport will encounter, given the assumptions about future trends in aviation and forecasts of the demand for flight services. The project alternatives consider various options for the expansion of the configuration of the runways (with a sixth and possibly even a seventh runway) and calculate which costs and benefits are involved under the same assumptions about developments in aviation and increasing demand for flight services. In the hypothetical case of a CBA for the global climate problem, a null alternative would be the continuation of the present status quo without further policies to reduce greenhouse gas emissions. This could act as a basis for calculating the costs and benefits of various options for a stricter global climate policy.

Of course, there are always different groups *of stakeholders* involved in the projects or plans that are the subject of a social CBA. The ideal situation is a result showing that an alternative plan under the CBA offers a welfare gain to all stakeholders. In that case, there are only winners; and the alternative, in the terminology of welfare economics, yields a real Pareto improvement. However, in reality, there will usually also be losers when the CBA shows a net benefit for the best alternative. In that case the *distribution problem* becomes much more compelling. This refers to the need for a societal balancing of the interests of stakeholders. If the net costs for the losers could be calculated in an unambiguous way and proved smaller than the net benefits of the winners, the winners could compensate the losers. In that case, the project or plan still yields an overall gain in social welfare. Instead of a Pareto improvement, we have a Kaldor–Hicks improvement. The weighing of the interests of winners and losers is a question of political preferences. Whether the CBA of a project or plan yields a positive or negative outcome may depend on a political assessment of the weights. This can be illustrated in a simple example where low incomes lose 100 units and high incomes gain 150. At equal weights, the project would, therefore, be implemented, but when the interests of the low incomes are valued twice as much as those of the high incomes, the implementation of the project brings about a welfare loss. Another problem is that the CBA should adequately identify which costs and benefits should be included in the calculation. Therefore, it is necessary to know *which* groups of stakeholders may face costs or obtain benefits from the project or plan.

After the various groups of stakeholders have been identified, their costs and benefits are calculated. It is relatively easy when all costs and benefits can be expressed directly in amounts of money. Then the question remains of whether the costs and/or benefits are of a temporary or permanent nature. In the latter case, the present value of the costs and benefits has to be calculated using a *discount rate*. In such cases a discussion may arise about what discount rate to use. In the case of projects or plans with a yield over a long period, as in the case of climate but also in the construction of a dam, it is argued that a discount rate of zero is most appropriate. A positive discount rate means a finite time horizon for the project or plan where the benefits and, in specific cases, the costs – think of the storage of nuclear waste – in the very long run are supposed to be zero. This discussion is not yet resolved.

10.1.3   Optimal Design of Regulation

This reference to cost–benefit analysis indicates that the wish to minimize the implementation costs of government regulation relates to the net costs of regulation. As a matter of fact, the best alternative in a cost–benefit analysis will always be the alternative where government regulation is designed in such a way that the net benefits are highest and the net costs relative to the null alternative (of, for example, no regulation) the lowest and negative. Only in the case of positive net benefits is it guaranteed that the welfare gain from the repair of market failure is higher than the costs of government failure associated with the distortion of the market caused by the regulation. It should be noted that such an optimal design of regulation does not automatically imply mild regulation or no regulation at all. In other words, it is not necessarily true that reducing the transaction costs of government always means deregulation. As the aim of regulation is to avoid negative externalities or promote positive externalities, the effects of such a regulation may only materialize in the long run, or in the form of a risk with a relatively small chance of materializing, but with significant negative consequences if it does. This aspect is sometimes forgotten by naïve lobbyists for deregulation.

A major example is the credit crisis of 2007–2010 and the consequent meltdown of the financial markets. The problem here is that supervision was very much focused on individual banks and too little attention was paid to macroprudential regulation (Den Butter, 2011b). This short-sighted avoidance of regulatory costs, as we now know, resulted in enormous costs because of the collapse of the financial markets and the consequent great recession. In general, in balancing the social costs and benefits in a cost–benefit analysis of regulation, the benefits of regulation (and thereby the net cost) depend largely on the warranted degree of risk aversion given the social preferences in this respect. An example of this balancing of risks is in environmental regulation, where it is reflected in the debate on no-regrets policies from the precautionary principle.

10.1.4 Summing Up

Regulations are not brought in without purpose. The view that no new regulation can be brought in unless another burden disappears is usually wrong and if followed through would expose society to unnecessary risk. Consequently, the next stage in the process of controlling the administrative burden may well be one of measuring not just the 'gross burden' but the net one too. That is, measuring the costs and the benefits. Therefore, a proper cost–benefit analysis should be a major element in the discussion on the administrative costs of regulation. In the case of a new regulation, benefits should exceed costs, and the regulation should be designed in such a way that, given the warranted scope of regulation, costs should be minimized. Obviously, these costs do not only comprise administrative costs in a narrow sense but include all kinds of transaction costs mentioned in this book. In addition, it shows that a target of, for example, merely reducing administrative costs by 25 per cent can be suboptimal from the perspective of welfare economics.

However, it is conceivable that a considerable reduction of the administrative costs and, even more so, the total transaction costs of government regulation is possible *given* the actual level of regulation. In that case, the way regulation is organized is suboptimal and can be improved by, for example, the better use of ICT and more efficient standardization. In such a case, minimizing transaction costs is the proper criterion for enhancing the welfare effects of regulation, assuming the level of regulation conforms to social preferences. In cases where actual deregulation is warranted – for example, lax rules or modest quality standards – again a fully-fledged cost–benefit analysis is in order. Here, the loss of benefits to society because of regulation – for example, allowing for higher risks or being less strict on internalizing negative externalities – should be smaller than the gains in terms of fewer transaction costs.

10.2 THE DUTCH 'POLDER MODEL' MAY REDUCE TRANSACTION COSTS

Apart from the implementation of government regulation as discussed in the previous section, transaction costs play a more general role in politics and public administration. Major examples in this respect are the design and set-up of the social security system and the various arrangements that lead to a sustainable public finance system in OECD economies now that they are confronted with problems of ageing and dejuvenation. The Dutch solution to keep costs low in the debate on policy measures to reduce budget deficits is the so-called 'polder model'. In this sense, the polder model can be considered a topical example of transaction management by the government. Apart from representing the spirit of the Dutch as traders, the painting 'The Syndics' by Rembrandt (Figure 1.1) also symbolizes the way consultations between stakeholders are organized in the polder model. This model of consultation- and compromise-seeking is a relic of the fragmentation of various social communities in the Netherlands. This country used to be very 'pillarized', that is various religious and political interest groups, such as the Catholics, Protestants, Dutch reformed, socialists and liberals, were living rather separately in their own communities, with their own values and norms. These were all minority groups. Therefore, to come to compromise agreements the leaders of these interest groups had to negotiate with each other. The way this negotiation was organized between these various groups is a key factor to the polder model. In the same way, almost all religious groups were represented in the commission of 'The Syndics' in the Golden Age of the Dutch Republic.

10.2.1   Tinbergen's 'Polder'

The institutionalization of (economic) decision-making – which is a form of governance – focuses on the dialogue between minorities, which tries to take into account, as much as possible, all minority interests. It was the first Nobel laureate in economics, Jan Tinbergen, who provided a major impetus to the current way of institutionalization of the process of economic policy preparation in the country. His idea was to have a clear separation in policy preparation between:

1.   Independent and *undisputed data* collection by an autonomous Central Bureau of Statistics (CBS);
2.   Trying to reach *consensus* on the working of the economy, as formalized in econometric models through the modelling and analysis of the Central Planning Bureau (CPB) (and today of other 'planning bureaus'); and
3.   Coming to a *compromise* agreement on policy goals between the various minority parties of the government in the Social and Economic Council (SER), which is an advisory body to the government with representatives from employer organizations, trade unions and independent experts.

The aim of this separation of responsibilities is to guarantee, as much as possible, the scientific quality of policy preparation and, at the same time, gain public support for policy measures so that implementation costs are kept low (see Den Butter, 2011a).

This separation of roles in the institutional set-up of policy preparation in the Netherlands, where the debate on the working of the economy is left to the experts as much as possible, reduces transaction costs because the polder consultations provide ample support for government policy. Moreover, the consultations between the parties are organized in such a way that, despite different stakes and interests, trust arises between the parties – and more specifically between the social partners in the SER. This trust reduces transaction costs (see for example Den Butter and Mosch, 2003a). However, the institutionalization of consultations in the polder model sometimes makes the decision-making process sticky and slow because of endless attempts to compromise, so that the benefits of this reduction in transaction costs no longer outweigh the costs of the postponement of important strategic decisions. Therefore, there seems to be some cyclicality in the appraisal of the way the SER, and more generally the 'polder' model, contributes to economic welfare in the Netherlands by reducing the implementation costs of policy measures. Sometimes, this institutional set-up is under pressure, but at other times it is widely praised, and even regarded as an example for other countries (the 'third' road).

10.2.2 Economic Effects of Calculations for Election Programs

Remarkable in this context is that, on the eve of parliamentary elections in the Netherlands, the CPB makes model-based calculations of the economic effects of the proposals in the election programs of the political parties. In the last elections of June 9, 2010, nine political parties asked the CPB to assess the effects of their programs. In this case, besides the CPB, the newly-established Netherlands Environmental Assessment Agency also contributed to the review by calculating the effects of the proposals on mobility, environmental quality and energy use (including greenhouse gas emissions). A main outcome of this exercise is that it provides, as objectively as possible, an assessment of the various political preferences of the parties. It is almost the fulfilment of Tinbergen's dream to have the assessment of the working of the economy – economic reasoning – separated from political preferences. This exercise was until recently unique in the world and characterizes the philosophy of the polder model. In 2010, the Institute of Fiscal Studies, on its own initiative, carried out a similar analysis with respect to the political programs for the UK general election.

The benefit of these kinds of exercises is not so much that it helps voters determine their choices, although that could be seen as the main objective. The most prominent advantage of the exercise is that it reduces transaction costs because it confines the discussion on the interpretation of proposals in election programs. All programs are compared under the same umbrella. In particular, this comparability, and the calculation of what policies lead with most efficiency to the warranted policy outcomes, makes the formation of a coalition government much easier. This is where the largest gain in transaction costs can be achieved, given the tradition in the Netherlands to have long-lasting negotiations before the government agrees on a coalition cabinet. By contrast, a disadvantage of this exercise is that the experts of the political parties, in writing their election programs, have learned which proposals give good results according to the models of the CPB. The consequence is that there is an emphasis on these proposals, whereas it overlooks other relevant policy changes that are outside the scope of the CPB models (see Graafland and Ros, 2003, for the pros and cons of this assessment; see CPB and PBL, 2010, for the assessment for the parliamentary elections of 2010).

10.2.3   'Matching Zones' as a Way to make Transaction Management in G2B Relationships Operational

The previous sections illustrate that the organization and institutionalization of coordination and consultation constitute an integral part of the implementation of public policies, and of the efforts to have the policies implemented at the lowest possible costs. This is true at the macro level for the polder of Tinbergen for policy measures that require parliamentary approval, but it also applies at a lower level, namely in reaching agreement on regulatory measures that affect the interests of certain groups or individuals. Here, in order to reduce transaction costs, it is important that the consultations and negotiations are institutionalized. This institutionalization in so-called *matching zones* can also be seen as a form of transaction management (Den Butter and Ten Wolde, 2011). Such matching zones can be described, in the principal/agent relationship between government and business or citizens, as arranging the meetings of the principal and (one or various) agents in a virtual or actual meeting place, in such a way that the transaction costs or operating costs in the principal/agent relationship are as small as possible. On the one hand, it is important that all relevant stakeholders participate in such consultations in the matching zone; but, on the other hand, coordination in the matching zone should not become too complex. In other words, it is advisable not to address too many issues and coordination problems simultaneously.

Apart from the design of the agenda in the matching zone, there is also the question of its optimal organizational size. This problem is similar to that of the optimal size of administrative units. At the macro level of the SER, there have also been ample discussions about which, and how many, stakeholders are to obtain a seat at the negotiation table.

Discussions and negotiations in the matching zone can, as mentioned before, be considered a form of 'polder' consultation that purports to create compromise between stakeholders with conflicting interests to obtain support for policy measures. In the case of matching zones, support is warranted for the regulatory legislation. The reduction of transaction costs that this consultation purports to reach should again be considered from the perspective of the principal/agent relationship. First, it may imply that the residual costs of imperfect policy coordination are reduced. Moreover, quantitative knowledge about the compliance costs of the industry and about the implementation costs for the government can be useful for a proper assessment of the various interests in the negotiations in the matching zone.

Here, the discussions in the matching zone can be seen as a game of negotiation where various alternatives with respect to the compliance and implementation costs, but also with respect to the benefits for the stakeholders, can be compared. As a first option, it is preferable that a compromise proposal involves a Pareto improvement with respect to the null alternative (present situation or a situation without regulation). In that case, the new situation is profitable for all stakeholders. This implies that the negotiation decides about which place will be reached on the contract curve, if there are still alternatives to do so (see the discussion on the Edgeworth box in Chapter 2). Now the negotiation is confined to the distribution of the net benefits from the new form of regulation. In other words, this is the case where two or more alternatives represent a Pareto improvement, but where one alternative is not Pareto superior relative to the other. The second possibility is that, in the 'best' alternative, the total transaction costs (= sum of costs for all stakeholders) decline, but that this implies a shift of costs between government and other stakeholders (for example, the cost reduction for the government is larger than the additional costs for other stakeholders). In that case, negotiations should consider compensation to come to a so-called Kaldor–Hicks welfare gain (see Box 10.2). Since government is a stakeholder in these kinds of negotiations it is recommended in such a matching zone to have an independent mediator chairing the negotiation in order to promote that the optimal equilibrium is reached.

A matching zone can also act as a platform where stakeholders meet regularly to discuss the implementation of government regulation and thereby can suggest improvements. In that case, the discussions in the matching zone obtain the character of a repeated game and exhibit similarities with the processing of government requests for advice in the SER. Such institutionalization as a repeated game can help avoid a hold-up situation where one of the parties obtains such a strong position that it can renegotiate the agreements to obtain a better position (see for example Den Butter and Mosch, 2003a). When trust-building in the institution-alizing of the negotiation as a repeated game results in avoiding such a hold-up situation, it may contribute to lowering the transaction costs of implementing regulatory measures.

10.3   AUTHORIZED ECONOMIC OPERATOR (AEO) AS AN EXAMPLE[1]

The AEO provides an interesting example of transaction management by the government that purports to reduce the implementation costs of government regulation in a G2B relationship. The AEO is a way of organizing regulation designed to reduce the transaction costs associated with the transit of goods through customs. This involves reducing the costs for the customs offices themselves – here it is also a welcome reduction in the workload of that organization – as well as the costs for importers and exporters, who sometimes have to wait several days before their goods can pass through.

In recent decades, the growth of trade combined with the reduction of trade barriers and the increasing threat of international terrorism has handed a different role to customs. Traditionally, customs offices focused on collecting tariffs and taxes. Today, they have to deal with the security of imports and exports, prevention of smuggling of drugs or weapons and registration of all trade flows. The role of customs is getting more and more complex because, on the one hand, global trade flows have become larger and, on the other hand, customs have increasingly limited resources to fulfil this expansion of their tasks. All these developments imply that customs-related transaction costs constitute a growing share of the total costs of goods transactions. A high level of trade control entails a high level of costs. Transaction costs arising from customs activities are enormously high, reaching as much as 15 per cent of the total value of goods traded. It is estimated that a 1 per cent reduction in transaction costs related to customs activities would yield gains of US \$40 billion worldwide (OECD, 2007; Willmott, 2007). Global governments are now trying to figure out a way to tackle this paradox, with effective control but lowered administrative burden from customs activities.

A number of initiatives have been taken to keep the executive role of the customs administration manageable and to affect world trade as little as possible. The AEO is such an initiative. The concept of the AEO has been developed within the EU. The idea of the AEO is that customs administration in each EU member state can establish partnerships with private sectors and certify them with AEO certificates. The involvement of these private firms in AEO will enhance the safety and security of international trade, and the certified AEOs will enjoy tangible benefits such as fast customs clearance and simplified procedures (for example, containers of AEO firms will not be inspected by customs when they pass EU borders) (European Commission, 2007). The AEO is in fact a new and enhanced customs control instrument (by applying the risk-based pre-selection of trusted trade parties and IT facilitation) without introducing any extra burden (but rather offering relief from the existing administrative burden) for both business and government. More specifically, the AEO reflects the 'win–win' philosophy that governments delegate major control responsibilities to the collaborative and trusted businesses themselves, while in return these businesses benefit from trade simplification.

Such a collaborative relationship means changing the G2B relationship from the traditional 'control and command' to a more 'trust-based' relationship, which includes replacing the traditional labour-intensive customs controls with businesses' 'self-control' on customs issues. To realize this transformation, the EU Directorate-General of Tax and Customs has made a major effort to develop and promote the concept of the AEO for European businesses (European Commission, 2007). The underlying idea is that if businesses can prove to the Tax and Customs Administration (TCA) that they are in control of the tax and security aspects of their own business processes, then they will be AEO-certified by the TCA, which brings them the benefits of fewer physical inspections, faster customs clearance procedures and trade facilitation by the TCA.

A crucial issue here is that the AEO certificate is quite unlike other governmental requirements; it is *voluntary* rather than mandatory: 'It requires . . . no obligation for economic operators to become AEOs, it is a matter of the operators' own choice' (European Commission, 2007). Firms can make their own decisions on whether or not to qualify for the AEO certificate based on firm strategy. In addition, in spite of the facilitations AEO firms may have, the AEO certificate is not cost-free. Firms have to make considerable investments (around €50 000 for small firms, up to a couple of million Euros for large firms) to obtain and maintain the certificate. Hence, AEO can be regarded as a free-will certificate 'market', with entry costs and associated benefits.

The problem here is that if the government cannot effectively differentiate firms from the two streams, a similarly adverse selection and signalling problem to that in the secondhand car market as described by Akerlof

(1970) may occur. The 'good' (trustworthy and compliant) firms are not willing to join when they see no fair value for them to participate. In this respect, a Netherlands-based international brewery remarked: 'We are already a compliant firm with a good reputation, and our current procedure is simpler than that of others anyway, why should we invest more to get the AEO certificate?' By contrast, the 'bad' (opportunistic and fraudulent) firms may see opportunistic benefits (less checking and a simplified procedure may create an opportunity for committing fraud) and relatively less compliance costs than 'good' firms (they can make a false compliance report to show the fulfilment of the requirements), and thereby are more willing to obtain the certificate.

The original aim of the government was to focus control effort on potentially fraudulent firms to limit the number of physical inspections and simplify the procedures for trusted firms with an AEO certificate. However, the consequences of the adverse selection problem may differ from the government's expectation. The situation may even deteriorate: if more 'bad' firms obtain the AEO certificate but commit fraud nevertheless, a market of 'lemons' (in the terminology of Akerlof) will be created and the public will lose trust in the government, thereby causing more societal loss.

10.3.1   AEO and Transaction Management by the Customs in the Netherlands

On 16 April 2008, the first AEO certificates were awarded to 19 Dutch firms. The introduction of the certificate provides both customs and businesses an opportunity to work more efficiently. Although a great effort has been made, because of the lack of experience in carrying out trust-based regulations and vague assessment guidelines, there still exists a big gap in the common understanding between businesses and government for AEO implementation. The TCA is recognized as one of the most innovative customs authorities in the world, especially in the field of trade facilitation. The Dutch AEO certificate assessment practice is perceived to be well established and effective by the European Commission.

The experience so far with introducing the AEO in the Netherlands shows that IT-enabled risk management may effectively eliminate the information asymmetry for G2B relationship building. The Dutch TCA has adopted risk management as part of its audit procedures. It views it 'as a structured process, consisting of well-defined steps, according to which a systematic identification, analysis, prioritization and treatment of risks is taking place, so as to support improved decision-making'. So-called IT-enabled risk management has two meanings. First, it means that IT and information systems are the focus for the assessment and, second, it refers to automated IT support, in the form of decision support systems, for the general risk management approach. In this case the Dutch TCA assesses the IT maturity level of firms and uses this assessment as one of its major decision criteria for AEO certification. Moreover, the Dutch TCA uses as much IT facilitation as possible to make risk management more efficient and effective.

The only way that the AEO certificate will become an efficient instrument of transaction management in G2B relationships is when it reduces the customs costs for businesses. Therefore, firms that apply for AEO certification will, given the considerations about signalling discussed above, require that the benefits of certification are larger than the costs. This means that customs-related transaction costs decrease, so that the productivity of the firm rises and its competitive position is strengthened. Therefore, both the costs and benefits of certification should be taken into consideration.

What are the costs for a firm that seeks certification? The costs for an AEO certificate can be divided into three categories:

1. Cost of the license application;
2. Expenses incurred for the firm to comply with the requirements raised by the customs authorities; and
3. Costs incurred in order not to lose certification.

The first two categories relate to sunk costs – that is, one-off costs that will still be incurred even if the firm ultimately does not gain certification. The third category consists of fixed costs, which typically have a recurrent nature.

What benefits does certification provide to firms? Here, a distinction can be made between direct benefits and indirect benefits. Direct benefits are the benefits arising from the simplification of customs procedures. Indirect benefits relate to cost reductions resulting from the conditions to be met by a certified firm, but which are not the direct result of simplified customs formalities. These benefits can largely be characterized as being a result of the reduction in soft transaction costs that certification may entail. A major part of the indirect benefits of an AEO certificate stems from the *reputation effect* of being an AEO-certified firm.

How does this reputation effect influence the soft transaction costs in trade between firms? A major aspect here is that the criteria for obtaining the AEO certificate give it the character of a quality standard (see Chapter 7). When firms do business together, the AEO certificate provides a guarantee that they are reliable business partners. The AEO certificate shows that the firm is trusted by the customs authorities. This gives a signal to other firms that they can trust the firm as well. Moreover, compliance with the criteria for a quality standard, regardless of the standardization authority that has imposed the criteria, provides a signal about the quality of the management of the firm. Obviously, the extent of the reputation effect is difficult to quantify. Yet, it is less difficult to observe which aspects determine the extent to which the reputation effect may influence the choice for firms that qualify as trading partners or not. The size of the reputation effect will to some extent also be reflected in insurance premiums for certified firms. Most probably these premiums will be lower than for non-certified firms.

The value of the reputation effect for a firm will depend on:

1. The extent to which certification is known and respected in the business community;
2. The reliability of the institution that issues and controls the certificate;
3. The effectiveness of controls; and
4. Recognition by the customs authorities of third-party countries.

The more firms that opt for certification, the more firms will know what being certified implies and to what criteria certified firms must comply. This is a self-reinforcing effect because certification can be regarded as a network externality. For example, if there is no knowledge about the criteria for obtaining a certificate, it will provide little information about how a firm handles its transactions and, therefore, little information about the reputation of that firm. However, when the criteria for being certified are commonly known, the certificate will provide the desired information about the reliability of the firm.

The government can play a major role in the start-up of this process by enhancing the reputational value of the certificate with information campaigns. The fact that the benefits are largest when the entire supply chain is certified will have a positive impact on the spread of the certificate. For the government this is part of exploiting the network externalities of certification, where the value of being licensed becomes larger when more firms are certified. More familiarity with the certificate means more certified firms resulting in a stronger reputation effect.

The reputation effect also depends on the reliability of the institution that issues and controls the certificate. In the case of the European AEO certificate, these issuers and controllers are the national customs authorities. When, for instance, the local customs authorities suffer from a rumour of being corrupt, the certificate will be a less effective means for a firm to judge the reliability of other firms. Therefore, a trusted authority is needed to control the AEO certificate and make it a signal of the quality of certified firms.

The same holds true for the effectiveness of controls. If the verification of compliance with the conditions for being an AEO-certified firm is not effective, then such a certification will be of little value to signalling the reputation of the firm. It is, therefore, in the interest of certified firms that other certified firms keep meeting the criteria, because a poor compliance with the criteria will downgrade the reputation of the certificate and thereby jeopardize the reputation of certified firms. However, when the control of the customs authorities is effective, it will be difficult for firms to circumvent the criteria unnoticed.

In general it holds true that the more customs authorities recognize the AEO certificate, the more valuable the reputation effect will be. This is because a firm that uses the reputation effect of certification will be able to connect with more international trading partners where their local customs authorities indirectly recognize that firm as a certified operator. It is for that reason that in the preparation of the AEO safety conditions, the international rules and conditions of the WCO are fully incorporated. Therefore, the more countries have their own AEO programs, and the more the certificates are mutually recognized in these countries, the greater the value for a firm to be certified. When more customs authorities recognize the certificate it will not only enhance the reputational value of AEO certification, but also the direct revenues, as a percentage of the costs of an application, will increase. This is because more transactions will be covered by the certificate, making it a true international standard. Here, it is assumed that the costs of obtaining and keeping certification will not increase when the certificate is recognized by more customs authorities. However, it is not yet clear whether such a global network of AEO certificates will become a reality in the future and what exactly the criteria for such a worldwide certification would be. But its existence would bring about a considerable reduction of transaction costs in world trade, and this would represent an important gain for AEO certification. Moreover, this gain would to a major extent be reflected in enhanced welfare and could not be allotted to individual firms. These indirect and social benefits are not part of the strategic decisions of individual firms based on comparing the costs and benefits of certification.

10.3.2 More Government Intervention is Warranted

From the perspective of positive externalities resulting from enhancing the reputational effect of certification and making certification global, the government can contribute to an increase in welfare by optimizing the design of the AEO certification. This is a core issue in the transaction management of the government in the special case of regulation in a G2B relationship. In this case, a well-designed government regulation brings about societal benefits that are much higher than those from a mere reduction – or in this case a shift – of administrative burden. Moreover, a well-designed and organized AEO certification process is also profitable for the government because it reduces its implementation costs.

However, for this 'win–win' situation to be realized, a better understanding must be obtained of the economic mechanisms that play a role in AEO certification and of the social costs and benefits that certification brings about. This applies particularly to the reputation effect and to the best way in which customs authorities can prevent fraud and the abuse of the certification. The above argumentation provides a first attempt to gain such an understanding from the perspective of transaction management.

To conclude, it should be noted that in practice there has been little progress in AEO certification. The number of applications is, especially internationally, still far below expectations. The result is that the discussed benefits of certification are hardly being realized. There seems to be a kind of deadlock: if few firms are certified, it is less attractive for firms to pursue certification. Moreover, in that case, the costs of loss of reputation in cases of cheating are low and the benefits of cheating may outweigh these costs. Therefore, it is recommended that governments should be more actively involved in promoting certification and making it worthwhile. There is a clear analogy with the government intervention needed to have XBRL as the generally accepted standard in business accounting (see Box 7.1). Yet, private service offices already fulfil a role of intermediary function and are the offices to which the application for AEO certification can be outsourced. Because these intermediaries have obtained experience with the application procedure, they reduce the transaction costs of the application. Thus, it provides another good example of transaction management.

NOTE

1. Based on Den Butter and Van Scheltinga (2008); Den Butter et al. (2012).

11. Conclusion

This chapter recapitulates the meaning and significance of managing transaction costs in nations where the focus is on the organization of production and on being competitive as a hub in international trade. These nations can be characterized as transaction (or orchestration) economies, and the skill of reducing transaction costs is labelled transaction management. This final chapter provides a kind of checklist of what knowledge is needed for effective transaction management, and how value can be created by exploiting the gains from the worldwide division of labour in this era of globalization.

This book outlines the pivotal role of the skill of reducing transaction costs in modern open economies where welfare creation depends on trade and the organization of production. First, the characteristics of a transaction economy (or orchestrating economy) are reviewed in a number of statements. Then, the role of transaction management as a key competence for government and industry in such a transaction economy is summarized.

11.1 CHARACTERISTICS OF A TRANSACTION ECONOMY

A precise definition, in one sweeping statement, of a transaction economy (or orchestrating economy) cannot be given. That is because transaction economies have different characteristics. For instance, Chapter 3 on the hub function of some selected transaction economies shows that The Netherlands and Belgium, nations with a long maritime tradition, act as purchasers in the world and as suppliers to the rest of Europe. Singapore has a similar role in East Asia. On the other hand, land-locked Switzerland, a big exporter of financial and business services, buys in Europe and sells to the rest of the world. Given these different characteristics, the major questions are: what *does* a transaction economy imply; and how will developed economies transform further to become transaction economies in the future? The following statements summarize the answers:

- A transaction economy is an economy where the opportunities of further specialization, division of labour and the fragmentation of production are fully grasped and exploited.
- In a transaction economy, the focus of economic activity is increasingly directed at the orchestration and organization of production rather than on the actual production processes themselves.
- A transaction economy is a high-tech knowledge economy supplemented with knowledge on how to reduce transaction costs.
- Knowledge workers in a transaction economy operate and cooperate at the scientific frontiers and global development of open standards and open innovation.
- A transaction economy provides excellent working conditions and a living environment for young knowledge workers from around the world, and thereby a good business climate for headquarters of international firms, where business strategies are developed and production is organized. Good accessibility, both physically and through modern communications, is a necessary condition for such an investment climate.
- In a transaction economy, businesses and financial and legal services aim for excellence and are internationally oriented.
- A transaction economy is open to cultural differences and knows how to exploit cultural diversity and convert it into creative collaboration.
- The government of a transaction economy is convinced of the importance of connecting innovation policy to trade policy.
- The government of a transaction economy knows, in education policy, how to proactively direct schooling towards the skills needed for organizing production and for outsourcing parts of production processes. It is the competence for the trade in tasks that matters.

These statements illustrate that much more sophistication and knowledge is needed to create value in organizing production and in trade than the connotation of the word 'trade' as just a simple bilateral exchange of goods or services may suggest. That is why:

- A transaction economy is not a distribution economy where economic activity primarily consists of trade and 'moving boxes'.
- A transaction economy is not an alternative for the knowledge economy: there is no need to choose.
- A transaction economy is not an economy where the manufacturing industry completely disappears.

● A transaction economy is not an economy where the only required skill is that of a savvy trader.

11.2 CHARACTERISTICS OF TRANSACTION MANAGEMENT

In contrast to a transaction economy, a definition of transaction management can be concisely given in one sentence. *Transaction management is the skill and ability to keep transaction costs as low as possible in all given circumstances.* However, this sentence does not really provide a clear picture of what transaction management actually is or of the reasons why it is an important method of strategic analysis in policy decisions for industry and the public sector. First, some possible misconceptions about transaction management are pointed out:

● Transaction management does not only relate to minimizing the transaction costs of financial transactions such as payment and administrative services. However, it is true that the way transaction management is elaborated in this book encompasses this original narrow connotation of transaction management.
● Transaction management is no panacea for all problems relating to the need to reduce costs: it is a means of analysis from a specific perspective, namely that of transaction costs.
● Transaction management does not solely seek to reduce existing transaction costs: there should be a good balance between existing and possible future transaction costs because of increased risks (for example, costs of safety). It is the combination of internal and external organization of production that matters in transaction management.
● Transaction management is not one of the many heuristic management principles or tools. It is based on the scientific theory of transaction cost economics, or more broadly: the theory of new institutional economics. This is a theory conveyed by Nobel Prize winners (Coase, North and Williamson) and that has been elaborated in articles in all leading economics journals.
● Transaction management does not lose relevance when transaction costs are reduced. On the contrary, thanks to good transaction management and the consequent reduction of transaction costs the globalized world has increasingly become more transaction-intensive; so the importance of transaction management has also increased. Transaction costs per transaction may decrease, but as transactions

become less expensive, it enables more fragmentation of production and trade in tasks, so that the ratio of transaction costs to sheer production costs ultimately increases.

This list already implies a number of characteristics of transaction management. What other aspects of transaction management are worth mentioning?

- Transaction management is a skill that creates great value, especially in a transaction economy. Therefore, it should be regarded as a key competence for the business sector in such transaction economies, and education and science policy should be aware of that crucial role.
- Managerial skills are valuable for transaction management but they do not suffice. In fact, for value creation through reducing transaction costs, an entrepreneurial spirit is of much greater importance. To a large extent, it is the intuition and the strong capability of estimating risks of the entrepreneur that matter in transaction management.
- Transaction management relates both to (horizontal) business transactions through the market and to (vertical) transactions through the hierarchy or through alliance agreements within or between firms.
- Transaction management is applicable: (i) within the industry (B2B); (ii) between government and industry (G2B); and (iii) within the government (G2G).
- Transaction management translates the theoretical knowledge of the economic theory of transaction costs (which combines parts of the macro-oriented theories of institutional economics, industrial organization and international economics) to a practical decision-making method for businesses and government.
- Transaction management creates value in a globalizing world by promoting the further fragmentation of production. This implies that firms in transaction economies will increasingly be engaged in the orchestration of production and in the 'make or buy' and location decisions with respect to outsourcing tasks.
- Transaction management creates value by making connections between various people (networks) and ideas (creativity, serendipity).
- The fact that transaction management acts as a key competence also means that trading nations remain an attractive location for foreign head offices from where the orchestrating function is performed.

11.3 CHECKLIST FOR TRANSACTION MANAGEMENT

This book presents an overview of the background and applications of transaction management and offers some primary examples of the application of the methodology. For further practical application to specific strategic decisions, it is useful to avail oneself of a list of the information needed successively to make the strategic decisions. A first step in developing the criteria of efficient transaction management is given below:

1. Do transaction costs relate to a (horizontal) transaction through the market or to (vertical) coordination within the firm? It should be noted that the choice between various ways of outsourcing and the 'make or buy' and location decisions depend on the comparison of marginal horizontal and vertical transaction costs.
2. On what kinds and types of transaction costs does the strategic decision depend? Here, the distinction is: (i) between internal and external causes; and (ii) between hard and soft transaction costs. Try to compile a comprehensive list of the relevant transaction costs based on the examples in this book. However, realize that forgotten or underestimated costs may lead to erroneous decisions (see Jongerius and Sie, 2010, for a prototype of such a list with respect to trade with China). These 'forgotten' costs mainly refer to what this book calls 'soft' transaction costs.
3. Distinguish between one-off transaction costs (which often are sunk costs) and transaction costs that have a regular and recurrent character.
4. Distinguish between costs: (i) to be made even if no transaction takes place (sunk costs); (ii) costs associated with the current transaction; and (iii) costs that (also) act as an investment in order to have lower transaction costs in the future (for example, investing in trust with a supplier, customer or employee, or costs of insurance and safety provisions).
5. Another categorization of the various types of costs relates to the question of whether the transaction costs to be made in the exchange relation are ex ante or ex post costs.
6. What alternatives are there to reduce costs? Find out whether the reduction of one type of costs (short-term) may lead to higher costs of another type (long-term).
7. Remember that standardization is an important way to reduce transaction costs. Here, it is essential to take into account the desired flexibility. A lack of flexibility limits the ability to reconcile specific needs

and preferences. By contrast, when the standard allows for too much flexibility, standardization may not be cost-reducing.

8. Trust and building a reputation of trustworthiness are other ways to reduce transaction costs. Trust can thereby serve as a substitute for detailed contracts, which will in fact never be 'complete' in the sense that they eliminate uncertainty in all future situations. It is advisable in a cooperative relationship based on trust to ensure that the cost of cheating (defying the trust relationship) is greater than the possible benefit of maintaining the trust relationship. This is a question of calculative trust. In such cases, it is advisable to institutionalize the trade relationship as a repeated game.

9. Risk involved in transactions require special attention. Here, a good balance is needed between the cost of avoidance and insurance, and the expected cost of the adverse event when the risk materializes. This risk assessment is best made by the party who has the most knowledge about the risk. Therefore, it is also desirable that the party with the best knowledge of the risk becomes the 'owner' of the risk.

10. Another balancing of transaction costs is in order when decisions about outsourcing tasks and splitting up the production chain have to be made. Here, the strategic decision relates to the 'make or buy' and the location decisions.

11. If relevant, assess whether there is a principal/agent relationship. In such a case, transaction costs can be categorized as the costs of: (i) implementation ('monitoring'); (ii) compliance ('bonding'); and (iii) failure when the objective of the principal is not met ('residual loss').

12. When assessing the welfare effects of a policy change, for example by a change in regulation or by introducing a new rule or institution, one should balance the benefits of reducing the costs in the new situation against the increased costs of the new situation including the transition costs. For instance, outsourcing leads to lower direct production costs but to higher transaction costs, or a merger or acquisition can lead to a cost reduction because of economies of scale but the transition costs are often underestimated.

Expanding this checklist and making it more specific for various cases of transaction management provides major scope for further research. Yet, in practice, the mere understanding of what types of transaction costs play a role in running a business, and simple costs adjustment from that perspective, may be sufficient to considerably enhance the efficiency of the organization of production. A similar consideration holds true for transaction management which aims at the optimal design of policy measures. Here, transaction management, when applied to practical cases, may bring about better regulation and public policy, and may thus lead to value creation which is beneficial to society in this era of globalization.

References

Akerlof, G.A. (1970), 'The market for "lemons": quality, uncertainty and the market mechanism', *Quarterly Journal of Economics*, **84** (3), 488–500.

Anderson, J.E. and E. van Wincoop (2004), 'Trade costs', *Journal of Economic Literature*, **42** (3), 691–751.

Antràs, P. and E. Rossi-Hansberg (2009), 'Organizations and trade', *Annual Review of Economics*, **1** (1), 43–64.

Arrow, K.J. (1969), 'The organization of economic activity: issues pertinent to the choice of market versus nonmarket allocation', in U.S. Joint Economic Committee (ed.), *91st Congress, The Analysis and Evaluation of Public Expenditure: The PPB System*, Vol. 1, Washington, DC: Government Printing Office, pp. 59–73.

Bakker, J. (2010), 'The effect of the ease of doing business on bilateral trade flows', MSc Thesis, Amsterdam: VU University, March.

Baldwin, R.E. and F. Robert-Nicoud (2010), 'Trade-in-goods and trade-in-tasks: an integrating framework', NBER Working Paper No. 15882, Cambridge, MA, April.

Beauvallet, G. and T. Houy (2010), 'Research on HRM and lean management: a literature survey', *International Journal of Human Resources Development and Management*, **10** (1), 14–33.

Beer, P.T. de (2001), 'Over werken in de postindustriële samenleving' ['On labour in the post industrial society'], Den Haag: Sociaal en Cultureel Planbureau, May.

Bénabou, R. and J. Tirole (2003), 'Intrinsic and extrinsic motivation', *Review of Economic Studies*, **70** (3), 489–520.

Berenschot Research (2005), 'Aard, omvang en effecten van verplaatsen bedrijfsactiviteiten naar het buitenland', Utrecht.

Berg, M. van den, K. van Buiren, T. van Giffen, P. Risseeuw, with collaboration of F.A.G. den Butter (2008), 'The Dutch trust industry; facts and figures', SEO-report nr. 2008-25. (See also Butter, F.A.G. den, P. Risseeuw and M. van den Berg (2008), 'De rol van trustkantoren in de Nederlandse economie' ['The role of trust offices in the Dutch economy'], *Economisch Statistische Berichten*, **93** (4542), 535–537.)

Blind, K. (2004), *The Economics of Standards*, Cheltenham, UK and Northampton, MA: Edward Elgar Publishing.

Boons, M.A.F.A. and F.A.G. den Butter (2011), 'Transactiemanagement en Lean management: kostenreductie vanuit een verschillend perspectief' ['Transaction management and Lean management: different perspectives on cost reduction'], *Maandblad voor Accountancy en Bedrijfseconomie,* **85** (6), 333–341. (See also Butter, F.A.G. den (2011), 'Cost reduction using transaction management: a complement to Lean management', *Review of Business and Economics*, **56** (3), 309–329.)

Brander, J.A. and B.J. Spencer (1983), 'Strategic commitment with R&D: the symmetric case', *Bell Journal of Economics*, **14** (1), 225–235.

Brander, J.A. and B.J. Spencer (1985), 'Export subsidies and international market share rivalry', *Journal of International Economics*, **18** (1–2), 83–100.

Bruce, M., L. Daly and N. Towers (2004), 'Lean or agile: a solution for supply chain management in the textiles and clothing industry?', *International Journal of Operations and Production Management*, **24** (2), 151–170.

Bruil, A., F.A.G. den Butter and P. Kee (2010), 'The definition of a job and the flow approach to the labour market; a sensitivity analysis for the Netherlands', Statistics Netherlands (CBS) Discussion Paper No. 10011, The Hague/Heerlen.

Butter, F.A.G. den (1999), 'Handelaartjes' ['Little traders'], *AVENIR-Economisch Bulletin*, **5**, nr. 5, p. 37.

Butter, F.A.G. den (2011a), 'The industrial organisation of economic policy preparation in The Netherlands', Ch. 10 in J. Lentsch and P. Weingart (eds), *The Politics of Scientific Advice; Institutional Design for Quality Assurance,* Cambridge: Cambridge University Press, pp. 177–214.

Butter, F.A.G. den (2011b), 'The macroeconomics of the credit crisis: in search of externalities for macroprudential supervision', Ch. 10 in E.F.M. Wubben (ed.), *Institutions and Regulation for Economic Growth? Public Interest Versus Private Incentives*, Cheltenham, UK and Northampton, MA: Edward Elgar Publishing, pp. 191–210.

Butter, F.A.G. den (2012), 'The transaction management perspective on procurement in the era of globalization', *International Journal of Procurement Management*, **5** (2), 123–139.

Butter, F.A.G. den and P. Corveleijn (2007), 'Standaardisering van het Europese effectenverkeer' ['Standardizing EU asset trade'], *Economisch Statistische Berichten*, **92**, 708–711.

Butter, F.A.G. den and R. Hayat (2008), 'Trade between China and the Netherlands; a case study of globalization', Tinbergen Institute Discussion Paper No. TI 2008-016/8, Amsterdam, February.

Butter, F.A.G. den and M.W. Hofkes (2006), 'A neo-classical economics view on technological transitions', in X. Olsthoorn and A.J. Wieczorek (eds), *Understanding Industrial Transformation: Views from Different Disciplines*, Dordrecht: Springer, pp. 141–162.

Butter, F.A.G. den and J. Hudson (2009), 'Standardization and compliance costs: relevant developments at the EU level', Ch. 10 in A. Nijsen et al. (eds), *Business Regulation and Public Policy: the Costs and Benefits of Compliance,* New York: Springer, pp. 141–155.

Butter, F.A.G. den and S.-G. Jo (2009), 'Pros and cons of "backing winners" in innovation policy', Tinbergen Institute Discussion Paper No. TI 2009-012/3, Amsterdam, February.

Butter, F.A.G. den and D. Leliefeld (2007), 'Van productie naar regievoering: IHC Holland Merwede als voorbeeld' ['From production to orchestration: IHC Holland Merwede as example'], *Maandblad voor Accountancy en Bedrijfseconomie,* **81** (10), 488–496.

Butter, F.A.G. den and K.A. Linse (2008), 'Rethinking procurement in the era of globalization', *MIT Sloan Management Review*, Fall 2008, **50** (1), 76–80.

Butter, F.A.G. den and O.K. van Megchelen (2005), 'Uitbesteden en innovatie in de bouw; het toenemend belang van de regie en handelsfunctie' ['Subcontracting and innovation in the construction industry; the increasing importance of trade and orchestration'], VU Research Memorandum, 2005-5.

Butter, F.A.G. den and R.H.J. Mosch (2003a), 'The Dutch miracle: institutions, networks and trust', *Journal of Institutional and Theoretical Economics*, **159** (2), 362–391.

Butter, F.A.G. den and R.H.J. Mosch (2003b), 'Trade, trust and transaction costs', Tinbergen Institute Discussion Paper No. TI 2003-082/3, Amsterdam, October.

Butter, F.A.G. den and C. Pattipeilohy (2007), 'Productivity gains from offshoring: an empirical analysis for the Netherlands', Tinbergen Institute Discussion Paper No. TI 2007-089/3, Amsterdam, November.

Butter, F.A.G. den and W.J. van Scheltinga (2008), 'Kosten en baten van AEO certificering' ['Costs and benefits of AEO certification'], Research report prepared for Trade Forum NV, VU University/RITM, Amsterdam, August.

Butter, F.A.G. den and S. ten Wolde (2011), 'The institutional economics of stakeholder consultation; reducing implementations costs through "matching zones"', Tinbergen Institute Discussion Paper, No. TI 2011-162/3, Amsterdam, November.

Butter, F.A.G. den, F. Lazrak and S.P.T. Groot (2007), 'Standaards als bron van welvaart' ['Standards as a source of welfare'], *Kwartaalschrift Economie*, **4** (2), 139–165.

Butter, F.A.G. den, J. Liu and Y.-H. Tan (2012), 'Using IT to engender trust in government-to-business relationships: the Authorized Economic Operator (AEO) as an example', *Government Information Quarterly*, **29**, 261–274.

Butter, F.A.G. den, J. Möhlmann and P. Wit (2008), 'Trade and product innovations as sources for productivity increases: an empirical analysis', *Journal of Productivity Analysis*, **30** (3), 201–211.

Casella, A. (2001), 'Product standards and international trade, harmonization through private coalitions?', *KYKLOS*, **54** (2–3), 243–264.

Cheung, S.N.S. (1987), 'Economic organization and transaction costs', *The New Palgrave: A Dictionary of Economics,* Vol. 2, pp. 55–58.

Choi, T.Y. and D.R. Krause (2006), 'The supply base and its complexity: implications for transaction costs, risks, responsiveness, and innovation', *Journal of Operations Management*, **24** (5), 637–652.

Coase, R.H. (1937), 'The nature of the firm', *Economica*, **4** (16), 386–405.

Coase, R.H. (2005), 'The institutional structure of production', Ch. 2 in C. Ménard and M.M. Shirley (eds), *Handbook of New Institutional Economics*, Berlin: Springer, pp. 31–39.

COM689 (2006), 'Measuring administrative costs and reducing administrative burdens in the European Union', European Commission, Brussels, November.

Combes, P.-P., M. Lafourcade and T. Mayer (2002), 'Can business and social networks explain the border effect puzzle?', CEPR Discussion Paper No. 3750, London, February.

Cooray, S. and J. Ratnatunga (2001), 'Buyer–supplier relationships: a case study of a Japanese Western alliance', *Long Range Planning*, **34** (6), 727–740.

Cox, A. and D. Chicksand (2005), 'The limits of lean management thinking: multiple retailers and food and farming supply chains', *European Management Journal*, **23** (6), 648–662.

CPB [Centraal Planbureau] (2006), *Macro Economische Verkenning (MEV) 2007* [*Macro Economic Outlook 2007*], The Hague: CPB.

CPB and PBL [Centraal Planbureau and Planbureau voor de Leefomgeving] (2010), 'Keuzes in kaart 2011–2015, effecten van negen verkiezingsprogramma's op economie en milieu' ['Choices mapped out 2011–2015, effects of nine election programmes on the economy and environment'], CPB Special Publication No. 85, The Hague, May.

Dalen, H.P. van and A.P. van Vuuren (2005), 'Greasing the wheels of trade: a profile of the Dutch transaction sector', *De Economist*, **153** (2), 139–165.

Deardorff, A.V. (1995), 'Determinants of bilateral trade: does gravity work in a neoclassical world?', NBER Working Paper No. 5377, Cambridge, MA, December.

De Nederlandsche Bank [DNB] (2007), 'Special financial institution – integrity risks caused by large cash flows', *DNB Quarterly Bulletin*, March, 61–64.

De Nederlandsche Bank [DNB] (2008), *Jaarverslag 2007 [Annual Report 2007]*, Amsterdam: DNB.

De Santis, R. and C. Vicarelli (2007), 'The "deeper" and "wider" EU strategies of trade integration: an empirical evaluation of EU common commercial policy effects', *Global Economic Journal*, **7** (4), Article 4.

Dewees, D.N. (1979), 'Estimating the time costs of highway congestion', *Econometrica*, **46** (6), 1499–1512.

DIN (2000), 'Economic benefits of standardization', Berlin: Beuth Verlag.

Dollar, D. and A. Kraay (2003), 'Institutions, trade and growth', *Journal of Monetary Economics*, **50** (1), 133–162.

Dreyer, C. and M. Willis (2006), 'Cheaper, smarter, faster: benefits to analysts from XBRL', *Professional Investor*, September, 10–16.

Dye, R.D. and S. Sunder (2001), 'Why not allow FABS and IASB standards to compete in the US?', *Accounting Horizons*, **15** (3), 257–271.

Dyer, J.H. (1997), 'Effective interfirm collaboration: how firms minimize transaction costs and maximise transaction value', *Strategic Management Journal*, **18** (7), 535–556.

Dyer, J.H. and K. Nobeoka (2000), 'Creating and managing a high-performance knowledge-sharing network: the Toyota case', *Strategic Management Journal*, **21** (3), 345–367.

Dyer, J., P. Kale and H. Singh (2001), 'How to make strategic alliances work', *MIT Sloan Management Review*, **42** (4), 37–43.

Eccles, R.G. (1981), 'The quasifirm in the construction industry', *Journal of Economic Behavior & Organization*, **2** (4), 335–357.

European Commission (EC) Directorate-General Taxation and Customs Union (2007), 'Authorised economic operators: guidelines', TAXUD/2006/1450, Brussels, June.

Farell, J. (1995), 'Arguments for weaker intellectual property protection in network industries', *Standard View*, **3** (2), 46–49.

Farell, J. (1996), *Choosing the Rules for Formal Standardization*, Berkeley: University of California.

Federico, S. (2010), 'Outsourcing versus integration at home or abroad', Banca D'Italia Working Paper No. 742, Rome, February.

Feenstra, R.D. (1998), 'Integration of trade and disintegration of production in the global economy', *Journal of Economic Perspectives*, **12** (4), 31–50.

Florida, R. (2002), *The Rise of the Creative Class: And How it's Transforming Work, Leisure and Everyday Life*, New York: Basic Books.

Frey, B.S. and R. Jegen (2001), 'Motivation crowding theory', *Journal of Economic Surveys*, **15** (5), 589–611.

Fukuyama, F. (1995), *Trust: The Social Virtues and the Creation of Prosperity*, New York: Free Press Paperbacks.

Gabriel, E. (1997), 'The lean approach to project management', *International Journal of Project Management*, **15** (4), 205–209.

Gattai, V. (2006), 'From the theory of the firm to FDI and internationalisation: a survey', *Giornale degli Economisti e Annali di Economia*, **65** (2), 225–262.

Gaulier, G., F. Lemoine and D. Ünal-Kesenci (2007), 'China's emergence and the reorganisation of trade flows in Asia', *China Economic Review*, **18** (3), 209–243.

Giddens, A. (1991), *Modernity and Self-identity: Self and Society in the Late Modern Age*, Cambridge: Polity Press.

Giovannini Group, The (2001), 'Cross-border clearing and settlement arrangements in the European Union', Brussels, November.

Gorter, J., P. Tang and M. Toet (2005), 'Verplaatsing vanuit Nederland; motieven, gevolgen en beleid' ['Reallocating out of the Netherlands; motives, consequences and policy'], CPB Document No. 76, The Hague, February.

Graafland, J. and C. Mazereeuw-Van der Duyn Schouten (2007), 'The heavenly calculus and socially responsible business conduct: an explorative study among executives', *De Economist*, **155** (2), 161–181.

Graafland, J.J. and A.P. Ros (2003), *Economic Assessment of Election Programmes: Does it Make Sense?*, Dordrecht/Boston: Kluwer Academic Publishers.

Greif, A. (1989), 'Reputation and coalitions in medieval trade: evidence on the Maghribi traders', *Journal of Economic History*, **49** (4), 857–882.

Greif, A. (1993), 'Contract enforceability and economic institutions in early trade: the Maghribi traders coalition', *American Economic Review*, **83** (3), 525–548.

Greif, A. (1994), 'Cultural beliefs and the organization of society: a historical and theoretical reflection on collectivist and individualist societies', *Journal of Political Economy*, **102** (5), 912–950.

Greif, A. (2000), 'The fundamental problem of exchange: a research agenda in Historical Institutional Analysis', *European Review of Economic History*, **4** (3), 251–284.

Greif, A. (2005), 'Commitment, coercion and markets: the nature and dynamics of institutions supporting exchange', Ch. 28 in C. Ménard and M.M. Shirley (eds), *Handbook of New Institutional Economics*, Berlin: Springer, pp. 727–786.

Groot, H.L.F. de, G.J.M. Linders and P. Rietveld (2005), 'Institutions, governance and international trade: opening the black box of OECD and GDP per capita effects in gravity equations', *IATSS Research*, **29** (2), 22–29.

Groot, H.L.F. de, G.J.M. Linders, P. Rietveld and U. Subramanian (2004), 'The institutional determinants of bilateral trade patterns', *Kyklos*, **57** (1), 103–123.

Grossman, G. and G. Maggi (2000), 'Diversity and trade', *American Economic Review*, **90** (5), 1255–1275.

Grossman, G.M. and E. Rossi-Hansberg (2006), 'The rise of offshoring: it's not wine for cloth anymore', *Federal Reserve Bank of Kansas City Proceedings*, 2006, 59–102.

Grossman, G.M. and E. Rossi-Hansberg (2008), 'Trading tasks: a simple theory of offshoring', *American Economic Review*, **98** (5), 1978–1997.

Harvard Research Group (2003), 'Clearing and settlement – making financial information flow', available at: http://www.hrgresearch.com/pdf/Clearing%20and%20Settlement.pdf.

Helpman, E. (2006), 'Trade, FDI and the organization of firms', NBER Working Paper No. 12091, Cambridge, MA, March.

Helpman, E. and P. Krugman (1985), *Market Structure and Foreign Trade*, Cambridge, MA: MIT Press.

Herrendorf, B. and A. Teixeira (2005), 'How barriers to international trade affect TFP', *Review of Economic Dynamics*, **8** (4), 866–867.

Hudson, J. and P. Jones (2003), 'International trade in "quality goods": signaling problems for developing countries', *Journal of International Development*, **15** (8), 999–1013.

Hunt, J. (2004), 'Trust and bribery: the role of the quid pro quo and the link with crime', NBER Working Paper No. 10510, Cambridge, MA, May.

Islam, R. and A. Reshef (2006), 'Trade and harmonization: if your institutions are good, does it matter if they are different?', World Bank Policy Research Working Paper No. 3907, Washington, DC, May.

Jacobs, D. and J. Waalkens (2001), *Innovatie²; Vernieuwingen in de Innovatiefunctie van Ondernemingen* [*Innovation²; Developments in the Innovative Role of Firms*], Deventer: Kluwer.

Jo, S.-G. (2010), 'Non-uniform strategic trade policy and aggregate profit creation effect', *Scottish Journal of Political Economy*, **57** (5), 645–662.

Jones, P. and J. Hudson (1996), 'Standardization and the costs of assessing quality', *European Journal of Political Economy*, **12** (2), 355–361.

Jongerius, L.J. and R.J.C. Sie (2010), 'A transaction cost analysis: outsourcing production to China', Stichting Handelsland Report, Amsterdam, September.

Kaufmann, D., A. Kraay and M. Mastruzzi (2009), 'Governance matters VIII: aggregate and individual governance indicators for 1996–2008', World Bank Policy Research Working Paper No. 4978, Washington, DC, June.

Kimura, F. and H.-H. Lee (2006), 'The gravity equation in international trade in services', *Review of World Economics*, **142** (1), 92–121.

Klamer, A. and D. McCloskey (1995), 'One quarter of GDP is persuasion', *American Economic Review* (*Papers and Proceedings*), **85** (2), 191–195.

Kok, K. (2004), 'Het UTA-personeel in de bouwnijverheid' ['The UTA-personnel in the construction industry'], Economisch Instituut voor de Bouwnijverheid, Amsterdam, July 2004.

Kox, H. (2005), 'Intra-EU differences in regulation-caused administrative burden for companies', *CPB Memorandum* No. 136, The Hague, December.

Krafcik, J.F. (1988), 'Triumph of the lean production system', *MIT Sloan Management Review*, **30** (1), 41–52.

Kuipers, B., G. Renes, M.J.P.M. Thissen and J.E. Ligthart (2003), 'De maatschappelijke betekenis van doorvoer; Een onderzoek naar de zuivere doorvoer van goederen door de Nederlandse zeehavens' ['The social significance of transit trade; an investigation of transit trade through Dutch ports'], TNO Inro rapport No. 2003-36, Delft, November.

Kuypers, F., A. Lejour, O. Lemmers and P. Rademakers (2012), 'Kenmerken van Wederuitvoerbedrijven' ['Characteristics of firms that focus on re-exports'], Webarticle CBS, 6-2-2012.

Landes, D.S. (1998), *Arm en Rijk* (translation of *Wealth and Poverty of Nations*), Utrecht: Het Spectrum B.V.

Levinson, M. (2006), *The Box: How the Shipping Container Made the World Smaller and the World Economy Bigger*, Princeton: Princeton University Press.

Liebowitz, S.J. and S.E. Margolis (1990), 'The fable of the keys', *Journal of Law and Economics*, **33** (1), 1–25.

Liebowitz, S.J. and S.E. Margolis (1994), 'Network externality: an uncommon tragedy', *Journal of Economic Perspectives*, **8** (2), 133–150.

Liebowitz, S.J. and S.E. Margolis (1996), 'Should technology choice be a concern of antitrust policy?', *Harvard Journal of Law and Technology*, **9** (2), 283–318.

Linders, G.J.M., H.L.F. de Groot and P. Rietveld (2005a), 'Institutional determinants of bilateral trade: an analysis according to product type', Tinbergen Institute Discussion Paper No. TI 2005-023/3, Amsterdam, February.

Linders, G.J.M., A. Slangen, H.L.F. de Groot and S. Beugelsdijk (2005b), 'Cultural and institutional determinants of bilateral trade flows', Tinbergen Institute Discussion Paper No. TI 2005-074/3, Amsterdam, July.

London Stock Exchange (2002), 'Clearing and settlement in Europe: response to the first report of the Giovannini Group', White Paper, London, February.

Matutes, C. and P. Regibeau (1996), 'A selective review of the economics of standardization. Entry deterrence, technological progress and international competition', *European Journal of Political Economy*, **12** (2), 183–209.

McAfee, R.P. (2004), 'The real lesson of Enron's implosion: market makers are in the trust business', *The Economists' Voice*, **1** (2), Article 4.

McCann, L. and K.W. Easter (2000), 'Estimates of public sector transaction costs in NRCS programs', *Journal of Agricultural and Applied Economics*, **32** (3), 555–563.

McCann, L., B. Colby, K.W. Easter, A. Kasterine and K.V. Kuperan (2005), 'Transaction cost measurement for evaluating environmental policies', *Ecological Economics*, **52** (4), 527–542.

Megchelen, O.K. van (2005), 'Sleutel voor inventief management; koerswijzer, eye-opener en startpunt voor slimmer bouwen' ['A key to innovative building: navigator/compass, eyeopener and starting point for a smarter building process'], Mimeo, Stichting Bouw Research, June.

Mellens, M.C., H.G.A. Noordman and J.P. Verbruggen (2007), 'Wederuitvoer: internationale vergelijking en gevolgen voor prestatie-indicatoren' ['Re-exports: international comparison and implications for performance indicators'], CPB Document No. 143. The Hague, April.

Ménard, C. (2005), 'A new institutional approach to organisation', Ch. 12 in C. Ménard and M.M. Shirley (eds), *Handbook of New Institutional Economics*, Berlin: Springer, pp. 281–318.

Ménard, C. and B. du Marais (2008), 'Can we rank legal systems according to their economic efficiency?', *Journal of Law & Policy*, **26** (55), 55–80.

Ménard, C. and J.M. Oudot (2010), 'Opportunisme ou équité? Le cas des contrats d'approvisionnement de défense', *Revue Française d'Economie*, **24** (3), 196–226.

Ménard, C. and M.M. Shirley (2005), *Handbook of New Institutional Economics*, Berlin: Springer.

Naghavi, A. and G.I.P. Ottaviano (2006), 'Outsourcing, contracts and innovation networks', CEPR Discussion Paper No. 5681, London, May.

Nijsen, A.F.M. (2008), 'SCM to measure compliance costs', Ch. 5 in A. Nijsen, J. Hudson, C. Müller, K. van Paridon and R. Thurik (eds), *Business Regulation and Public Policy: The Costs and Benefits of Compliance*, New York: Springer, pp. 61–82.

Nijsen, A.F.M. (2012), 'SCM 2.0, an argument for tailored interpretation', in A. Alemanno et al. (eds), *Better Business Regulation in a Risk Society*, New York: Springer, forthcoming.

Noguer, M. and M. Siscart (2005), 'Trade raises income: a precise and robust result', *Journal of International Economics*, **65** (2), 447–460.

North, D.C. (1990), *Institutions, Institutional Change and Economic Performance*, Cambridge, MA: Cambridge University Press.

North, D.C. and J.J. Wallis (1986), 'Measuring the transaction sector in the American economy: 1870–1970', in S. Engerman and R. Gallman (eds), *Long Term Factors in American Economic Growth*, Chicago: Chicago University Press, pp. 95–161.

North, D.C. and J.J. Wallis (1994), 'Integrating institutional change and technical change in economic history: a transaction cost approach', *Journal of Institutional and Theoretical Economics*, **150** (4), 609–624.

Nunn, N. (2007), 'Relationship-specificity, incomplete contracts and the pattern of trade', *Quarterly Journal of Economics*, **122** (2), 569–600.

OECD (2007), 'Policy brief October 2005, the costs and benefits of trade facilitation', in P. Wilmott, 'A review of the European Commission's plans for an electronic customs environment', *World Customs Journal*, **1** (1), 11–17.

Ouchi, W.G. (1980), 'Markets, bureaucracies and clans', *Administrative Science Quarterly*, **25** (1), 129–141.

Oxley, J.E. (1997), 'Appropriability hazards and governance in strategic alliances: a transaction cost approach', *Journal of Law, Economics & Organization*, **13** (2), 387–409.

Oxley, J.E. (1999), 'Institutional environment and the mechanisms of governance: the impact of intellectual property protection on the structure of inter-firm alliances', *Journal of Economic Behavior & Organization*, **38** (3), 283–309.

Peter, K.S., J. Svejnar and K. Terrell (2004), 'Distance to the efficiency frontier and FDI spillovers', CEPR Discussion Paper No. 4723, London, November.

Piercy, N. and N. Rich (2009), 'The implications of Lean operations for sales strategy: from sales-force to marketing-force', *Journal of Strategic Marketing*, **17** (3–4), 237–255.

Portes, R. and H. Rey (1999), 'The determinants of cross-border equity flows', NBER Working Paper No. 7336, Cambridge, MA, September.

Prusak, L. and L. Weiss (2007), 'Knowledge in organizational settings; how organizations generate, disseminate, and use knowledge for their competitive advantage', in K. Ichijo and I. Nonaka (eds), *Knowledge Creation and Management, New Challenges for Managers*, Oxford: Oxford University Press, pp. 32–43.

Putnam, R.D. (1993), *Making Democracy Work: Civic Traditions in Modern Italy*, Princeton, NJ: Princeton University Press.

Putnam, R.D. (2000), *Bowling Alone: The Collapse and Revival of American Community*, New York: Simon and Schuster.

Rauch, J.E. (1999), 'Networks versus markets in international trade', *Journal of International Economics*, **48** (1), 7–35.

Rauch, J.E. (2001), 'Business and social networks in international trade', *Journal of Economic Literature*, **39** (4), 1177–1203.

Rauch, J.E. and V. Trindade (2002), 'Ethnic Chinese networks in international trade', *Review of Economics and Statistics*, **84** (1), 116–130.

Rose, A.K. (2005), 'Which international institutions promote international trade?', *Review of International Economics*, **13** (4), 682–698.

Sena, V. (2004), 'The return of the prince of Denmark: a survey of recent developments in the economics of innovation', *Economic Journal*, **114** (496), F312–F332.

Shah, R. and P.T. Ward (2003), 'Lean manufacturing: context, practice bundles and performance', *Journal of Operations Management*, **21** (2), 129–149.

Sijpersma, R. (2004), 'Onderaannemingsbedrijven op de bouwplaats' ['Subcontractors at the construction sites'], EIB, Amsterdam, May.

Simon, H.A. (1983), *Reason in Human Affairs*, Oxford: Basil Blackwell.

Suyker, W. and H.L.F. de Groot (2006), 'China and the Dutch economy: stylised facts and prospects', CPB Document No. 127, The Hague.

Sztompka, P. (1999), *Trust: A Sociological Theory*, Cambridge: Cambridge University Press.

Tinbergen, J. (1962), 'An analysis of world trade flows, the Linder Hypothesis and exchange risk', in J. Tinbergen (ed.), *Shaping the World Economy*, New York: The Twentieth Century Fund.

Trefler, D. (1995), 'The case of missing trade and other mysteries', *American Economic Review*, **85** (5), 1029–1046.

UK Government (2008), *25 Ideas for Simplifying EU Law*, London: Crown Copyright.

Visser, H. (2005), 'Leveren uitgaande directe buitenlandse investeringen een bijdrage aan productiviteitsverbetering, innovatie en economische groei in de binnenlandse economie?' ['Does outgoing FDI contribute to productivity growth, innovation and economic growth in the domestic economy?'], Ministry of Economic Affairs Research Series No. 05BEB06.

Volberda, H.W., F.A.J. van den Bosch, J.J.P. Jansen, A. Szczygielska and M.W. Roza (2007), *Inspelen op Globalisering; Offshoring, Innovatie en Versterking van de Concurrentiekracht van Nederland* [*Anticipating Globalization; Offshoring, Innovation and Strengthening the Competitiveness of the Netherlands*], SMO: The Hague.

Vor, M.P.H. de (1994), 'Meting van transactiekosten in de Nederlandse economie' ['Measuring transaction costs in the Dutch economy'], *Maandschrift Economie*, **58** (3), 166–177.

Wang, C., Y. Wei and X. Liu (2010), 'Determinants of bilateral trade flows in OECD countries: evidence from gravity panel data models', *The World Economy*, **33** (7), 894–915.

Watts, R.W. and J.L. Zimmerman (1990), 'Positive accounting theory: a ten year perspective', *The Accounting Review*, **65** (1), 131–156.

Wechsberg, J. (1966), *The Merchant Bankers*, New York: Bedminster Press.

Williamson, O.E. (1975), *Markets and Hierarchies: Analysis and Antitrust Implications,* New York: Free Press.

Williamson, O.E. (1985), *The Economic Institutions of Capitalism*, New York: Free Press.

Williamson, O.E. (1993), 'Calculativeness, trust, and economic organization', *Journal of Law and Economics*, **36** (1), 453–486.

Williamson, O.E. (1996), *The Mechanisms of Governance*, Oxford: Oxford University Press.

Wilmott, P. (2007), 'A review of the European Commission's plans for an electronic customs environment', *World Customs Journal*, **1** (1), 11–17.

World Bank (2008), *Doing Business 2009*, Washington, DC: The World Bank.

WRR [Wetenschappelijke Raad voor het Regeringsbeleid] (2003), *Nederland Handelsland – Het Perspectief van de Transactiekosten* [*The Netherlands as a Trading Nation: The Perspective of Transaction Costs*], Den Haag: SDU.

Zandvliet, K. and L. Blussé (2002), *De Nederlandse Ontmoeting met Azië, 1600–1950* [*The Dutch Encounter with Asia, 1600–1950*], Zwolle: Rijksmuseum Amsterdam en Waanders Uitgevers.

Index